John Dewey and the Lessons of Art

John Dewey and the Lessons of Art

Philip W. Jackson

Yale University Press

New Haven and London

Set in Adobe Garamond and Stone Sans types by The Composing Room of Michigan, Inc., Grand Rapids, Michigan.

Printed in the United States of America.

Library of Congress Cataloging-in-Publication Data

Jackson, Philip W. (Philip Wesley), 1928–

    John Dewey and the lessons of art / Philip W. Jackson.

       p.   cm.

    Includes bibliographical references and index.

    ISBN 0-300-07213-9 (alk. paper)

     1. Dewey, John, 1859–1952—Aesthetics. 2. Aesthetics, American. 3. Aesthetics, Modern—19th century. 4. Aesthetics, Modern—20th century. 5. Art—Study and teaching. I. Title.

B945.D4J33   1998

700'.1—dc21   97-34861

A catalogue record for this book is available from the British Library.

The paper in this book meets the guidelines for permanence and durability of the Committee on Production Guidelines for Book Longevity of the Council on Library Resources.

10 9   7 6 5 4 3 2 1

For Adam, Nancy, David, Steven, and Hannah

"The collecting of poetry from one's experience as one goes along is not the same thing as merely writing poetry."
—*Wallace Stevens*

Contents

Acknowledgments, ix

Introduction, xi

1 Experience and the Arts, 1

2 The Spirituality of Art-Centered Experiences, 68

3 Experience as Artifice: Putting Dewey's Theory to Work, 121

4 Some Educational Implications of Dewey's Theory
of Experience, 165

References, 197

Index, 201

Acknowledgments

I am grateful to the Board of the Spencer Foundation and to its president, Patricia Alberg Graham, for the foundation's generous support of this project. This is not the first time that I have been fortunate enough to benefit from the foundation's generosity. I remain deeply indebted for the backing that it has given my work over the years.

The Department of Education at the University of Chicago, which has been my academic home for more than forty-two years, has provided much more than a comfortable place to work and a host of stimulating colleagues. The department's students in particular have been a continuing source of intellectual stimulation and reward. A group of those students, having developed a special interest in Dewey, formed a discussion group that has met off and on at my house for quite some time. The regulars attending the sessions include Desha Baker, Catie Bell, David Granger, Kenneth "Buzz" Hunter, Elizabeth Meadows, and Wendy Naylor. I have profited greatly from our lively discussions.

In addition to the students with whom I currently work, I am extremely fortunate to have among my treasured friends several former students, a number of whom helped in one way or another to see me through this project. Those whose help warrants special mention include René Arcilla, with whom I have a continuing debate over the merits of Dewey's philosophy and in whose company I have spent many delightful hours viewing works of art in museums around the country; Craig Cunningham, my computer guru and fellow admirer of Dewey's metaphysics, who is as interested as I am in the educational applications of Dewey's thought; Mary Driscoll, who shares my love of poetry and whose droll stories of her Catholic childhood and her Irish relatives have never failed to lift my spirits, even when they have not been down; David Hansen, with whom I have regularly taken leisurely Sunday walks through Wooded Island, discussing the progress of this book, among many other things; Lauren Sosniack, my faithful E-mail correspondent, whose almost daily messages of encouragement and support have done much to sustain me over the years.

I thank Jim Garrison, editor of *The New Scholarship on Dewey* (1995), who invited me to write on Dewey's aesthetics when my ideas on the subject were just beginning to form and whose generous reading of an earlier draft of this manuscript contributed to its being accepted by Yale University Press. To the acquiring editor at the press, Gladys Topkis, I owe thanks for her enthusiastic endorsement of the manuscript from the start. I thank Mary Pasti for the benefits of her editorial acumen and her many helpful queries.

My friend Jerry Hausmann has played a special role in the preparation of this book. He and I have had lunch together once a month for several years. During lunch we regularly discuss the arts, and I have often reported on this book's progress. Jerry has been a wonderful listener and a helpful critic. His deep knowledge of the visual arts has proved to be an invaluable resource. In addition, he has graciously read the entire manuscript in draft form and has offered detailed suggestions for its improvement. Whatever faults remain are, of course, of my own making.

My debt of thanks to my wife, Jo, remains, as always, far greater than I can describe, much less repay.

This book is dedicated to my son-in-law, my three children, and my grand-daughter—affectionately referred to as "the kids."

Introduction

This book deals with what the arts have to teach us about how to live our lives. It concentrates on a very important but largely overlooked answer to that question, one having less to do with any single art than with the arts in general, and less to do with art objects or performances as isolated entities than with the experiences that they sometimes engender. It also treats the subsidiary question of how teachers of all kinds might make use of art's "lessons" (understood in experiential terms) to improve their teaching. The answer that it gives to both questions draws chiefly on the writings of John Dewey, whose standing as one of the preeminent philosophers of the twentieth century is universally acknowledged and whose reputation as an educational thinker and reformer is of equal renown. It does not, however, presume any familiarity with Dewey's writings on the part of its readers.

Dewey turned to a systematic consideration of the arts late in his career. His only book on the subject, *Art as Experience,* was published in 1934, the year he turned seventy-five. By that time, however, his influence within philosophy had begun to wane, as had his prominence in the public eye. Though the aesthetician Monroe Beardsley, some thirty years after the book's publication, declared *Art as Experience* to be "by widespread agreement, the most valuable work on aesthetics written in English (and perhaps in any language) so far in our century" (Beardsley 1966, 332), it was not terribly well received at the time of its publication and therefore garnered far less attention nationwide than had several of his earlier works. Even today, I would wager, far more people have heard of Dewey the pragmatist or Dewey the educator or even Dewey the social critic than have heard anything at all about his views on the arts. My sense that such was the case prompted the decision to write this book.

Another reason for thinking a book of this kind worth writing was that not everything Dewey had to say about the arts is contained in *Art as Experience.* His thoughts on the subject are scattered throughout his works, sometimes in articles and books that have little to do with the arts per se. By drawing upon those scattered observations (and on other material as well) I hoped to fill in the picture of Dewey's view of the arts in a way that could not be done by relying solely on what he has to say in his chief work on the subject.

My wish to address teachers and professional educators in particular, along with a more general audience, reflects my own longstanding interest in teaching as a professional practice and as a human endeavor. To that was added my awareness that Dewey himself never bothered to discuss educational matters in *Art as Experience.* He did insert a remark here and there that might be said to have special relevance for those who teach, but overall he ignored the subject. The word *education* does not appear in the book's index, nor do its correlatives *teaching* and *learning.* Given Dewey's deep involvement in educational affairs and given also the fairly close connection between the arts and education at the level of public opinion, those omissions must seem strange to readers accustomed to hearing from Dewey the educator. One reader who found them so was Sir Herbert Read, the celebrated British advocate of the arts and a longtime admirer of Dewey. Unable to explain why Dewey said so little about education in *Art as Experience,* Sir Herbert could but remark, "I regard it as one of the curiosities of philosophy that when John Dewey, late in life, came to the subject of aesthetics, he nowhere, in the course of [his] imposing treatise, established a connection between aesthetics and education" (Read 1943, 245).

I share Sir Herbert's puzzlement, but not entirely. My own guess as to why Dewey chose to overlook educational matters in *Art as Experience* focuses chiefly on the issue of size. To have included a thorough discussion of such material would have made his book far too long and unwieldy in content. But I also suspect a further reason, for he could well have chosen to write yet another book on the subject, an "applied" version of *Art as Experience*. I think that Dewey may have chosen not to discuss the educational implications of his theory of the arts chiefly because he had not yet thought them through to his own satisfaction. He also lacked the time and means to do so. To embark upon such a project at his stage of life and without a school of his own in which to experiment and try out ideas was more than he was willing or able to do. Or so I surmise. He thus left that task for others to accomplish.

Though strongly tempted to try, I do not take up that challenge in this book. I avoid doing so for a number of reasons, among them the fact that I, too, lack the means of testing whatever ideas might occur to me. Additionally, I suspect that classroom applications of Dewey's ideas about the arts are best thought about with a particular context in mind. Each practitioner must undertake that kind of thinking on his or her own.

What I do here instead is consider how Dewey's theorizing about the arts might help each of us to live life differently. My assumption is that teachers and other educational practitioners stand to gain as much from such an exploration as anyone else. To accomplish that task I draw upon suggestions contained in two instructional books in the arts and one in popular psychology (Kent and Steward 1992; Franck 1973; Kabat-Zinn 1994). None of these self-help books mentions Dewey's ideas directly, but all three seem to me Deweyan in spirit. Each offers concrete advice that accords well with what Dewey has to say about the development of perceptual acuity, a key notion in his thinking about the arts.

I turn from general considerations to the demands of teaching and to the ways those demands might be elucidated by Dewey's emphasis on the forces that give unity to a situation. I begin with a brief account of Dewey's early work at the University of Chicago Laboratory School to set the stage for a subsequent examination of two unsavory extremes of educational practice, each of which might have been avoided or at least remedied by adhering to one or more of Dewey's precepts. That Dewey himself serves as one of those examples adds poignancy to the analysis. It also raises questions that remain to be pursued. In Chapter 3 I take up the task of putting Dewey's theory to work. In Chapter 4 I address teachers specifically.

Having decided upon those two goals—presenting an overview of Dewey's thinking about the arts and saying something about its practical implications for the general reader and especially for educators—I was set to undertake the writing of this book. One question, however, remained. It had to do with whether Dewey's views on the arts might be outdated. After all, a lot has happened in the world at large and in the artworld in particular since 1934, when *Art as Experience* appeared. What further prompted me to raise that question was my personal acquaintance with some of the ways art itself has changed in recent years. I knew, for example, that many of today's leading artists and critics have created and celebrated works of art that have called for quite different kinds of responses on the part of viewers or readers or listeners than did the works that Dewey typically used to elucidate his theory.

The works of art that Dewey mentions in *Art as Experience* are for the most part paintings and poems that were thoughtfully designed and executed. Their appreciation by others calls for a corresponding degree of thought and reflection. That means, among other things, paying attention to the internal structure of the work, noting how its parts fit together or how the work as a whole temporally unfolds. Much of today's art, however, seems *not* to call for the kind of analysis that Dewey's conceptual apparatus, with an emphasis on unity, wholeness, and balance, encourages one to make.

I initially feared that the inappropriateness of the Deweyan categories to the analysis of many contemporary works would extend to their use outside the arts. Were that so, the power of Dewey's theory to shed light on everyday experience might be correspondingly reduced. I have since come to see that my fear was unfounded and that Dewey's analytic categories are just as helpful in understanding what goes on when we encounter a Duchamp readymade, let us say, or a painting by Andy Warhol as when we analyze a Rembrandt or any other classic work. In this book I try to make clear why that is so. On the way to arriving at that conviction, however, I came upon another set of issues that I found intriguing and far more pertinent to my overall project than the up-to-date-ness of Dewey's theory. These had to do with the power of art to be genuinely transformative, to modify irrevocably our habitual ways of thinking, feeling, and perceiving. Changes of that magnitude may occur infrequently, true enough, but when they do, they leave no doubt in the mind of the experiencer that something significant, perhaps even spiritual, has taken place.

What got me thinking about such matters were the published accounts of several artists and art critics who report having had at least one such transformative experience in connection with the very kind of artwork that I feared Dewey's theory might have difficulty handling. I realized then, more keenly than before, that the criteria of unity and wholeness that Dewey so frequently invoked when discussing the properties of an *art-centered* experience (a term I ultimately settled on to use in referring to experiences in which a work of art is central) need by no means be limited in their reference to formal properties internal to the work itself, even though that internal-to-the-work perspective was the one that Dewey chiefly employed in *Art as Experience*. Those same criteria, I came to see, could as easily refer to art-centered experience as a whole and to the relation among its elements. In fact, Dewey's theory of experience not only allows for that possibility but actually mandates it, as I also hope to show.

It is experience, in other words, to which all such criteria of judgment must ultimately be applied. Art-centered experiences include a work of art by definition, a work that, again by definition, occupies a central position in the exchange. But there is nothing about its centrality that dictates what properties the work must have in order for the experience in which it figures to be aesthetically satisfying and fulfilling. Thus, someone can undergo an experience whose properties are aesthetically satisfying in one way or another while interacting with an art object that itself is lacking in balance, coherence, continuity, and other unifying qualities. Conversely, someone can have a totally unsatisfying experience in connection with a work of art or any other object whose internal properties exemplify those same qualities of balance, coherence, and so forth. An example of the latter possibility (one that involves Dewey himself) figures prominently in Chapter 4.

In the process of determining whether Dewey's theory could accommodate some of the latest developments within the arts I was brought to realize something else. I came to see that the ongoing controversy among today's artists and art critics over whether art (chiefly painting and sculpture) has somehow reached the end of its own history is related to a much broader and older controversy having to do with whether the arts as a whole might one day outlive their usefulness. The latter question, in turn, sounded to me uncomfortably akin to Dewey's notion of the arts serving to exemplify what it takes for an experience to be rich and fulfilling. The connection between Dewey's view and the older controversy can be summarized in the form of a question: Once we have learned from the arts what it takes for all of experience to be rich and fulfilling, what further need would we have of them? We might still find them immediately enjoyable, true enough, but even as sources of passing pleasure their value would be greatly diminished, for we would have less need of such escapist delights if all of life could be made more artlike. That line of reasoning, though blatantly flawed, has sufficient appeal to make a proper Deweyan nervous. I decided that it needed to be addressed.

My looking into questions having to do with the transformative power of the arts and the end-of-the-arts controversy was tangential to my main purpose of making Dewey's views accessible to a wider audience. At the same time it yielded information that broadened the applicability of Dewey's theory, shedding light on issues that Dewey himself could not have anticipated. I found that information interesting and worth sharing with others. I therefore decided to devote a section of the book exclusively to the outcome of those explorations and to have it serve as a bridge between the exposition of Dewey's ideas in Chapter 1 and my reflections on how those ideas might be to work, in Chapter 3. This middle section, entitled "The Spirituality of Art-Centered Experiences," comprises all of Chapter 2.

Finally, a word about the book's title. What the arts have to teach us, which includes everything we might learn from them, goes far beyond the "lessons" brought to light by Dewey and given prominence in this book. Dewey would surely concur with that statement. The fruits of our encounters with individual works of art are endless in their bounty. Dewey's theory of experience helps to explain why. At the same time, Dewey would also insist on there being more to art than can be gleaned from individual works closely observed. Some of art's features are best viewed from a distance and in the company of works from diverse media. Such was Dewey's perspective and such is the one that predominates in this book. In Chapter 2, however, I temporarily lay aside Dewey's bird's-eye view in order to explore the many ways in which individual works leave an enduring impact on the lives of artists and audience alike. In the final analysis, as I hope this book will make clear, the lessons of art derive from both its general and its specific features as each contributes to the enrichment of life.

John Dewey and the Lessons of Art

Chapter 1 Experience and the Arts

John Dewey's *Art as Experience* (1934) begins by sidestepping the arts completely, even though *art* stands as the first word in the title. The book opens instead with an extended commentary on experience, its traits and preconditions. There is an important reason for this order of things. For Dewey, ordinary experience is historically prior to its evolved variants. All of the more specialized forms of experiencing, such as those that we encounter in the arts or the sciences or religion, made their appearance secondarily. These more highly evolved forms of interaction derived from experiences in everyday life. They could never have come into being if ordinary experience were not the way it is. In short, Dewey wants to reflect upon what common experience is like before moving on to consider its more specialized and derivative forms.

Dewey's sidestep makes good sense, but it has drawbacks. One is that the qualities being looked for are not immediately evident. Though ordinary experience is commonplace, its attributes are not apparent. Its underlying structure, traits, and preconditions do not stand out for all to see. Dewey put it this way: "It is not experience which is experienced, but nature—stones, plants, animals, diseases, health, temperature, electricity, and so on. Things interacting in certain ways *are* experience; they are what is experienced" (LW1, 12). To talk about experience requires a kind of stepping back from a consideration of its contents in order to say something about its form.

But we remain locked within experience even when we step back. Thus the view that we are trying to develop conforms to the same structures and circumstances that we are seeking to describe. If we find, for example, that the substance of experience is always contingent upon the situation as a whole, so too must be our declarations about it. What we have to say about experience is, perforce, situated as well. In other words, there is no privileged position outside experience from which to make our observations, no neutral ground on which to stand. This means, among other things, that our pronouncements about the nature of experience must be provisional. They must remain open to revision in the light of subsequent experience.

Another difficulty resides in the widespread belief that we already know what experience is like generically, even though we may seldom speak of it in those terms. As part of mastering a language and learning to communicate with others we each develop a perspective on what it means to be human, one that contains any number of tacit assumptions and beliefs about the nature of experience. Some of these tacitly held beliefs are built directly into our language and become part of our way of thinking without our even realizing it. Others are transmitted more explicitly. Both kinds can be immensely helpful. As part of what we usually call common sense, they save us from having to construct a worldview entirely from scratch. They enable us to communicate with one another. They also, however, turn out to be a liability when we entertain alternative perspectives. Whatever appears commonsensical to us also usually seems incontrovertible. We typically are unwilling to give it up without a struggle.

Dewey was painfully aware of these difficulties and was almost defeated by them. After struggling for years to clarify his conception of the generic components of experience, he came close to throwing in the towel. In what was to have become the introduction to a revised edition of his seminal work, *Experience and Nature,* a project that he did not live to complete, Dewey announced that if he were to rewrite the book, he would change its title, eliminating the word *Experience* and replacing it with *Culture.* As he explained, "I would abandon the term 'experience' because of my growing realization that the historical obstacles which prevented understanding of my use of 'experience' are, for all practical purposes, insurmountable" (LW1, 361). The historical obstacles to which Dewey refers consisted chiefly of inherited ways of looking at things: the way we have of separating subjects from objects, for example, or facts from values, or even past from present and present from future. Dewey readily acknowledges the usefulness and even the necessity of such distinctions. He has no difficulty with our continuing to employ them as instruments of thought. The trouble, as he sees it, lies in assuming that these useful distinctions, which we have come to recognize through reflection, were there to begin with and, therefore, constitute reality pure and simple. The danger, in other words, lies in treating an intellectual invention as the discovery of an unquestionable truth. Dewey found that error to be so pervasive throughout history and particularly throughout the history of philosophy that he branded it *the* philosophical fallacy (LW1, 34).

Applied to the way we traditionally think of experience, our tendency to commit *the* philosophical fallacy usually takes the form of placing experience well inside the experiencer, making it something that each of us can report on to others but can never share directly with them. This makes it a very personal and private affair. Over the centuries we have come to treat experience as though it were exclusively a psychological concept, a mental state of some sort, forced on us by obdurate Nature.

Dewey invites us to think of experience differently. He asks us to abandon the convention of looking upon experience as something that happens exclusively within us, that is, as an essentially psychological concept. In its place he would substitute a conception far more inclusive, one that embraces what is being experienced as well as the experiencer. Here is the way he puts it: "Instead of signifying being shut up within one's own private feelings and sensations, . . . [experience] signifies active and alert commerce with the world; at its height it signifies complete interpenetration of self and the world of objects and events" (LW10, 25). Experience, in other words, is transactional. It is not just what registers on our consciousness as we make our way through the world but includes the objects and events that compose that world. The objects and events are as much a part of experience as we are ourselves. When we are fully immersed in experience, its components so interpenetrate one another that we lose all sense of separation between self, object, and event. It is when situations become problematic—when something goes wrong or when for some other reason we pause to reflect upon the circumstances at hand—that such distinctions become evident. Then we start to isolate this or that element within experience so that we might better deal with the situation as a whole.

Another of Dewey's major points about the nature of experience calls attention to its temporality. Dewey urges us to recognize that experience exists in time and changes over time. It always has a history. "An instantaneous experience is an impossibility, biologically and psychologically," Dewey tells us. "An experience is a product, one might almost say a by-product, of *continuous* and *cumulative* interaction of an organic self with the world" (LW10, 224, emphasis added).

Changes that occur within experience over time may or may not be intentional. Chance and accident often play as large a part as ideas and intentions do. What this means from the standpoint of the experiencer is that things do not always turn out as planned. Some experiences proceed smoothly from beginning to end precisely as intended, but not all do. Indeed, in examining a lifetime of experiences we likely would find that predictable and smoothly unfolding experiences are the exception rather than the rule.

Dewey had a special way of discussing segments of ordinary experience marked by a sense of wholeness and unity and often accompanied by feelings of fulfillment and delight. He spoke of them singly, declaring each one to be *an* experience, a discrete unit with discernible boundaries distinguishing it from the general flow of events. Here is the way he described such occurrences:

> We have *an* experience when the material experienced runs its course to fulfillment. Then and then only is it integrated within and demarcated in the general stream of experience from other experiences. A piece of work is finished in a way that is satisfactory; a problem receives its solution; a game is played through; a situation, whether that of eating a meal, playing a game of chess, carrying on a conversation, writing a book, or taking part in a political campaign, is so rounded out that its close is a consummation and not a cessation. Such an experience is a whole and carries with it its own individualizing quality and self-sufficiency. It is *an* experience. (LW10, 42)

Dewey points out that the arts provide us with exemplary instances of *an* experience. They do so, moreover, viewed from the standpoint of either the artist or the audience. From the artist's point of view the experience is chiefly one of making or doing something that culminates in an art object or a performance. From the viewpoint of the audience or the reading public the task is one of interpretation, of making sense of the artist's accomplishment. The audience's transaction with the work culminates in a state of appreciative understanding. In either case, the experience, when successful—when it truly is *an* experience—is characterized at its close (and often periodically during its course) by feelings of satiety and fulfillment. What is fulfilling from either perspective is not simply the object or the performance, although we often speak as though it were. At the close of such an experience we say things like "I really enjoyed that play" or "I find that painting very satisfying." This way of speaking, however, with its clear-cut separation of subject and object, is but an instance of the commonsensical view of experience that Dewey wants us to abandon. Actually, it is the audience's encounter with the object or performance, or the artist's wrestling with the stuff of its making that proves to be the source of their enjoyment or suffering. The true work of art is not the object that sits in a museum nor the performance captured on film or disc. Rather, it is the experience occasioned by the production or the experience of appreciating objects and performances. For the artist, those two forms of experiencing are one.

Does every encounter with an art object or an artistic performance necessarily culminate in *an* experience? Certainly not. There are countless reasons why such experiences may be fragmentary and unsatisfying for both artist and audience. Perhaps, for example, the artist failed, the art object or performance was poorly executed and lacked unity. Think of the novel that has a weak ending or the play that is poorly acted. The audience could also be at fault. Perhaps its members lacked the background to appreciate what the artist was trying to do or did not try hard enough to fathom the work's meaning or took insufficient time to do so. Consider here the speed with which the average museum-goer moves from one exhibited object to the next. The ruination of experience can also come from the outside. Some readers may recall the famous visitor from Porlock who interrupted Coleridge's composition of "Kubla Khan." Interruptions may also occur mundanely in the form of overhead planes at an outdoor performance, talkativeness on the part of other patrons in the darkened theater, crinkling candy wrappers in the concert hall.

When conditions are just right or very close to it, the resultant transaction between self and surroundings constitutes *an* experience. What is special about such occurrences is not simply that their parts or phases hang together to form a whole. Nor is it simply that we find them to be momentarily satisfying. What adds to their importance are the enduring changes that they produce. They leave in their wake a changed world. The contents of the world have been increased by one more painting or poem or piece of music, and, more important, both the experiencer, whether artist or art appreciator, and the object experienced have changed. The experiencer changes by undergoing a transformation of the self, gaining a broadened perspective, a shift of attitude, an increase of knowledge, or any of a host of other enduring alterations of a psychological nature. The object of experience changes through the acquisition of new meanings. These meanings, once disclosed, are potentially communicable to everyone. They thereby augment the fund of interpretive possibilities available to all who subsequently come upon the same object or event.

Another way of thinking about these interchanges with art objects that result in enduring changes in both the experiencer and the experienced is to label them educative. They are so, Dewey would say, because of their liberating effect on future experiences. An educative experience, he explains, is one that does "something to prepare a person for later experience of a deeper and more expansive quality" (LW13, 28). Conversely, "any experience is mis-educative that has the effect of arresting or distorting the growth of further experience" (LW13, 11). To say that encounters with art objects, works of literature, and theatrical performances often leave us better able to deal with future events is, however, not to claim that such experiences are the only ones worthy of being called educative. Many other objects and many other forms of encounter also yield educational dividends.

Yet successful encounters with art objects and artistic performances are set apart from other experiences of educational worth. What special something sets them apart? What do the arts give us that other forms of experience do not?

The arts, Dewey tells us, reveal the rewards of bringing an experience to fruition. They reveal what it takes to fashion works whose form and structure are holistic and unified, yielding a reaction on the part of both artist and audience that is at once satisfying and fulfilling. In this way they hint at what life might be like if we sought more often to shape ordinary experience in an artistic manner. They thus offer indirect lessons about fashioning the more mundane aspects of our lives.

The distinction between experiences connected with the arts and those connected with life in general is by no means absolute. This too is a crucial part of Dewey's message. The arts, he insists, are not the sole source of aesthetic pleasure. They are not the only repository of the holistic and the unified. Nor are they the only place to go when we are looking for a sense of satisfaction and fulfillment. Any job well done yields rewards akin to those associated with the production or appreciation of art. Instead of being unique in experiential terms, what the arts offer are but refinements of qualities to be found in ordinary experience. "The esthetic," he proclaims, "is no intruder in experience from without. . . . [Instead] it is the clarified and intensified development of traits that belong to every normally complete experience" (LW 10, 52–53).

Dewey's emphasis on the primacy of ordinary experience, together with his insistence that the arts be looked on as a natural development within experience, serves to define the task ahead. With the ordinary as our starting place, we must first identify those traits that belong to every normally complete experience. These include not only the defining characteristics of such experiences—whatever it is that prompts us to call them complete—but also associated traits that normally complete experiences share with the rest of our experiencing.

THE GENERIC TRAITS OF *AN* EXPERIENCE

What are the traits of every normally complete experience that the arts serve to clarify and intensify? Dewey never treats them systematically, but he does say enough about them to enable us to piece together a fairly comprehensive picture of all they might include. The most prominent trait is the quality of completeness or cohesion that serves to name the kind of experience that we are talking about.

Completeness

What makes *an* experience complete? A partial answer was quoted earlier: "We have *an* experience when the material experienced runs its course to fulfillment." Dewey goes on to say that such an experience "is so rounded out that its close is a consummation and not a cessation." Both statements focus attention on what happens at the close of such an experience. Each refers to a state of affairs acknowledged by the participant to be an ending rather than a point where matters inexplicably grind to a halt or where an ongoing activity is broken off. One natural ending is childbirth. Like the pregnancy that culminates in a successful delivery, complete experiences are ones that have been brought to term.

It is not just the ending of an experience that makes it complete. Dewey describes completed transactions as being "integrated within" and as "demarcated in the general stream of experience from other experiences" (LW10, 42). The ending of a complete experience relates organically and dynamically to the circumstances preceding it, the way the phenomenon of birth relates to the prior conditions of gestation. Childbearing constitutes an entity whose historical integrity and internal structure cause it to stand apart, enabling it to be identified as *an* experience.

Pregnancy may be too dramatic to stand for all forms of complete experiences. Among the examples that Dewey mentions are several whose internal structures are not nearly as well integrated and demarcated as are the biological processes and bodily changes connected with motherhood. Eating a meal, playing a game of chess, carrying on a conversation—these too, Dewey tells us, can on occasion be so rounded out that their close comes as a consummation and not a cessation.

Dewey's inclusion of prosaic examples helps us to see something that we might otherwise have overlooked. The traits that we are trying to identify (those of every normally complete experience) are not present or absent in an all-or-nothing way. They vary in amount. Eating a meal may constitute a complete activity most of the time, but some meals—a banquet, say—are more rounded out than others. Thus there exist degrees of completeness (also called internal integration or demarcation) among those experiences that, overall, we might want to call complete.

What makes this variability important is its demonstration that the connection between art and ordinary affairs is relative rather than absolute. This means that we need not look upon art as qualitatively apart from the rest of life. Instead, we need to see it as a refinement, a clarification, and an intensification of those qualities of everyday experience that we normally call complete.

Uniqueness

Though wanting us to appreciate the commonalities that unite all of experience, Dewey also wants us to understand that every normally complete experience is unique. Each is "a whole" that "carries with it its own individualizing quality and self-sufficiency" (LW10, 42). "An experience has a unity that gives it its name. The existence of this unity is constituted by a single *quality* that pervades the entire experience in spite of the variation of its constituent parts." It is this unity that enables us to speak of the experience as a whole. Yet, as Dewey points out, "this unity is neither emotional, practical, nor intellectual, for these terms name distinctions that reflection can make within it" (LW10, 44).

What kind of a unity can it be that gives an experience its name yet is neither emotional, practical, nor intellectual? Let me answer that question with an illustration. Imagine that you attended a birthday party yesterday at a friend's house. Attendance-at-a-birthday-party-at-so-and-so's-house becomes, in effect, the name of the experience. It is what you say when asked what you did yesterday. What Dewey wants us to understand, as I read him, is that such a birthday-party experience is characterized by an "individualizing quality," as he calls it—that not only differentiates it from what went before and after, causing it to stand out as a unified event within a field of other happenings, but also makes it utterly unique, unlike any other birthday party that you have ever attended or ever will attend.

When you are asked, "Well, how was it?" or "What was it like?" the "it" that the questioner is asking about is that single *quality* that pervades the entire experience in spite of the variation of its constituent parts. The questioner is inviting commentary on the whole experience, leaving it open for the person who is doing the reporting to decide what form that commentary might take.

The intriguing aspect of this singular quality is that we cannot talk about it or describe it, at least not directly. The best we can do when reflecting on the experience as a whole is to speak of it in emotional, practical, intellectual, or other terms by making distinctions within it. We can describe the setting, name the people in attendance, list the gifts received. We can prattle on about how we felt about things that occurred at the party. We can describe memorable aspects of all that took place and tell what was said by whom and to whom. We can even register our reaction to the event by vowing never again to attend such a party or by expressing the hope that we will be invited back next year.

What we cannot do is to recapture the vibrant immediacy of the experience. Indeed, we cannot even come close. To say that we are close to describing the whole is to imply that we already know the whole and that it can be used as a standard against which to judge how close we have come with our description. But Dewey's point is precisely that we have no prior knowledge of what comprises the whole (even after having been a part of it), save as we make differentiations reflectively within the experience itself. We therefore cannot say how near or how far we are from such a standard, for its limits cannot be articulated. A description of the experience can only be given reflectively and is not the experience itself. The description does not exist until we bring it into being through language.

Our incapacity to provide an exhaustive description of *an* experience may appear to be contradicted by the finite number of things we have to say when asked to report on an event. Ultimately we reach a point where we have nothing more to add. Our stock of memories and impressions stands empty. It would be a mistake, however, to treat that inevitable state of affairs as evidence of our having exhausted all there is to say about the experience, much less to read it as our having captured the individualizing quality that made the experience unique. To do so would be to fall into the trap that Dewey warns us against: that of interiorizing experience, of treating it as what goes on within us and nothing more or, even more narrowly, as what remains interiorized—in the form of memories and such—after the experience has ended.

My focus on the fitness and naturalness of a complete experience is not meant to imply that the details of its closure can always be predicted. Often they cannot. Like fiction, life is full of surprise endings. And happily so. Indeed, it may well be that the most satisfying completions of all are those containing an element of surprise. Even as rudimentary a pleasure as watching a sunset can bring unexpected delights—a blaze of color, the silhouetted flight of birds against the sky—despite our knowing in very general terms how the experience will unfold. Yet if unexpected endings are to contribute to the sense of fulfillment that accompanies a normally complete experience, they too must conform to prior conditions within the experience itself. They must satisfy as much as surprise. If they do not, if we find them to be totally unexpected and inexplicable, we are apt to feel disappointed.

I have already addressed a portion of what it means to call an experience consummatory and self-sufficient. What I have not yet explicitly noted is that such experiences are at least to some degree enjoyable in their own right. This is not to say that we engage in them for their sake alone. It is simply to insist that every such experience is partially an end in itself. It contains its own rewards. It is intrinsically worthwhile.

Among the examples of complete experiences that Dewey mentions, eating a meal and playing a game of chess clearly have consummatory and self-sufficient aspects. Food is almost always enjoyable to its consumer; so too is a game of chess to its participants, even though one may win and the other lose. Each activity offers its own form of consummatory gratification, which contributes to its distinctiveness as *an* experience.

Unifying Emotion

"Experience," Dewey tells us, "is emotional but there are no separate things called emotions in it." That statement, which readers may find puzzling, comes at the end of a paragraph in which Dewey discusses the place of emotion in experience. What precedes it is the following: "We are given to thinking of emotions as things as simple and compact as are the words by which we name them. Joy, sorrow, hope, fear, anger, curiosity, are treated as if each in itself were a sort of entity that enters full-made upon the scene, an entity that may last a long time or a short time but whose duration, whose growth and career, is irrelevant to its nature. In fact, emotions are qualities, when they are significant, of a complex experience that moves and changes. I say when they are *significant*, for otherwise they are but the outbreaks and eruptions of a disturbed infant" (LW10, 48).

Dewey claims that our customary way of thinking about emotions divorces them from their context. We think of them as states of pure feeling, and in so doing we may forget the circumstances that gave rise to them and the particularity of what gives them meaning. He reminds us that we never experience joy or fear or any other emotion divorced from its context. We undergo each emotion in connection with particular circumstances. "There is no such thing as *the* emotion of fear, hate, love. . . . The *unique, unduplicated* character of experienced events and situations impregnates the emotion that is evoked" (LW10, 73, emphasis added). Moreover, those feelings alter as conditions change. "All emotions," Dewey tells us, "are qualifications of a drama and they change as the drama develops" (LW10, 48).

Though emotions fluctuate in response to changed conditions, they also serve to unify experience. Emotion holds the elements of an experience together. It causes them to cohere. Dewey calls emotion "the moving and cementing force." He adds: "It selects what is congruous and dyes what is selected with its color, thereby giving qualitative unity to materials externally disparate and dissimilar. It thus provides unity in and through the varied parts of an experience" (LW10, 49). The problem here is that he is ascribing agential force to emotion, as though emotion itself were capable of reaching out and selecting this or that element for inclusion or exclusion within *an* experience. What Dewey means, I believe, is that emotion works like a filter through which perceptions are screened. It allows some features of the environment to stand out and others to fade away, often to the point of disappearing. When gripped by a positive emotion we perceive our world positively. The reverse occurs when our feelings are negative. The underlying emotion that permeates *an* experience has its ups and downs and may in fact undergo such a transformation that we wind up feeling very different at its close than we did at its start. Those changes, however, form a coherent whole. Their trajectory constitutes the emotional history of the experience.

Dewey wants us to understand that emotional unity is fundamentally aesthetic. It gives experience an aesthetic quality even when the tenor of the experience is not predominately aesthetic. Thus, all normally complete experiences may be said to have an aesthetic quality.

The emotion at work within *an* experience "belongs of a certainty to the self," as Dewey readily acknowledges. It is psychological in the conventional sense of the word. But it belongs to a self that is engaged in the situation, the self, as Dewey says, "that is concerned in the movement of events toward an issue that is desired or disliked" (LW10, 48). Without that emotional cement of caring about outcomes, without that sense of engagement, the experience would lack unity and would fail to be *an* experience in the fullest sense of the term.

Dewey draws yet another helpful distinction in his explication of how emotion works within experience. He distinguishes between primary and secondary emotions. Primary emotions are those that "qualify the experience as a unity" (LW10, 49); secondary emotions are "evolved as variations of the primary underlying one" (LW10, 50). To clarify this difference Dewey asks readers to imagine an interview between someone who is applying for a job and an interviewer who controls the final decision. The primary emotion on the part of the applicant "may be at the beginning hope or despair, and elation or disappointment at the close" (LW10, 49). Minor fluctuations within that transition from hope to disappointment or from despair to elation constitute, for Dewey, the secondary emotions. The subtlety and nuances of those variations can be astonishing even within something as mundane as a job interview. "It is even possible," Dewey says, "for each attitude and gesture, each sentence, almost every word, to produce more than a fluctuation in the intensity of the basic emotion; to produce, that is, a change of shade and tint in its quality" (LW10, 50). Although Dewey doesn't say so, we might expect the fine fluctuations in the secondary emotions to vary with the strength and depth of the primary emotion that provides unity to the experience as a whole. Thus, in the job interview the emotional ups and downs of the applicant may be far more varied and subtle than those of the interviewer because, for the former, more hangs in the balance.

An Experience Versus Experience in General

Having identified several of the traits of a normally complete experience, we are in a position to see how those traits might apply to run-of-the-mill experiences, for as Dewey points out, "even a crude experience, if authentically *an* experience, is more fit to give a clue to the intrinsic nature of esthetic experience than is an object already set apart from any other mode of experience" (LW10, 16, emphasis added). Let us take Dewey up on his suggestion and imagine something as simple as taking an stroll to the mailbox. The question is, Under what circumstances might we want to call such a common event normally complete? As we think about that question we need stay alert to the kinship between such a mundane occurrence and those experiences that center on works of art.

My walk to the mailbox has a narrative structure that provides unity. It forms a brief story with a beginning, a middle, and an end. Let us assume that it also terminates successfully. and that its parts unfold harmoniously. I start at home, walk to the box, drop in the letter, and return home. The experience is rounded out.

My walk is readily identified as self-contained. I might easily include it in a report of what I did during the day. "I mailed my application to Harvard," I might tell a friend, or "I finally mailed my income tax." To make the event worth reporting it would have to be special in some way, of course. I would hardly bother doing so, otherwise.

By introducing the criterion of being special I have interjected something about the emotional significance of the experience. If the posting of the letter is of special significance, the experience is emotionally charged. The charge may be weak. I may care little about whether the letter gets mailed tonight or tomorrow. I also may think that not much is at stake should it become lost in the mail. I may even have cared so little about the outcome of my journey that I became lost in thought along the way and found myself back home a few minutes later with the letter still in hand. But if the letter did go unmailed, giving to my story an unhappy (or at least comic) ending, I presumably would laugh at myself or curse myself for having forgotten the point of my errand. In other words, the experience would remain tinctured with emotion. I might still look on it as a normally complete experience, even though the ending was more of a surprise than I might have wished.

Whatever the circumstances, the point is that a unifying emotional state, a state of conscious concern over whatever is at issue, is indeed the cement, as Dewey calls it, that holds the experience together, giving it coherence. To look on my walk to the mailbox as *an* experience does not require remaining aware of what I am doing at each and every moment, but it does require caring at some level about what I am doing. It requires being emotionally set on attaining a particular goal.

Can feelings fail to register? Can I care about something without knowing that I care? Dewey does not directly address those questions. But he does come close to doing so. He acknowledges that "attitudes and meanings derived from prior experience" can exist subconsciously and can be aroused into activity where they "become conscious thoughts and emotions." He also speaks of "a self not consciously known" (LW10, 71). Thus he allows for the possibility of being emotionally responsive to a situation without fully realizing it, which is to say, without bringing those feelings to a level of conscious awareness. This possibility bears importantly on the question of what transforms a disjointed experience into *an* experience. It suggests that by becoming more closely attuned to the emotional dimensions of experience, by pausing to consider how we feel about the situation that we are in, no matter how dim that feeling, we effectively contribute to its transformation.

Becoming more keenly aware of the emotional dimension of experience is not the same as becoming narcissistically absorbed. On the contrary. Though the emotions that we feel may belong to the self, they are complexly attached to the situation as a whole. Thus the question How do I feel? when asked by the person who is immersed in what he or she is doing, is really a shorthand way of asking, How does this situation make me feel? How are my feelings related to it? Identifying the feeling is only the first step. One must then ask, What about this complex set of conditions makes me feel this way?

Let us see where the walk to the mailbox has taken us in our attempt to draw together Dewey's observations about what constitutes *an* experience. Whether I judge my stroll to have been *an* experience in a Deweyan sense depends chiefly on its cohesiveness, on how it hangs together. This in turn rests on how I feel about it, on how fully it engages me intellectually and emotionally. Can something as inconsequential as a trip to the mailbox ever be fully engaging? Not ordinarily perhaps, but it is easy enough to imagine circumstances under which it might come close—if, for example, the letter constituted a decisive step in some larger and more important undertaking.

There is another point to be made about the mailbox example. Even though my walk may stand out experientially from what came before and what comes after, it remains connected in countless ways with both past and future events. Though we may speak of it as *an* experience in Deweyan terms, its contextuality remains. The advantage of viewing it as a discrete experience is that by doing so I isolate its eventfulness, giving the stroll an integral quality that it would not otherwise have. The capacity to consider *an* experience as discrete, lacking a past and a future, is of particular importance in coming to appreciate art objects, as will soon be evident.

THE ROLE OF MEANING IN *AN* EXPERIENCE

The primary distinction that Dewey draws in establishing how meaning operates has to do with referencing. If the meaning refers to something outside the object, event, or situation under scrutiny, meaning is said to be *extrinsic*. If it refers to the object, event, or situation itself, to qualities that inhere, *intrinsic*. Returning to the mailbox example, we might say that the chief extrinsic meaning of the evening stroll lay in its instrumental effectiveness in sending the letter on its way. Its intrinsic significance resided chiefly in its symbolic value. What it meant emotionally to the sender to have that letter on its way gave the event whatever affective coloration it may have had.

Yet we must be careful not to equate the extrinsic with the instrumental, nor the intrinsic with the affective. As Dewey points out, extrinsic meaning, which is always the product of reflection, has a way of becoming intrinsic. Moreover, the transformation from extrinsic to intrinsic meaning serves to enrich human life immeasurably. As he explains,

> In reflection, the extrinsic reference is always primary. . . . In the situation which follows upon reflection, meanings are intrinsic; they have no instrumental or subservient office, because they have no office at all. They are as much qualities of the objects in the situation as are red and black. . . . And *every reflective experience adds new shades of such intrinsic qualifications.* . . . [It enriches] the immediate significance of subsequent experiences. And it may well be that this by-product, this gift of the gods, is incomparably more valuable for living a life than is the primary and intended result of control, essential as is that control to having a life to live. (MW10, 330, emphasis added)

Dewey's reason for calling this enrichment of meaning a gift of the gods is easy to understand. The added meaning is not sought. It happens effortlessly and without notice—like a bolt from the blue. Yet in the long run, as Dewey points out, those unsought increments in intrinsic meaning may far exceed in value the instrumental payoffs on behalf of which the extrinsic meaning was initially and reflectively derived. In short, as extrinsic meaning becomes intrinsic, the meaningfulness of experience in general is correspondingly enriched. This is not to say that the expansion of either kind of meaning is always welcome. Situations, objects, and events can be fearsome as well as attractive. Added meaning may bring pain as well as joy. Even when distasteful, however, the extended meaning is often of service. It teaches us what to avoid, thereby reducing life's irritants.

Situations Versus Objects and Events

Until now I have been treating situations, objects, and events as though they were three equivalent classes of things to which meaning becomes attached. Dewey, however, differentiates between situations on the one hand and objects and events on the other. In so doing he further explicates how meaning operates.

Situations, for Dewey, constitute the "larger system of meaning" within which objects and events emerge as mere elements. He says, "By the term situation . . . is signified the fact that the subject-matter ultimately referred to in existential propositions is a complex existence that is held together, in spite of its internal complexity, by the fact that it is dominated and characterized throughout by a single quality. By 'object' [or event] is meant some element in the complex whole that is defined in abstraction from the whole of which it is a distinction" (LW5, 243). Our sense of the situation that we are in broadly determines which objects and events stand out within the enveloping whole. It causes us to pay attention to some things while ignoring others. As Dewey puts it, "The situation controls the terms of thought; for they are *its* distinctions, and applicability to it is the ultimate test of their validity" (LW5, 247). Elsewhere he remarks that our sense of what the situation is all about "suffuses, interpenetrates, colors what is now and here uppermost" (LW1, 231).

Returning to the mailbox example, we can easily see how the situation as a whole dictated the emergence of certain objects and events that contributed to the situation's resolution. At the same time, that selective awareness blocked out peripheral matters. The letter to be mailed, the mailbox as destination, and the physical task of getting there and back were key to the journey's success. So, too, were the sender's thoughts about what the mailing of the letter signified in an instrumental sense (i.e., how it contributed to the furtherance of a chain of events) and what it symbolized expressively (i.e., what it stood for as a singular event). Other aspects of the physical surroundings—the buildings along the way, the cloud cover, the street lights, the cracks in the sidewalk, the pause for a car to pass in order to cross the street—all of these were only peripherally attended if they were noticed at all. The same is true for any stray thoughts that might have occurred and other transient psychological states that had little or no bearing on the errand's accomplishment.

Having established that situations contain objects and events and having also begun to show how objects and events selectively emerge, Dewey's explication of the meaningfulness of situations takes an unexpected turn. He proceeds to insist that our sense of the situation in which we are currently immersed—no matter what its content—"is not and cannot be stated or made explicit." Instead, its meaning "is taken for granted, 'understood,' or implicit in all propositional symbolization. It forms the universe of discourse of whatever is expressly stated or of what appears as a term in a proposition." We must be cautious, however, in interpreting that statement, for as Dewey goes on to point out, "to call it 'implicit' does not signify that it is implied. It is *present throughout* as that of which whatever is explicitly stated or propounded is a distinction" (LW5, 247, emphasis added).

The notion of being situated without being able to say what one's situation is all about—that is, what one takes to be its sense or its meaning—doubtless sounds counterintuitive to readers unaccustomed to Dewey's way of thinking. As conventionally understood, the task of describing the situation that we are in presents no problem. All that we need do to accommodate anyone seeking such information is to depict the setting in some generic manner (naming its most relevant objects, perhaps) and then say a few words about what is going on, which, in Dewey's terms, means naming or describing the pervasive quality that yields a sense of the whole. (That pervasive quality is what makes the situation unique, what makes it this situation rather than that one.)

But Dewey's point is that such a description can only be offered proleptically; we can speak of it only after the fact. As soon as we begin to offer a description of the situation we are in, we have exited that situation (by transforming it into an object) and entered another one. The one that we now occupy may closely resemble the one that we have left. Indeed, the two might be physically identical. However, as enveloping wholes they differ radically. The new situation is dominated by a pervasive quality that remains its own, not matter how closely it may resemble the preceding one. Dynamically, the preceding situation is no longer an inhabited situation in the strict sense of the term. Instead, it has become an object, temporally distant from the current setting.

The writer Annie Dillard provides an example of what it means to leave one situation and enter another without so much as moving a finger. Dillard's account is worth quoting at length. She describes herself stopping at sunset to purchase fuel at a small gas station in Nowhere, Virginia. As she drinks a cup of coffee and watches the sun descend behind the mountains, a beagle puppy belonging to the station attendant comes sniffing at her shoes. Dillard continues: "I set my coffee beside me on the curb; I smell loam on the wind; I pat the puppy; I watch the mountain" (Dillard 1974, 78). And then,

> My hand works automatically over the puppy's fur, following the line of hair under his ears, down his neck, inside his forelegs, along his hot-skinned belly.
>
> Shadows lope along the mountain's rumpled flanks; they elongate like root tips, like lobes of spilling water, faster and faster. A warm purple pigment pools in each ruck and tuck of the rock; it deepens and spreads, boring crevasses, canyons. . . . The air cools; the puppy's skin is hot. I am more alive than all the world.
>
> This is it, I think, this is it, right now, the present, this empty gas station, here, this western wind, this tang of coffee on the tongue, and I am patting the puppy, I am watching the mountain. *And the second I verbalize this awareness in my brain, I cease to see the mountain or feel the puppy. I am opaque, so much black asphalt.* But at the same

second, the second I know I've lost it, I also realize that the puppy is still squirming on his back under my hand. Nothing has changed for him. . . .

I sip my coffee. I look at the mountain, which is still doing its tricks, as you look at a still beautiful face belonging to a person who was once your lover in another country years ago: with fond nostalgia, and recognition, but no real feeling save a secret astonishment that you are now strangers. Thanks. For the memories. . . . I get in the car and drive home.

. . . That I ended this experience prematurely for myself—that I drew scales over my eyes between me and the mountain and gloved my hand between me and the puppy—is not the only point. After all, it would have ended anyway. I've never seen a sunset or felt a wind that didn't. (1974, 79, emphasis added)

Dillard's point is that it was not consciousness alone that tore her from her wordless interaction with the breathtaking scenery and the appreciative puppy relishing the idle affection of a passing stranger. It was a special kind of consciousness—self-consciousness—that nudged her from one situation to another. She goes on to say,

Consciousness itself does not hinder living in the present. In fact, it is only to a heightened awareness that the great door to the present opens at all. Even a certain amount of interior verbalization is helpful to enforce the memory of whatever it is that is taking place. The gas station beagle puppy, after all, may have experienced those same moments more purely than I did, but he brought fewer instruments to bear on the same material, he had no data for comparison, and he profited only in the grossest of ways, by having an assortment of itches scratched.

Self-consciousness, however, does hinder the experience of the present. It is the one instrument that unplugs all the rest. So long as I lose myself in a tree, say, I can scent its leafy breath or estimate its board feet of lumber, I can draw its fruits or boil tea on its branches, and the tree stays alive. But the second I become aware of myself at any of these activities—looking over my own shoulder, as it were—the tree vanishes, uprooted from the spot and flung out of sight as if it had never grown. (Dillard 1974, 81)

Dillard may not be right about self-consciousness being the one instrument that unplugs all the rest. but she is surely accurate in her description of what it feels like to be wrenched from an absorbing situation by the intrusion of a wayward thought.

In an essay entitled "Experience," Ralph Waldo Emerson makes a point akin to Dillard's. "It is very unhappy," he says, "but too late to be helped, the discovery we have made, that we exist. That discovery is called the Fall of Man. Ever afterwards, we suspect our instruments. We have learned that we do not see directly, but mediately, and that we have no means of correcting these colored and distorting lenses which we are, or of computing the amount of their errors" (Emerson 1983, 487). Emerson sees self-consciousness as engendering those forms of philosophical skepticism that in the extreme lead to doubts about the existence of the material world and even cause their victims to question the presence of other minds.

It is not always self-consciousness, however, that pulls us away from a situation. We can depart for many other reasons, as ultimately we must do. As Dillard notes, musing on the abrupt termination of her rapt absorption with the dog and the setting sun, "It would have ended anyway. I've never seen a sunset or felt a wind that didn't." The point is not simply that all situations come to an end, which is, by itself, hardly worthy of notice. Rather, it is that another sure way of exiting a situation (besides by becoming self-conscious) is by trying to describe it. *As long as we remain immersed in a situation, we cannot describe it.* That is Dewey's point. The same point forces us to see Dillard's description of her initial situation (before her self-consciousness set in) as artistically deceptive or, perhaps we should say, deceptively artistic.

Her use of the present tense in describing the scene before her eyes (prior to the point where self-consciousness takes over) makes it sound as though the description and the immediate experience of taking it in occurred simultaneously. "I set my coffee beside me on the curb"; she begins. "I smell loam on the wind; I pat the puppy; I watch the mountain." If Dillard was saying those words to herself while performing the actions, she would already have been a victim of the self-consciousness that she describes as having ultimately intruded upon her attentiveness. The detail that follows the opening sentences is also presented in the present tense, which helps to extend the illusion. But there, too, it is hard to imagine her finding just the right words to capture the scene before her eyes while remaining totally engaged in that scene. The effect that she seeks is to have her readers feel as though they were present at the scene themselves, witnessing what she witnessed. Yet if we pause to think of the two events—the scene as witnessed and the scene as later described—we quickly see that they could not have taken place at the same time.

Some readers might object that it seems quite possible for a person to be totally within a situation while describing it or, more generally, quite possible for a person to inhabit more than one situation at the same time. "Imagine," one might say, "that you are the host of a party and you receive a phone call from an out-of-town friend. Through the phone the friend hears background noise and asks what is going on. You explain that a party is in progress and the friend asks for more details, whereupon you begin to name the people in attendance, describe what some of them are wearing, what they are currently doing, and so forth. Meanwhile, several of the party-goers nod to you in passing and you nod back or point helplessly at the telephone and make a wry face, thereby signaling your wish to hang up. Under such circumstances aren't you participating in the party and describing it at the same time?"

Dewey would surely allow that such could happen. But he would probably go on to insist that our telephoning party host is not inhabiting two situations at once. Instead, the situation that he is in, talking-on-the-telephone-while-attending-a-party, makes competing demands on him. He must divide his attention between the person at the other end of the line and what is going on in front of him. The unity that holds that situation together is a form of disunity. The two foci of interest vying for the host's attention threaten to pull apart, causing him to abandon one of them, at least temporarily, a move that would result in a redefinition of the situation, giving it greater cohesion. Unless or until that happens, our host is in the uncomfortable position of having to juggle two tasks at once. As Dewey points out, "Confusion and incoherence are always marks of lack of control by a single pervasive quality. The latter alone enables a person to keep track of what he is doing, saying hearing, reading, in whatever explicitly appears" (LW5, 247).

Some people are better than others at coping with situations that call for divided attention. It may be that certain individuals prefer such situations to ones that allow for total absorption in a single task or activity. Many of today's teenagers, for example, listen to the radio or watch television while doing their homework. Such preferences do not alter Dewey's claim about situations being dominated by a single pervasive quality. They merely show that, for some, the pervasive quality that is actively sought (at least part of the time) is one that calls for divided attention.

The meaning that Dewey associates with pervasive qualities of situations is one he calls *sense*. It is not the same as *feeling*, although the two concepts are closely allied. "Sense is distinct from feeling," he explains, "for it has a recognized reference; it is the qualitative characteristic of something, not just a submerged unidentified quality or tone" (LW1, 200). Sense refers to the situation itself and not simply to the feeling that the situation engenders. Moreover, the way sense operates referentially also differentiates it from *signification*, which yields a different kind of meaning. "The latter," Dewey explains, "involves use of a quality as a sign or index of something else, as when the red of a light signifies danger, and the need of bringing a moving locomotive to a stop.

The sense of a thing, on the other hand, is an immediate and immanent meaning; it is meaning which is itself felt or directly had" (LW1, 200).

The immediacy and immanence of the meaning associated with the sense of a situation connects to the broader concept of *qualitative immediacy*, which plays a central role in Dewey's theory of experience and in his aesthetics. It is important, therefore, that we get straight what Dewey is driving at when he talks about a meaning that is felt or directly had. A good way of doing that is through the distinction he makes between feeling as a psychological state, on the one hand, and making sense of a situation, on the other. Here is how he formulates that distinction:

> It is to be remarked that a situation is a whole in virtue of its immediately pervasive quality. When we describe it from the psychological side, we have to say that the situation as a qualitative whole is sensed or *felt*. Such an expression is, however, valuable only as it is taken negatively to indicate that it is *not*, as such, an object in *discourse*. Stating that it is felt is wholly misleading if it gives the impression that the situation *is* a feeling or an emotion or anything mentalistic. On the contrary, feeling, sensation and emotion have themselves to be identified and described in terms of the immediate presence of a total qualitative situation. (LW12, 73–74)

What Dewey is saying is that we sense or feel the situation we are in without thinking of it per se, without it becoming an object of reflection. Yet the situation cannot be reduced to the feelings that it engenders. On the contrary, as Dewey takes pains to point out, we can only identify and describe whatever feelings we might have by relating them to the immediate presence of the situation in which we find ourselves.

At times, however, the feeling that a situation arouses is bafflement. Under those circumstances the situation lacks coherence. In the extreme case we might say that it makes no sense whatsoever. When those conditions hold, we are led to search for elements and relations within the situation that will reveal its meaning, thereby causing it to make sense. Here is the way Dewey describes the process: "When we are baffled by perplexing conditions, and finally hit upon a clew, and everything falls into place, the whole thing suddenly, as we say, 'makes sense.' In such a situation, the clew has signification in virtue of being an indication, a guide to interpretation. But the meaning of the *whole* situation as apprehended is sense." He then points out that "whenever a situation has this double function of meaning, namely signification *and* sense, mind, intellect is definitely present" (LW1, 200, emphasis added). The meaning that feeling and sense alone contribute—the condition that Annie Dillard described as "living in the present"—is deepened or added to by the increments of meaning that reflection supplies. Dillard too, as we have seen, comments on the benefits that come with reflection. "Consciousness itself does not hinder living in the present. In fact, it is only to a heightened awareness that the great door to the present opens at all." She goes on to point out that the dog at her side "may have experienced those same moments more purely than [she] did but he brought fewer instruments to bear on the same material, he had no data for comparison, and he profited only in the grossest of ways, by having an assortment of itches scratched."

Dillard's observation fits nicely with Dewey's explanation of how the sense of a situation—the meaning directly had—becomes enriched by the meaning that signification supplies. Here is Dewey's description of the process: "In the course of experience, as far as that is an outcome influenced by thinking, objects perceived, used and enjoyed take up into their own meaning the results of thought; they become ever richer and fuller of meanings" (LW4, 134). The dynamics of that richer and more meaningful experience is what we are seeking to understand.

The Emergence of Objects and Events

We are ready now to look a little more closely at the process of signification and at the way objects and events emerge from within the confines of situations. A good place to start is with the recognition that objects and events are always contextualized. Though they may stand out within an experience, they do so because of their bearing on the direction that experience is currently taking— that is, because of the guidance given it by the experiencer's sense of the situation. Here is the way Dewey tells it.

> In actual experience, there is never any such isolated singular object or event; *an object or event is always a special part, phase, or aspect, of an environing experienced world*—a situation. The singular object stands out conspicuously because of its especially focal and crucial position at a given time in determination of some problem of use or enjoyment which the *total* complex environment presents. There is always a *field* in which observation of *this* or *that* object or event occurs. Observation of the latter is made for the sake of bringing out what that *field* is with reference to some active adaptive response to be made in carrying forward a *course* of behavior. (LW12, 72)

Objects and events, as Dewey refers to them, have both place and origin in a perceived world. They become objects and events as they figure into the ongoing activity of an experiencer. Prior to becoming perceived as objects and as events, they were but brute existences, things whose bearing on the course of behavior was either unperceived or nonexistent. Thus the lamp in my study, the pencil on my desk, the flight of a bird past my window, and all manner of other things in my immediate environment (including not just physical entities but ideational ones as well—facts that I might look up or memories that I might recall) are not objects for me, save as I attend to them. Moreover, I attend to them only as objects or events, Dewey insists, when I have some reason for doing so, that is, when they intrude upon my presence against my will (the way the passing bird just did) or when they promise to serve some purpose of mine, some end of use or enjoyment (or possibly both).

Another of Dewey's key points is that objects are invariably the product of inquiry, which is how we come to know them as objects. We test their properties. We experiment with them. We put them to use. We speak to others about them and others do the same to us. As we come to know objects in this way they acquire the kind of settled yet multifaceted meaning that enables us to employ them as means of obtaining new knowledge and of experiencing fresh enjoyment. "Objects," Dewey says, speaking again proleptically, "are the *objectives* of inquiry" (LW12, 122).

The inquiry entailed in the transformation of brute existences into objects need not be undertaken afresh by each experiencer. As I gaze at the lamp across from my desk its objecthood appears to me a given. I recognize it at once for what it is: a lamp. I know its properties. I know how to turn it off and on. I can replace its bulb, unplug its cord from its socket, or move it about the room. There is little that I need to do to ascertain its overall purpose or learn more about its usefulness. With respect to this familiar object, which might well stand for almost everything else I can point to in my present environment, inquiry seems superfluous.

But Dewey wants us to understand that the only reason I need not experiment with the lamp or my pencil or any other familiar thing is that others have already done so. As a beneficiary of that long history of inquiry, as someone who long ago became acquainted with lamps and their functions, I am released from having to inquire about them on my own. This does not mean that I need to recognize instantly every lamp I encounter. Under special circumstances I may still be puzzled by the identity of an object and have to figure it out on my own ("Oh, it's a *lamp*"). Nor does it mean that I need not bother to experiment with those lamps that have become a familiar part of my environment ("How would this lamp look if I moved it to the end table?"). All it means is that I am not perpetually puzzled by the sights and sounds that surround me nor by the thoughts that occur to me. (Dewey speaks of thoughts as "rational" objects.)

Most of the things that I encounter, whether rational or physically extant, I have encountered before and have treated as objects in this or that situation. It takes no effort, therefore, to re-cognize them as objects when I come upon them afresh.

Events as Objects, Objects as Events

Dewey often treats objects and events as though the two were virtually inseparable, as indeed they turn out to be from his perspective. What makes them so, Dewey proclaims, is that every object has a history. It has a past and a future. Therefore, it is an event. It is so even though we may seldom recognize its eventful character. We are unaccustomed to thinking of the cup on the table or the house across the way as events, yet that is the way Dewey wants us to see them. He wants to force upon us the awareness that all existences—including the existences of material things like cups and houses—have a beginning and an end. The same holds for rational objects, such as ideas, memories, and theories. Each is temporally situated. Each is buffeted by the winds of change.

Yet objects, whether material or ideational, are not events plain and simple. They are not, in other words, brute existences. Instead, they are events with meaning, events whose character has been transformed through inquiry. Whereas once they may have stood in relation to us as nothing more than unacknowledged existences, they now, as objects, are available to play an instrumental role in the conscious shaping of future experience. Every event, Dewey insists, has the potential of undergoing that kind of transformation.

Another aspect of the event-object relation deserves mention. It is that those existences that we normally think of as events—the passage of the bird outside my window, for example, or the constellation of events that we refer to as World War II—can also become objects, no less so than those existences (events), like cups and houses, that are materially embodied. Indeed, the former (like the latter) must become objects if they are to be known and used by us. This condition relates to what I was saying earlier about one's inability to describe the situation one finds oneself in at any moment in time. It is only as one steps outside that situation (event) and looks back on it retrospectively, thereby transforming it into an object, that one becomes capable of making statements about it and of linking it to other events and objects in one's life.

The Inexhaustible Meaning of Things

To objectify an event is to give it meaning. It is to bring certain of its properties into conscious awareness while ignoring others. It is to treat those acknowledged properties as as signifying something. Meaning in this sense is a function; it is, in Dewey's terms, "that office of one thing representing another, or pointing to it as implied; the operation, in short, of serving as a sign" (MW10, 329).

We must keep in mind that the potential meaning that we might ascribe to an event is virtually limitless and is not confined to the particular meaning that we might happen to assign to it. An object is always an abstraction. It is like a sketch of the thing itself, a sketch in which certain features are highlighted and others overlooked. The event with meaning (i.e., the object) is not to be mistaken for the event itself. Dewey puts it this way: "What a thing means is another *thing;* it doesn't mean a meaning" (MW8, 75). That other thing—what it means—is not to be confused with the thing to which it refers, though there is always the danger of doing just that. We are tempted to treat existences as objects whose properties are completely known and understood, rather than as objects possessing properties that we might also have considered. Ordinarily this oversight has no serious consequences. It is even efficacious in that it prevents us from getting tangled up in irrelevancies when time is of the essence. It can, of course, have serious consequences if it leads to systematically ignoring the expressive properties of things.

The Complementarity of Use and Enjoyment

Why bother to identify objects within situations? Why ascribe meaning to events? The first answer is that we have no choice; we can't help doing so. Soon after birth the newborn starts to become aware of being immersed in a world that is full of objects. The developing child discovers that people employ speech and that things have names and, with that discovery, is launched on the path not only of learning a language but, more important, of transforming the world of the infant—famously described by William James as "one great blooming, buzzing confusion" (James 1890, I:488)—into an environment of recognizable sights and sounds.

There are two additional explanations for the human inclination to pick out objects within the environment and invest them with meaning. The first is that doing so turns out to be useful; the second is that it is enjoyable. When we use objects to help resolve problematic situations (i.e., situations whose properties we wish to see changed), the objects become, as Dewey says, "*means* of obtaining knowledge of something else" (LW12, 122). Seen in this light, they are primarily instrumental. In another formulation of the same idea Dewey says, "An object . . . is a set of qualities treated as *potentialities* for specified existential consequences" (LW12, 132). Another way of talking about the instrumental function of objects is to speak of them in relational terms, to see the object as having connections with other elements within the environment, to see how it bears on other things. The useful object becomes a link within a chain of actions. It becomes integrated into a method, which comprises a form of use.

The things that we treat as useful objects—that is, as tools for the attainment of desired ends—are also events to be enjoyed (or suffered through) in their own right. The same is true of objects that serve no use save as impediments to progress. The enjoyment (or the dislike) of things, Dewey reminds us, "is a declaration that natural existences are not mere passage ways to another passage way, and so on *ad infinitum*" (LW1, 74). In addition to being useful or unuseful, things are what they are. They have meaning and value (or disvalue) in and of themselves. As Dewey puts it: "In every event there is something obdurate, self-sufficient, wholly immediate, neither a relation nor an element in a relational whole, but [something] terminal and exclusive" (LW1, 85). Further along in the same passage he speaks of "those irreducible, infinitely plural, undefinable and indescribable qualities which a thing must *have* in order to be and in order to be capable of becoming the subject of relations and a theme of discourse" (LW1, 74).

The immediacy of existences (like that of situations) yields a form of meaning that is sensed rather than signified. According to Dewey, these are "meanings that present themselves directly as possessions of objects which are experienced." "Here there is no need for a code or convention of interpretation; the meaning is as inherent in immediate experience as is that of a flower garden" (LW10, 89).

The Expressiveness (Immediacy) of Objects

Another way of speaking of those meanings that are directly possessed by objects is to call them *expressive*. What do they express? According to Dewey, they express "that quality which is one with the character of an object." They render its character "distinct by emphasis" (LW10, 207). What Dewey means by an object's character is that combination of qualities that gives the object its distinctiveness, that makes it one of a kind. In these terms, every object in its uniqueness possesses expressive meaning, awaiting our perception.

Our perception of an object's uniqueness is not something we customarily dwell on. It does not always register on us, not even in the case of those objects with which we have frequent commerce. In fact, it may be that such familiar objects are precisely the ones whose expressive qualities (i.e., whose character and uniqueness) we most frequently overlook. Why should that be so? Because in the normal course of events we are usually absorbed in the instrumental properties of such objects, in what they can do for us, in how they might further our immediate needs and interests. So absorbed, we tend to overlook their immediacy. We respond to them indifferently, treating them not as singularities but as one of a kind or even one of many. Over time, Dewey says, "apathy and torpor conceal this expressiveness by building a shell about objects" (LW10, 109).

Herein lies an important aspect of the mission of art. One of its ultimate purposes, in Dewey's view, is to reawaken our sensibilities, causing us to see once again what we have come to overlook. "Art," Dewey tells us, "throws off the covers that hide the expressiveness of experienced things; it quickens us from the slackness of routine and enables us to forget ourselves by finding ourselves in the delight of experiencing the world about us in its varied qualities and forms. It intercepts every shade of expressiveness found in objects and orders them to a new experience of life" (LW10, 110).

Another aspect of how meaning operates within Dewey's system of thought concerns the way meanings multiply. The more we know about an object, the more we discover about its connections with other worldly things, the richer its meaning becomes. Moreover, this increased richness applies not only to the *instrumental* meaning of an object, which has to do with its explicit usefulness. It also extends to what Dewey calls its *expressive* meaning. How this happens is not entirely clear in Dewey's account, as we have already seen, though he says enough to provide a rough idea of how it occurs. Essentially, his notion is that those aspects of meaning that are reflectively attained (i.e., the ones reached through inquiry) gradually become absorbed by the objects themselves. Thereafter, those objects are altered in their qualitative immediacy. We perceive them as possessing those meanings that experience has added on. Once I have learned how a hammer functions, for example, I no longer look upon it as a strange wooden object with an oddly shaped piece of metal at one end. I see it immediately as an object of use, ready to be grasped and put to work. The hammer's usefulness is no longer something I need to discover or empirically test. It belongs to the hammer as surely as the hammer's name does—even more so, for the hammer's name changes from one language to another, whereas an understanding of its use transcends linguistic barriers.

Meaning and Value as Inferential, Imaginative Constructions

To attach meaning or value to an event (i.e., to transform it from a mere existence into an object) adds to its significance. That extension of meaning (or significance) takes place inferentially and imaginatively. It requires that we acknowledge something beyond the immediately given—something, that is, beyond the here and now. To name an event is to set that imaginative process in motion, for, as Dewey points out, "events when once they are named lead an independent and double life. In addition to their original existence, they are subject to ideal experimentation: their meanings may be infinitely combined and re-arranged *in imagination,* and the outcome of this inner experimentation—which is thought—may issue forth in interaction with crude or raw events" (LW1, 132, emphasis added). That act of imagination constitutes for Dewey both the essence of consciousness and the heart of thought. "All *conscious* experience has of necessity some degree of imaginative quality," he says. "The experience enacted is human and conscious only as that which is given here and now is extended by meanings and values drawn from what is absent in fact and present only imaginatively" (LW10, 276).

Inference enters the picture from the start, but it grows in significance as we seek to imagine what would happen if we did thus and so with the event in question. Again from Dewey: "The business of reflection is to take events which brutely occur and brutely affect us, to convert them into objects *by means of inference as to their possible consequences*" (LW1, 245, emphasis added). In most instances involving real-life problems those inferences, imaginatively drawn, are empirically tested by us or by others. We use them as scientists might use hypotheses, as guides to action in a continuing effort to rearrange the situation that we are in to better suit our needs. The fruit of that experimentation, summed over countless situations and transmitted to others through myriad channels, constitutes what is known about the object in question. Thus, "we may not need to do any thinking now when some event occurs, but if we have thought about it before [or have benefited from the thinking of others], the outcome of that thinking is funded as a directly added and deepened meaning of the event." Dewey concludes that "the great reward of exercising the power of thinking is that there are no limits to the possibility of carrying over *into* the objects and events of life, meanings originally acquired by thoughtful examination, and hence no limit to the continual growth of meaning in human life" (LW8, 128, emphasis added).

Dewey distinguishes between extrinsic and intrinsic meaning. The same distinction applies, he avers, to the dual concepts of significance and value. *Extrinsic* meaning (likewise, significance or value) refers to what an object or event signifies. It has to do with the subservient and instrumental role that the object or event plays in the attainment of some end. *Intrinsic* meaning (likewise, significance or value) inheres within the object or event itself. It intrinsically characterizes the thing experienced. Intrinsic meaning is also instrumental, but in a different way than extrinsic meaning is. It is not put to use directly. Instead, it serves to enrich the immediacy of subsequent experience. That enrichment Dewey looks on as being so wonderful and yet so fortuitous as to be called a gift of the gods.

Intrinsic meaning is consummatory and final. It is meaning enjoyed for its own sake, as opposed to having a practical or utilitarian force. It is also expressive. Those situations or experiences in which such meaning predominates Dewey calls *aesthetic.* "Esthetic experience is imaginative," but he quickly points out that "all *conscious* experience has of necessity some degree of imaginative quality" (LW10, 276), a fact that sometimes gets obscured in discussions of how the arts work. The difference between aesthetic experience and ordinary experience lies in the relative predominance of the imaginative element. It predominates in aesthetic experience, Dewey explains, "because meanings and values that are wider and deeper than the particular here and now in which they are anchored are realized by way of *expressions* although not by way of an object that is physically efficacious in relation to other objects" (LW10, 277).

Another Elementary Example: A Breakfast Teaspoon

Let me review the distinctions that Dewey makes with respect to meaning. He distinguishes between the extrinsic and intrinsic meanings of objects and events. The former deal with meanings in use, the latter with meanings-divorced-from-use (at least in the conventional sense). All meanings are initially imaginative; they refer inferentially to what is not present. And intrinsic meanings are expressive, final, consummatory. The situations in which they predominate are classified as aesthetic. To see how these distinctions might apply within a lifelike setting, let us imagine the gradual unfolding of yet another ordinary event, much like the walk to the mailbox, but this time a mundane encounter with an ordinary teaspoon at the breakfast table.

At the start I look about for something to stir my coffee. My gaze falls on the spoon that lies beside my plate. Its meaning and value at that instant are both extended and imaginative in that they draw upon knowledge that is absent in fact and present only imaginatively (i.e., my knowledge of what spoons are for, my recognition that this particular object is a spoon, my judgment that it is capable of doing the job, and so forth). The spoon's meaning for me at this moment is what Dewey would call extrinsic. It is restricted to meaning-in-use. Moreover, the particular use to which the spoon will be put is both narrow and conventional. (I could as easily have thought of using the edge of the spoon to crack a soft-boiled egg, for example, in which case the spoon would still have been looked upon as instrumental, though rather less conventionally so.) At this point, the spoon's meaning is essentially cognitive to the extent that I am conscious of thinking of it at all, which means that I am not particularly conscious of feeling one way or another about the spoon.

Let us next imagine that as I lay the spoon in the cup's saucer, having used it to stir my coffee, I become momentarily aware of its intrinsic worth as a manufactured object. I note how carefully it is crafted, admire its luster and its shape, the simplicity of its lines, the balanced feel of holding it. All of those properties refer to qualities intrinsic to the spoon itself. They have little or nothing to do with its instrumental value. These intrinsic aspects of the spoon's meaning are consummatory and final. I enjoy them for their own sake. They are also expressive and aesthetic. They were presumably put there by the silversmith or the spoon's designer. They have been realized by way of expression, as Dewey puts it, and they are now anchored in the object itself.

All of those intrinsic qualities can be modified. The spoon can lose its luster. It can become dented or stained. Even its overall spoonness can be made to disappear, as would happen if the spoon was grossly bent out of shape or if it was melted down in order to reuse the metal for some other purpose. At least for the time being, however, those extensions of meaning belong to the spoon. They do not exist solely in the eyes of the beholder. They are as real as any other of the spoon's properties.

The separation between my instrumental use of the spoon and my appreciation of its intrinsic worth need not be nearly as sequential and as clear-cut as I have made it here. I could have become aware of the spoon's beauty while stirring my coffee. Had I done so, I might then have been aware of the spoon's instrumental value and its intrinsic worth simultaneously. Such a dual focus, the flip-flopping back and forth from the instrumental to the expressive, characterizes a broad class of experiences in which well-crafted tools play a significant role.

Let us return to our imaginary breakfast table, where I next recall how I came to own the spoon. This aspect of the spoon's meaning—its status as, say, a wedding gift—also has little to do with the object's use as a utensil. Its status, too, is intrinsic to the spoon, or expressive, final, and consummatory—though not in the same way as the other qualities that I have mentioned. What does the spoon express nonmaterially? It expresses a friend's thoughtfulness and perhaps also her good taste. Why is that aspect of the spoon's meaning final and consummatory? It is so because at this particular moment the spoon's meaning is enjoyed for its own sake.

Knowledge of the spoon's history as a gift increases the object's worth for its owner (and perhaps for its giver as well) but not necessarily for anyone else, making such an extension of meaning and value *personal* or even *sentimental*— thus introducing yet another set of categories into which meanings might be classified. We must, however, keep those newly introduced designations separate from the ones that we have been discussing, even though certain of the resemblances between the two may prompt us to collapse them. An object that is of great personal or sentimental value to someone is, by definition, replete with expressive meaning for that person. Yet that same object might also be appreciated for possessing qualities that others might readily discern. Its expressive meaning, in other words, might be either private or public, or both. The same applies to its instrumental meaning. That, too, may be either privately understood or widely shared.

Let us add a final layer of complexity to our spoon example and imagine the spoon to be an antique and a very special one at that. Let us suppose that it was once owned and handled by Queen Victoria. What does that piece of information add to the spoon's meaning? Shall we call that extension of meaning instrumental or expressive? It could be called either or both, depending on the circumstances. When I gaze at the spoon and thrill at the thought that Queen Victoria may have stirred her tea with it, just as I am using it now for my coffee, its historical meaning is being expressively undergone. If, however, I make use of that same knowledge to bolster a historical argument of some kind, I am treating it instrumentally. I could conceivably be doing both at the same time.

What does that added knowledge of the spoon's history do to the experience that I have with the object? It extends and deepens it. It does so, moreover, in each of the three ways that we have been discussing. The spoon's instrumentality now includes its power to evoke thoughts of Queen Victoria, a power unlike that of any other spoon in my possession. The aesthetic quality of the experience that I have with the spoon is likewise enhanced. My enjoyment as I look on it has noticeably increased. This is not to say that the spoon has become more beautiful or more elegant in design or more perfect in balance. But it is to acknowledge an added source of pleasure and pride occasioned by the thought of my being the spoon's present owner. That added pleasure, Dewey would insist, is fundamentally aesthetic in nature. It is so because it is immediate and final. The spoon, perceived aesthetically, is what it is and nothing more. It is enjoyed for its own sake.

The spoon's expressiveness has been added to by my knowledge of the spoon's history. I now see the spoon not just as a beautiful work of art or as a gift from a friend but as a historical object. It is now "Queen Victoria's spoon," a designation that belongs to the spoon itself, much as does its elegant design, its balance, and its worthiness as a memorable gift. The spoon's royal lineage is not physically embedded in its form and structure in the same way as is its luster and balance, but it belongs to the object all the same. It is part of its history, and those who know of its past find it an extension of the spoon's expressive meaning.

I will stop here with the example of the spoon. There is no end to the layers of meaning that could be added. That, too, is one of Dewey's major conclusions. As he points out, "Any experience, however trivial in its first appearance, is capable of assuming an indefinite richness of significance by extending its range of perceived connections" (MW9, 225).

Still, an additional point remains to be extracted from the teaspoon example, namely, that the boundaries of a situation can vary perceptually in both breadth and depth. Under certain conditions the boundaries can be so narrowed as to include little more than a single physical object and the range of meanings that it evokes. When used to stir a beverage, the spoon was one object among many others, including the cup, the sugar bowl, the stirring motion required to dissolve the sugar, and so forth. As soon as I began to concentrate on the spoon itself, those other useful objects faded in importance. They became insignificant. The spoon alone (and all that it stood for) commanded my attention. Spatially, I centered my attention on it.

This shift of focus I have characterized as a move from an initial concern with the spoon's instrumental meaning to a concern in which its expressive meaning predominated. The shift was also from practical to aesthetic concerns. As my focus changed, the spoon was transformed. It went from being an ordinary tool to an art object, a treasured gift, and, ultimately, a rare historical artifact.

That transformation entailed a temporary withdrawal from the situation with which the example began and to which its enactment in real life might ultimately return. For the space of a few seconds at least, I inhabited a different situation, one in which more practical considerations dropped away. Discussing such conditions, Dewey says, "There are situations in which self-enclosed, discrete, individualized characters dominate. They constitute the subject-matter of esthetic experience; and every experience is esthetic in as far as it is final or arouses no search for some other experience. . . . The fine arts have as their purpose the construction of objects of just such experiences" (LW4, 188).

My absorption in the spoon's beauty, its status as a gift, and its historical significance merits the term *aesthetic* in Dewey's lexicon. Yet such brief interludes of being absorbed with an object hardly add up to an aesthetic experience in the fullest sense. To qualify for the latter designation I would need to undergo a more extended and self-sufficient experience than the one with the spoon allowed. Here is where the arts come in. Their purpose is the construction of just such experiences. We now turn to Dewey's conception of how the arts contribute to that end.

DEWEY'S VIEW OF HOW THE ARTS WORK

Dewey sees the arts as serving three major functions. They first lead to consummatory experiences that often stand unrivaled in their intensity and meaningfulness. "Experience in its integrity" is his way of referring to the holistic nature of such encounters (LW10, 278). Our interactions with art objects epitomize what it means to undergo *an* experience, a term with a very special meaning for Dewey.

The arts do more than provide us with fleeting moments of elation and delight. They expand our horizons. They contribute meaning and value to future experience. They modify our ways of perceiving the world, thus leaving us and the world itself irrevocably changed. Those enduring changes constitute the second of Dewey's conceptions of how the arts potentially serve us. Their dynamics derive from his account of how experience operates in general. He explains: "The world we have experienced becomes an integral part of the self that acts and is acted upon in further experience. In their physical occurrence, things and events experienced pass and are gone. But something of their meaning and value is retained as an integral part of the self" (LW10, 109). That residue of our encounters with art objects—the record of their impact that lingers in the form of enduring changes within the self—might be said to comprise art's *instructional* function, if we take that term to refer broadly to the fruit of all life's lessons, whether explicitly taught or casually learned. The arts refresh our sensibilities. They aid in the reconstruction of old habits. They teach us new ways of thinking, feeling, and perceiving.

A third function that the arts may serve is in a way synonymous with Dewey's mission as a philosopher in *Art as Experience*. What he tries to do in that book is to adopt a bird's-eye view of aesthetic experience. He gazes down on it from a high level of abstraction. His purpose in doing so is to come up with something like an aerial map of the terrain below. Such a perspective "may be of assistance to the direct experience of others, as a survey of a country is of help to the one who travels through it" (LW10, 313).

Dewey's method provides yet another a way of learning from the arts and of teaching others what they have to offer. It, too, is instructional in its outcome, just as direct encounters with particular art objects are (or can be). Yet his method differs significantly from those individual lessons in that it is a way to teach us something about aesthetic experience in general—its generic features—rather than a way to engage us in the immediacy of an encounter with a particular art object. In Dewey's own words, his goal is to reveal "what a work of art is as an experience: the kind of experience which constitutes it" (LW10, 313).

What good is such a lesson? What can we hope to gain from it? There are two major domains of application. One pertains directly to the arts, the other to life in general. With respect to the arts, becoming acquainted with the generic properties of an aesthetic experience promises to enrich our future encounters with individual works of art. As Dewey puts it, "Stating what a work of art is as an experience, may render particular experiences of particular works of art more pertinent to the object experienced, more aware of its own content and intent" (LW10, 313). If, for example, we come to understand that successful art objects or performances cohere expressively or that most exhibit a balance among their constituent parts, we might ask how this or that work manages to comply with those demands. These generic properties become what Dewey calls criteria of judgment; they might serve as the basis of criticism for either the artist at work or her audience. Dewey warns against looking on such criteria as standards of measurement or as rules or prescriptions, but he clearly sees them as instrumental in judging individual works.

The same criteria can be applied to experience in general. Once we have identified the distinguishing characteristics of an experience centered on an outstanding work of art, we can inquire into the presence or absence of the same properties in ordinary experience. We then may proceed to ask how such properties might be brought into being where and when we find them missing. This is not to say that all of life may come to exhibit experience in its integrity, nor is it to say that we necessarily would relish such a condition were it possible. It is to suggest that more of life might be made more meaningful than we find it to be if only we would bend our individual and collective wills in that direction. What holds true for experience in general may also apply to more specialized forms of experience, such as those occurring within schools and classrooms.

Here I seek to present Dewey's conception of the generic traits of those experiences that are *distinctively* aesthetic. I stress the qualifier because Dewey does not restrict the adjective *aesthetic* to experiences that clearly warrant such a label. In his view *all* of experience has an aesthetic component, even though that component may often be overlooked or ignored. Some experiences, however, are predominantly aesthetic and are acknowledged as such. It is these experiences that concern us here.

Another distinction needs be made. It is not one that Dewey himself explicitly makes, though I expect he would condone my making it, for he seems to take its application for granted throughout *Art as Experience*. It is the distinction between aesthetic experiences that have nothing to do with art objects of any kind and those that are specifically focused on such objects. The former experiences take many forms and typically occur somewhat unexpectedly. They might be occasioned by almost any set of conditions—a walk in the woods, a swim in the lake, the sight of children playing in the park, the sound of birdsong at dawn. They are the kind of experience that Emerson famously described in *Nature* when he wrote, "Crossing a bare common, in snow puddles, at twilight, under a clouded sky, without having in my thoughts any occurrence of special good fortune, I have enjoyed a perfect exhilaration. I am glad to the brink of fear" (Emerson 1983, 10). Though such experiences are obviously aesthetic in character, they are not designedly so. The second category of aesthetic experiences, those involving art objects, entail purposeful design. The enjoyment derived from them, on the part of either their creators or others, is intimately connected with that design. So, too, is the extension of meaning and value that eventuates from the experiences.

As a way of acknowledging this distinction, I shall use the term *art-centered aesthetic experiences* or, more commonly, *art-centered experiences* to refer to experiences that focus on art objects. The others I will speak of as *aesthetic experiences in general* or as *naturally occurring aesthetic experiences*. Because Dewey is chiefly concerned with art-centered experiences in *Art as Experience*, the naturally occurring kind will hardly be mentioned at all.

How does an art-centered experience differ from one that is equally fulfilling but has some other focus? Dewey's ready answer, as we have already seen, is that the two do not differ, at least not fundamentally. Aesthetic experiences, whether involving art objects or not, resemble satisfying experiences in general. All such experiences are marked by a unity of form and content. Each is characterized by a single pervasive quality. They all exhibit some degree of expressiveness. They all unfold temporally. They all possess meaning and value. They all exhibit rhythm and balance of one kind or another. The list of their common properties could go on.

Yet, for Dewey, experiences involving art objects stand apart in the intensity and clarity of those properties that mark integral experiences. They also come across as being more concentrated in their impact and more integrated in their cohesiveness than do most other encounters with the world, even those that we find to be fulfilling in other ways. Describing their integral quality, Dewey says, "The uniquely distinguishing feature of esthetic experience is exactly the fact that no such distinction of self and object exists in it, since it is esthetic in the degree in which organism and environment cooperate to institute an experience in which the two are so fully integrated that each disappears" (LW10, 254). Nor is the wiping out of the self-object distinction the only form that integration takes within an art-centered experience. Dewey adds: "In art as an experience, actuality and possibility or ideality, the new and the old, objective material and personal response, the individual and the universal, surface and depth, sense and meaning, are integrated in an experience in which they are all transfigured from the significance that belongs to them when isolated in reflection" (LW10, 301). I will have more to say later about the dualities that Dewey mentions.

Selection and Rejection in the Service of a Qualitative Whole

How do art-centered experiences achieve the qualities of intensity, clarity, concentration, and integration that Dewey identifies? A large part of the answer lies in the two terms *selection* and *rejection*. Art, Dewey tells us, "is a selection of what is significant, with rejection by the very same impulse of what is irrelevant, and thereby the significant is compressed and intensified" (LW10, 211). Reduced to a rule of thumb, the artist's task boils down to this: Retain the essential and get rid of everything else. Strict adherence to that advice can have only one outcome: a finished work of art, stripped of all irrelevancies, pristine in its freshness and purity. Nothing could be simpler, nothing more assured. The trick, of course, lies in putting that rule into practice.

What controls or guides the artist's process of selection and rejection? Dewey refers to the guiding force as an "impulse." Elsewhere, as in the following, he speaks of the artist's (or the art appreciator's) sense of the qualitative whole. "The logic of artistic construction and esthetic appreciation is peculiarly significant because they exemplify in accentuated and purified form the control of selection of detail and of mode of relation, or integration, by a qualitative whole" (LW5, 251). The point is not that other forms of *an* experience are lacking in selection and rejection on the part of the experiencer. All of perception, and therefore all of conscious thought, entails selective attention and its correlate, inattention. So, too, a sense of an enveloping whole plays a guiding role in ordinary experience, much as it does for artists and their audiences. We have already seen how that sense operates to define a situation. Recall, for example, the way certain objects stood out in the hypothetical walk to the mailbox while others faded into the background. Art-centered aesthetic experiences are by no means unique in either of these ways.

The difference is more one of degree than of kind. While at work, the artist selects and rejects more self-consciously and more intently than do most people most of the time. She does so, moreover, more than in other moments of her own life. The artist at work is also more keenly attentive than usual to the emerging sense of an enveloping whole, a sense of the whole that guides the selection and placement of component parts. The person who comes to appreciate a work of art (someone other than the artist) must somehow take the thoroughness and the sensitivity of the artist's selection and rejection into account. Likewise, the art appreciator comes to grasp the work's overarching unity in a manner akin to (but not the same as) the artist's.

To speak of the artist as working intently and as being guided by an overall conception of the work is not to say that she must be capable of articulating from the start what the finished product will sound or look like. Nor must she be able to say where she is headed each step of the way. That sense of the whole lying behind or beneath artistic decisions may only register intuitively. However, it is the acuity and the prominence of that feeling of what fits or what is called for that serves to differentiate much of what the artist (or the earnest art appreciator) does from actions or decisions that shape our everyday world.

Yet being more perceptually acute than most others and being subservient to a sense of the whole tell but a part of the story. The artist's heightened sensitivity to what fits cannot operate in isolation, nor can her grasp of what constitutes the whole. Both must inevitably be influenced by her background of experience—her funded intelligence, as Dewey might say—which includes not only her mastery of technique but also her knowledge of the artistic tradition within which she works or from which she seeks to depart. Knowledge of the tradition can often be of decisive help. As Dewey points out, "Even the work of an original temperament may be relatively thin, as well as tending to the bizarre, when it is not informed with a wide and varied experience of the traditions of the art in which the artist operates" (LW10, 269).

To take but one instance of how those traditions operate, consider the problem of how to present a work of art in a way that maximizes its integrity as a freestanding object. Ultimately, a work's cohesion and self-sufficiency depend on the relation among its component parts. The relational criteria remain internal to the work itself, but they receive strong support from the conventions of presentation that have come to be taken for granted within the traditions associated with each art form. In painting, for example, works are usually mounted in frames and often are lighted in ways that help to separate them from their surroundings. Musical works are likewise performed in settings that are made as free of extraneous sounds as possible, thus allowing a work to be heard clearly and distinctly. The hush that falls over the audience before the music begins and the applause that comes afterward frame the work no less than wood and gilt frame paintings. Plays, operas, ballets, and other theatrical events have their own traditions of staging and presentation in which the dimming and raising of houselights, the opening and closing of curtains, and the use of other devices play a significant role in readying the audience for what is to come, in marking significant junctures, such as scenes and acts, and in drawing the event to a close. Even written works are packaged and designed in ways that make them stand out as entities.

There are also standardized physical dimensions associated with various genres of artworks. A sonnet has fourteen lines. A novel is usually three or four hundred pages long. A symphony typically has four movements. A modern play conventionally has three acts. These and other conventions help to establish audience expectations for what constitutes a whole and complete work. They contribute in no small measure to the sense of fulfillment that a successful work provides.

All of this is a way of pointing out that the achievement of a whole and self-contained quality that we commonly associate with a completed work of art does not occur solely as a result of the artist's having been sensitive to the fit of things within the work. The latter attribute is crucial, of course. The artist is aided, however, in accomplishing that sense of the whole by a vast array of conventions, and customs associated with each artistic genre.

Before turning from this discussion of the role played in aesthetic undertakings by the artist's sensitivity to detail and her concern with the fit of things, I must say a word about those works of art that appear to contradict what has just been said—those in which attention to detail and other manifestations of artistic fastidiousness are conspicuously lacking. This topic will come up again when treating the larger question of whether Dewey's conception of how art-centered experiences truly operate is hopelessly outdated. For the present I will restrict my attention to that aspect of the question that has to do with selection and rejection in service of an enveloping whole.

The arts today include many works in which the principle of selection and rejection as laid out in the preceding few paragraphs seems almost to be ignored, if not consciously violated. Indeed, some of the most sought-after works in recent years have the look and sound—at least to the uninitiated—of having been almost haphazardly constructed. Paint dribbles and drips down the surface of canvases. Street noises are incorporated into musical works. Words selected at random are offered as poems. What shall we say about such practices? What do they imply about the principle of selection and rejection? Has that principle ceased to operate in the construction of today's art? If so, does not its abandonment undermine Dewey's emphasis on unity and coherence right from the start? I believe the answer to that question is no, and I will try to explain why in Chapter 2. For now I will make do with the assertion that artists who incorporate chance elements into their work and even those who allow their work to take on a rough or unfinished appearance have by no means abandoned the principle of selection and rejection as Dewey intends it to be understood. Indeed, if Dewey is correct, that choice does not belong to them. It is not something that artists can avoid doing. Selection and rejection are mandated by the conditions in which the artist works (the artist herself being a part of those conditions, of course). Choice enters the picture not because the artist selects to choose (or selects to refrain from choosing) but simply because there is no conceivable alternative. The inevitability of choice is what makes selection and rejection the hallmark of art-centered experiences.

Selection and rejection takes place throughout experience, as already noted. It is chiefly the way the artist goes about selecting and rejecting, the thoroughness and sensitivity that she brings to those tasks, that distinguishes what she does while at work from what goes on elsewhere. So the question becomes, Do those works that appear to be spontaneously executed evince an absence of attention to the work as a whole or even a failure to consider detail? Do they reveal the artist to have been asleep at the job? To see why the answer to that question is usually no, we must broaden our understanding of the field of choice in which selection and rejection operates. We must see it as extending far beyond the sheer physical materials out of which the art object is constructed. That field includes the artist herself and all she brings to the work. It also includes the external forces that impinge on the work and that threaten or promise to leave their mark upon it. These forces include uncontrolled forces whose intrusions we variously ascribe to chance, accident, and error.

This conception of the influences at work in the construction of an art object enables us to see that the apparent inattention to detail or the inclusion of chance events and accidental occurrences may themselves have been chosen by artists. What at first may look like evidence of inattention or nonchalance turns out, on closer scrutiny, to be a way of conveying a different message entirely, a way of saying that what really counts in this work is not its neatness and its polish but something quite different, something having little or nothing to do with that conception of what art is all about.

Materials and Media

Dewey makes much of the fact that all art objects have a physical existence. They involve material—physical stuff of one kind or another—that is worked on by the artist. In the process of that work, two things happen. First, the raw stuff is transformed into something else. It becomes a *medium,* a mode of language, an organ of expression and communication. Second, when the work is successful, the material adds something of its own to the communication. Its value as *material* contributes to the work of art. It is as though the making of the art object has managed to bring the material to life, helping it to realize its potential. Dewey summarizes this transformation thus: "The abiding struggle of art is thus to convert materials that are stammering or dumb in ordinary experience into eloquent media" (LW10, 233).

To say that physical material becomes a medium of expression means that it becomes a means of communication, a way in which meaning is conveyed. It also means that the material itself becomes inextricably entwined in the work's meaning. As Dewey puts it, "Not all means are media. There are two kinds of means. One kind is external to that which is accomplished; the other kind is taken up into the consequences produced and remains immanent in them" (LW10, 201).

The repeated use of the words *means, meaning,* and *medium* in my own statement and in the brief quotation from Dewey may be confusing to some. To clarify matters, I need to say a bit more about Dewey's two kinds of means, even though doing so requires a return to a set of distinctions already made in connection with the way meaning operates in *an* experience.

The first of Dewey's two kinds of means works like a shovel or a pipeline. It transports meaning from here to there but is not itself altered in the process (save for normal wear and tear, as happens to physical objects like shovels and pipelines). The means is, as Dewey says, external to that which is accomplished. We also call such a means instrumental. It is a way of getting something done. Not only is it external to what is accomplished, but it also pales in significance when placed beside that accomplishment.

The second of the two kinds of means, the one to which Dewey attaches the term *media*, cannot be separated from the meaning that it conveys. The meaning is, as it were, embedded within the object. Moreover, the union is irrevocable. The last remnants of sand can be wiped from a shovel, and the residual film of oil can be wiped from the pipeline, but embedded meaning is there to stay. To acknowledge the permanence of that fusion we speak of the material as having been qualitatively transformed. It has now become a medium.

The meaning embedded within an art object is expressive. The finished product is always a medium of expression. It is so, in part, because of what the artist does in working with the material at hand and, in part, because of what she brings of herself to the task of construction. As Dewey says, "Objective material becomes the matter of art only as it is transformed by entering into relations of doing and being undergone by an individual person with all his characteristics of temperament, special manner of vision, and unique experience." It is this meshing of the objective material with the personal history and characteristics of the artist that leads Dewey to declare that "the medium of expression in art is neither objective nor subjective" (LW10, 292). Nor is it one *and* the other. It is a fusion of the two.

The way a work of art helps to bring its physical material to life requires explanation, for that aspect of a medium's constitution is not always apparent, not even to artists themselves. One need only attend a student art show from time to time in order to see how the expressive potentiality of the material being used is often overlooked. The aspiring artist does not take advantage, in other words, of what the raw material has to offer. A reminder of how easy it is for that to happen became forcefully evident to me recently while attending an exhibition featuring works in glass by student artists around the nation. As I wandered through that exhibit I thought often of Dewey's remarks about material that is stammering and dumb being transformed into eloquent media. That transformation, it seemed to me, was present in some of the works but conspicuously missing in others.

If we think of what glass is like as material, several of its key properties come quickly to mind. It can be opaque or transparent; it can be made as flat and thin as a sheet of paper or as delicately elongated as a strand of human hair; it can also be as thick and clunky as a cement block or as large and rough-hewn as a boulder; it can be made to splinter or shatter; it can be cut, ground, etched upon, polished, melted, and spun; it can be given an edge as sharp as a razor's; it can be mixed with pigments that give it color, or it can remain colorless; it can be painted or stained; when in a near molten state, it can be twisted and bent into forms that retain their shape when cooled; when used as a lens, it can magnify, shrink, or distort whatever is looked at through it; it can be made to give off a musical tinkle or a resounding crash when struck. Perhaps most important of all from the standpoint of its artistic use are the properties that glass exhibits in the presence of light. When faceted, it can become an object that glistens and glitters, giving off starlike bursts of refracted and reflected light; used as a window, it can allow light to pass through unimpeded, becoming nearly invisible itself, or it can effectively block light, as might a mirror. It can even reflect light while remaining transparent, making it possible for a viewer to choose between looking at the reflected image or at what lies beyond the glass.

Several of these properties of glass were highlighted and used effectively by several of the student artists. Objects of delicate shape and color were made even more delicate by the fragility of the material out of which they were made. There were intricate pieces of sculpture, for example, whose gossamer quality made them seem suspended in air and almost too fragile to touch. There were works that featured the transparency of glass and others that took advantage of its opacity. Some constructions were made to peer into; others threw back reflected light. There were even several objects that made ironic or humorous use of glass's transparency—clear windows that looked out on nothing, for example, and tiny boxes with glass tops whose unlikely contents (an apple seed, dried garlic skins) seemed designed to tease or confuse the curious viewer. All of those different works did indeed incorporate the physical material of construction into the work as a whole and did so in a way that took advantage of one or more of the characteristic properties of glass.

In the same exhibit, however, were other works whose creators seemed to have given little thought to the distinctive properties of the material with which they worked. There were lifelike objects—sculpted animals, for example, and miniature human figures, including a prizefighter made of garish red glass, his left arm cocked to throw a blow—each looking as out of place as a hot dog at a banquet. There were hunks of melted glass that looked as though they had been scraped from the floor of a glass furnace at the close of a working day. Odd shapes and colors, true enough, but little more than that. Did they have anything to do with glass per se? If so, I could not say what it was, save, perhaps, that the residue extracted from a glass furnace is no less attractive than any other form of industrial waste.

These examples of highly successful and less successful ways of integrating the physical material into a work of art illustrate how in a successful work the material contributes something of its own to the work's power. In works that are less successful the physical material is irrelevant to the effect being sought, or, even worse, one fights the other, creating a struggle between what the artist is trying to achieve and what the physical material allows. The examples involving glass generalize to the use of other materials. Each has its distinctive properties that lend themselves to some artistic endeavors but not to others. The artist's sensitivity to that potential, her feel for the material that she is using, cannot but affect the final product.

Thus far I have focused almost exclusively on physical materials, the brute stuff—paint, marble, glass, clay—out of which artwork is constructed. I have also noted how that physical stuff, when worked on by the artist, is gradually transformed, becoming a medium of expression. We must remember, however, that Dewey does not restrict the term *materials* to physical entities. The artist, he points out, works with ideas. These, too, are materials, Dewey insists, as much so as the objects of paint, stone, and clay. Dewey calls the former *inner* materials to distinguish them from the *outer* materials that we have been talking about. He includes among them "images, observations, memories, and emotions." The inner materials "are also progressively re-formed [in the process of constructing a work of art]; they, too, must be administered" (LW10, 81).

Dewey's extension of the notion of materials to include images, observations, and the like helps to clarify what he means when he says "the medium of expression in art is neither objective nor subjective" (LW10, 292). Instead of operating in isolation, the two forms of material work on each other reciprocally: "The physical process develops imagination, while imagination is conceived in terms of concrete material." Dewey sums up the significance of that reciprocity as follows: "Only by progressive organization of 'inner' and 'outer' material in organic connection with each other can anything be produced that is not a learned document or an illustration of something familiar" (LW10, 82). The reason why a learned document could be produced without such an interaction is that it is composed almost exclusively of inner materials (ideas, knowledge, etc.). The same is true of an illustration of something familiar. Both entail the use of outer materials (pen and paper, drawing implements, etc.), as well as inner ones, but there is no progressive organization of the two domains. They do not vitally inform each other.

Symmetry, Balance, Form, Rhythm, and Structure

Toward the middle of *Art as Experience*, Dewey devotes three full chapters to what might be called the internal organization of aesthetic experiences. There he treats notions such as symmetry, balance, form, rhythm, and structure—key ideas whose treatment has long been standard fare in courses and textbooks on art appreciation. The same topics reappear elsewhere in Dewey's text, though less prominently than in those three central chapters.

Dewey's treatment of these standard topics remains far from textbookish, however. He does not approach them systematically, taking up each in turn and giving it its due before moving on to the next. Instead, he interweaves them the way a weaver of cloth might work a variety of colored threads into the design of a fabric. A key idea is introduced, discussed at some length, then laid aside, only to be picked up again in a slightly different way a few paragraphs or pages later. As a result, each idea, though seemingly simple at the start, becomes more and more complex. Moreover, the relation between and among ideas grows in complexity as Dewey's exposition moves along.

As disorienting as such interweaving may be to some readers, particularly to those looking for sharp definitions and quick answers. Dewey's goal is not to create discomfort. Nor does he write this way in order to be seen as an artful conjoiner of disparate materials. His subject demands it. The integral nature of an aesthetic experience forces him to twist and turn as he goes along. If there is a single truth about such experiences, it is that its elements merge to form a unified whole. During the process of initially experiencing them they are not even distinguishable as elements. We discern them as being so only as we shift to an analytic mode of perception. And even then the distinctions we make gradually blend with others and tend to disappear when our backs are turned.

What we conceive to be form from one angle may be looked on as structure from another. Rhythm, for example, can be static or dynamic. We can view it as the relation among the parts of a work, in which case we are inclined to concern ourselves with notions like balance and harmony, or we can treat it as a quality of the experience itself, in which case the pulsations of doing and undergoing, of acting and reflecting, come to the fore and provide the basis of judgment and evaluation. Corresponding complexities emerge as each of the other conventional categories undergoes analysis.

Because it is impossible to recapture the richness and complexity of Dewey's theory without going into more detail than present circumstances allow, I have chosen to concentrate on a single strand of thought that runs through Dewey's exposition in *Art as Experience* and appears in other of his works as well. Its focus is the temporality of an aesthetic experience. *Temporality,* as the term will be used here, refers to the way an experience unfolds over time, as well as to the way it relates to past, present, and future events. Dewey looked on this temporal process as key to understanding what an aesthetic experience, particularly an art-centered one, is all about. I will try to make clear why he did so.

Dewey's Formal Conditions of Aesthetic Form

Dewey identifies five characteristics that he refers to as "formal conditions of aesthetic form" (LW10, 143). In the order he names them, they are continuity, cumulation, conservation, tension, and anticipation. He implies that other terms could be added to that list, and, indeed, a few pages beyond the introduction of those five he does name a sixth condition, fulfillment, which he includes along with four of the others (continuity is missing), this time referring to them as the "formal characteristics of an esthetic experience" (LW10, 149). Having already discussed the concept of fulfillment in connection with the explication of *an* experience, I will postpone a return to that concept for the time being. Each of the others, however, stands in need of explication to make its meaning clear. Crudely speaking, continuity has chiefly to do with the before and after of experience—with its past, in other words, and its future. Cumulation, conservation, tension, and anticipation all have to do with the internal dynamics of experience, with what happens during its unfolding.

Continuity. In its broadest meaning, continuity refers to what is stable in experience, to that which continues. Employed in this way, it contrasts with *flux.* As Dewey says, "Nature and life manifest not flux but continuity, and continuity involves forces and structures that endure through change; at least when they change, they do so more slowly than do surface incidents, and thus are, relatively, constant" (LW10, 327). Among the various forces and structures that provide continuity to experience, some are physical; others, ideational. Central among the physical forces are the materials that the artist manipulates to give a work its characteristic shape and form—stone, for example, or paint and clay. Central among the ideational forces are the predilections and proclivities that the artist (and her audience) brings to the work in the form of habits, attitudes, and dispositions. These, too, as we have seen, constitute materials with which the artist works. They, too, give stability to experience. They do so by linking present with past and past with future.

Among the terms referring to the artist's inner materials, *habit* is the most inclusive. It refers, as Dewey explains, to "that kind of human activity which is influenced by prior activity and in that sense acquired; which contains within itself a certain ordering or systematization of minor elements of action; which is projective, dynamic in quality, ready for overt manifestation; and which is operative in some subdued subordinate form even when not obviously dominating activity" (MW14, 31). We humans are indeed creatures of habit, as the saying goes, but, according to Dewey, not for the reasons usually given—not because we do the same thing again and again, responding automatically to whatever challenges or opportunities might come our way. Rather, we are creatures of habit because we bring to each new challenge and to each new opportunity a vast array of resources in the form of attitudes, interests, skills, and other acquired characteristics—each of them a habit in Dewey's lexicon and each ready to be put to use. In short, to call us creatures of habit simply means, for Dewey, that we are the repositories of our own experiential history and of portions of that larger history that constitutes the culture in which we live. We each have a past to draw upon, one whose resources we selectively bring to bear upon the present.

To conceive of the past affecting the present, as the operation of habit allows, tells only part of the story. There is far more to the concept of continuity than that. Habits, though representing stability, are themselves modified in use. Thus the transaction between past and present moves in both directions. Not only does the past affect the present but the present also affects the past. It does so by altering whatever of the past we bring to it, from the broadest of outlooks to the narrowest of skills. Dewey applies the term *reconstruction* to these alterations. Thus, attitudes and interests (to name but two of the forms that structural stability of an inner sort commonly takes) are inevitably reconstructed in either major or minor ways when put to use. Additionally, the environing conditions undergo a corresponding set of changes as a result of what is done to them. This means that the future is modified along with the present and the past. The future will inevitably contain all of those reconstructions, both inner and outer, that result from the ongoing exchange. Here is Dewey's summary of the process: "The basic characteristic of habit is that every experience enacted and undergone modifies the one who acts and undergoes, while this modification affects, whether we wish it or not, the quality of subsequent experiences. . . . [T]he principle of continuity of experience means that every experience takes up something from those which have gone before and modifies in some way the quality of those which come after" (LW13, 18).

The trouble with the concept of continuity as so far explained is that it is too broad to serve as a criterion of judgment within the domain of experience in general. It applies to all experiences, whether good, bad, or indifferent. It thus fails to offer a basis for differentiating between those experiences in which the principle of continuity operates beneficially and those in which it has detrimental effects. To aid in making that distinction, Dewey introduces the concept of *growth*.

Human growth, for Dewey, is more than physical. It is also moral and intellectual. It is a form of development, an opening up or an unfolding of potentialities. It entails an increase in the organism's power to perceive differences and to engage effectively with its environment. It results in an expansion of meaning and value. Yet growth of a moral and intellectual kind does not occur automatically. It requires learning, which means the creation of new skills, attitudes, and abilities (all of them habits in Dewey's terminology). This in turn calls for the reconstruction of prior modes of responding, as spelled out in my prior explication of the principle of continuity. Those changes evince continuity at its best, continuity as ideally conceived, not as it normally occurs. As Dewey points out, "There is no paradox in the fact that the principle of the continuity of experience may operate so as to leave a person arrested on a low plane of development, in a way which limits later capacity for growth" (LW13, 20). Since continuity in and of itself may have either good or bad effects, it is always reasonable to ask what those effects have turned out to be in any particular situation. Often we may even plan ahead so that the likelihood of positive (i.e., growth-enhancing) outcomes is maximized. We must note, however, that continuity, as Dewey speaks of it, is not to be avoided or circumvented. Experience is always linked to a past whose influence continues to operate in the present. It also is always linked to a future in which the outcome of what is going on at present will continue to operate. That reciprocity of past, present, and future is what the principle of continuity teaches.

Unlike continuity, which deals chiefly with relations that link an aesthetic experience with circumstances lying outside its own boundaries—that is, with resources from the past that it draws upon and with the future consequences of the changes that it occasions—the formal characteristics of cumulation, conservation, tension, and anticipation (the four remaining categories) refer chiefly to what goes on within the confines of the experience itself. They relate, in other words, to the internal dynamics of what takes place between the onset of the experience and its culmination. They also are closely interrelated, as Dewey makes clear: "There can be no movement toward a consummating close unless there is a progressive massing of values, a cumulative effect. This result cannot exist without a conservation of the import of what has gone before. Moreover, to secure the needed continuity, the accumulated experience must be such as to create suspense [tension] and anticipation of resolution" (LW10, 142). With this interrelation in mind, let us proceed to the four remaining characteristics.

Cumulation. The buildup that attends the temporal unfolding of an aesthetic experience is its cumulation, which is evinced in a variety of ways depending on perspective and on the specifics of the situation. Emotionally, the increase may be felt as tension or anticipation. Intellectually, it may be undergone as an increase in the internal complexity of the work or as a deepening of its meaning. The buildup may be experienced as an increased sense of worth— what Dewey calls "a progressive massing of values" (LW10, 142). From the point of view of the artist, cumulation extends to the physicality of the work. As the work progresses, it increases in size: pages pile up, the blank canvas becomes covered with paint. The work's history is evinced physically as well as ideationally.

Regardless of its manifestation, cumulation tells us this: Without a buildup of some kind, there can be no fulfillment. And without fulfillment there can be no aesthetic experience.

Conservation. Dewey offers two explanations of how conservation works. In one of them he explains it in terms of the *energies* that operate within the experience as a whole; in the other he emphasizes what happens to *meaning.* Each calls attention to a different aspect of a complex set of conditions.

Dewey's explanation in terms of energy goes like this: For anything to constitute a whole there have to be energies resisting each other. Without such resistances whatever was on its way to becoming a whole would promptly collapse, explode, or otherwise dissipate. Some of those opposing energies are internal; others are external.

This requirement of oppositional forces within and without is as true of those wholes that we call experiences as it is of entities in the physical world. This last point is important to Dewey, for he insists that each of the energies at work in experience (some physical and others not) is very real indeed. Starting with his depiction of the energy at work in experience, he describes each opposing force as entailing movement. The balance of those forces fluctuate. They often do so rhythmically. Movement in one direction is followed by movement in another. Here is the way Dewey depicts that fluctuation. "Each [energy source] gains intensity for a certain period, but thereby compresses some opposed energy until the latter can overcome the other which has been relaxing itself as it extends. Then the operation is reversed, not necessarily in equal periods of time but in some ratio that is felt as orderly." Then Dewey offers the key to an understanding of one way conservation operates. "Resistance accumulates energy; *it institutes conservation* until release and expansion ensue" (LW10, 159, emphasis added).

What gets conserved is energy itself. That pent-up energy builds to a point where its force exceeds that of its opposition. Then comes its release, or "expression." The energy whose resistance has been temporarily overcome has been correspondingly conserved.

From the standpoint of meaning, what gets conserved is, as Dewey says, "the import of what has gone before" (LW10, 142). A bit later on he points out: "Thinking consists in ordering a variety of meanings so that they move to a conclusion that all support and in which all are summed up and conserved. What we perhaps are less cognizant of is that this organization of energies to move cumulatively to a terminal whole in which the values of all means and media are incorporated is the essence of fine art" (LW10, 176).

In the arts, as in thinking in general, meanings are summed up and conserved. Yet there is a difference between the two. Here is how Dewey describes what goes on in thinking: "In most intellectual work, in all save those flashes that are distinctly esthetic, we have to go backwards; we have consciously to retrace previous steps and to recall distinctly particular facts and ideas. Getting ahead in thought is dependent upon these conscious excursions of memory into the past." Here is what he says about conservation as it works in the arts: "Only when esthetic perception is interrupted (whether by lapse on the part of artist or perceiver) are we compelled to turn back, say in seeing a play on the stage, to ask ourselves what went before in order to get the thread of movement. What is retained from the past is embedded within what is now perceived and so embedded that, by its compression there, it forces the mind to stretch forward to what is coming" (LW10, 187).

In other words, in an aesthetic experience the conservation of meaning occurs almost unconsciously. When reading a book or watching a play we normally do not have to stop and think about what happened in the last act or the last chapter. We remember enough of it to allow us to proceed. We carry that memory with us not as something to consult from time to time, the way a scholar might return to her notes, but as part of the living present, as a vital, embedded component of all that we currently perceive. Even with works that lack a clear narrative structure—many musical performances, for example— the same capacity to hold on to a portion of what has passed works to our advantage. We recognize the return of themes and motifs from earlier sections of the work. We hear variations as variations of passages performed earlier.

What if the conservation of meaning did not occur at all? Quite simply, life could not go on. Actions would be meaningless. Art would not exist.

Tension. Like the concept of conservation, tension has more than one referent for Dewey. Most of the time it refers to the opposition of energies within the experience as a whole. In these terms, tension results from a compression of energy seeking release. During compression the condition of intensity dominates. During release the shift is to extensity. The difference is not just a play on words. Dewey explains: "The connection of intensity and extensity and of both with tension is not a verbal matter. There is no rhythm save where there is alternation of compressions and releases. Resistance prevents immediate discharge and accumulates tension that renders energy intense. Its release from this state of detention takes necessarily the form of a sequential spreading out" (LW10, 184).

The rhythmic interplay of compression and release gives life to experience. The same pulsations move life forward, for, as Dewey points out, "the more there is compressed . . . the more intense the forward impulsion" (LW10, 186).

Dewey's conception of tension as a form of energy seeking release posits the existence of an opposing force. One force blocks the other. The struggle between them constitutes the source of the tension. To this overview Dewey adds an important complication. He points out that tension itself can be an energizing force, something we might seek rather than try to avoid. As he puts it, "That tension calls out energy and that total lack of opposition does not favor normal development are familiar facts. In a general way, we all recognize that a balance between furthering and retarding conditions is the desirable state of affairs—provided that the adverse conditions bear intrinsic relation to what they obstruct instead of being arbitrary and extraneous" (LW10, 66). In other words, we actually benefit from encountering difficulties on our way to either creating or understanding (appreciating) a work of art, provided that those obstructions in the course of either activity derive from the work itself and are not just intrusions from the outside.

The way Dewey treats the benefits of tension within an art-centered experience also helps to clarify the relation between experiences that are principally intellectual and those that are principally aesthetic. Both kinds of experience make use of intelligence as a guide to action. They both call for reflection of one kind or another. Resistances of various kinds crop up in both. In aesthetic experiences, as contrasted with those of a more intellectual cast, the tensions undergone and the problems encountered are, however, more immediate than instrumental. They deal principally with what Dewey calls "the proper reciprocal adaptation of parts" within the experience itself (LW10, 143). They are chiefly concerned, in other words, with the integral nature of the experience rather than with conditions that lie beyond its temporal boundaries. Intellectual experiences, on the other hand, are focused more on problems whose source lies elsewhere and whose solution promises to be of maximal value when put to use in future contexts.

Not only does the artist encounter tensions and problems in the course of an aesthetic experience but her audience must do so as well. Dewey says: "The perceiver as well as the artist has to perceive, meet, and overcome problems; otherwise, appreciation is transient and overweighted with sentiment." (To that he adds: "For in order to perceive esthetically, he must remake his past experiences so that they can enter integrally into a new pattern. He cannot dismiss his past experiences nor can he dwell among them as they have been in the past" (LW10, 143).

The true appreciator of an art object, for Dewey, is not the casual listener or viewer. Rather, he is someone who has spent time with a work, has found it engaging, stimulating, puzzling, perhaps even troubling, and, as a result of his sustained exploration of it, has undergone a significant change of some kind. His encounter with the object or performance forces him to modify his former habits, his old ways of looking at things. The new and the old become integrated. They form a new pattern, a new way of perceiving.

The tensions and problems that the artist encounters resemble in some ways those encountered by the art appreciator, yet the two sets of resistances are by no means identical. It is quite possible, for example, for the artist to struggle with her materials and to overcome countless difficulties without the finished product containing a trace of her having done so. Those transient problems remain unknown to later viewers or listeners. At the same time it is also possible for perceivers of the art object to encounter difficulties with the work that the artist herself did not foresee. These may arise because the work is from a different culture or a different historical period than that of its audience. Or the artist may have neglected to remove obstacles to understanding.

Not only does an artist sometimes fail to remove difficulties that emerge in a work spontaneously, but she sometimes builds difficulties into the work. There are times, in other words, when the artist consciously tries to make the work difficult for those who will later encounter it. The ways of accomplishing this end and the motives for doing so can be quite varied and will depend on the kind of work that is being produced. In writing a traditional detective story, for example, the author may seek to throw his readers off track and keep them guessing who did it till the very end. In some of the so-called higher literary forms, such as poetry and the "serious" novel, the writer may allow the work to become obscure from time to time in order to test the limits of meaning or to reinforce an atmosphere of uncertainty and doubt or even to reveal to readers one of the central purposes of a work of art. The poet Wallace Stevens, for example, characteristically resisted offering explanations of some of his more difficult poems. He did so, he later explained, for purely aesthetic reasons: "Things that have their origin in the imagination or in the emotions very often take on a form that is ambiguous or uncertain. It is not possible to attach a single, rational meaning to such things without destroying the imaginative or emotional ambiguity or uncertainty that is inherent in them and that is why poets do not like to explain" (Stevens 1990, 249). Milton Bates, author of a prominent study of Stevens's poetry, elaborates: "Stevens disliked explaining because he feared that readers would lose interest in poems they could comprehend fully. It was not a question of mystification. Rather, he understood that pure poetry succeeds when it detaches the reader from reason and reality and lifts him by the most tenuous of threads to another plane of experience. To explain is to make the reader overly conscious of those filaments and so to subvert their function. When that happens, something more valuable than understanding is lost." (Bates 1985, 145).

Yet the asymmetry between artist and audience in the tensive quality of their experiences with a work of art leaves sufficient room for overlapping concerns as well as for differences. Within the region of overlap we find similarities in the problems faced by the artist and her audience as each reflects upon a particular piece. With those similarities go differences as well. The artist's involvement with the problems that come up in the making of a work is typically direct and consequential, whereas the audience's subsequent participation in the solution of the same problems must by definition remain indirect and vicarious.

Dewey stressed the importance of the shared sense of problems that links the artist and her audience. One role of the critic, in his judgment, was to help a work's audience to understand and to share in the difficulties that its creator had successfully encountered and overcome. As he points out, "We lay hold of the full import of a work of art only as we go through in our own vital processes the processes the artist went through in producing the work. It is the critic's privilege to share in the promotion of this active process" (LW10, 328).

Anticipation. The anticipation associated with an art-centered experience divides conveniently into two temporal phases. The first occurs before the experience has formally begun. The second characterizes what goes on during the experience. Dewey has almost nothing to say about the first phase. He has relatively little to say about the second one either, at least directly. He does, however, twice acknowledge the place of anticipation as a formal characteristic of all aesthetic experiences. Moreover, his lengthy discussion of how such experiences work contains sufficient detail for us to piece together a fairly satisfying account of how he sees anticipation fitting within the overall picture.

Concerning the form of anticipation that typically precedes an art-centered experience, Dewey perhaps has very little to say because he saw that such a condition does not have to exist. In any case, as viewers-to-be, readers-to-be, or listeners-to-be we commonly start to ready ourselves for art-centered experiences far in advance. We buy tickets to the theater ahead of time, we work out plans to visit the art museum with a friend, we purchase a book on the strength of a review of it that we have read, we choose to go to a movie because a neighbor has recommended it or because we have seen it advertised, and so on. We commonly approach such experiences in an anticipatory mood.

Unfortunately, our expectations often exceed what the experience delivers in the way of pleasure or enjoyment. As a consequence, we feel let down. Fortunately, however, the reverse also happens. At times our expectations are more than fulfilled, in which case we find ourselves pleasantly surprised. These mismatches between what we anticipate and the event itself help to reinforce what has already been said about the continuity of experience. The ensuing consequences of disappointment or unexpected pleasure reveal the dynamic interplay between what we bring to an experience and the quality of the experience itself. When what we bring includes an anticipation of what the experience will be like as an experience, the stage is set for a judgment to be made.

The typical way we look forward to art-centered experiences—the ubiquity of the sense of anticipation that precedes an experience—also helps to highlight the central importance of Dewey's concept of qualitative immediacy. Although we may plan to go to the theater or read a book or visit a museum, what we are anticipating is not something we can describe in advance, save in the most vague and general terms. What we actually look forward to under such circumstances is the thrill of the experience, the feel of it, the undergoing of it. Such descriptions come as close as we can get to what Dewey repeatedly speaks of as the qualitative immediacy of experience.

The anticipation that Dewey acknowledges to be an integral part of an aesthetic experience grows out of the emerging conditions of the experience itself, which may be one reason for his giving it far less attention than the other formal properties that we have discussed. Once meaning has begun to pile up and tensions to build, anticipation follows as a matter of course. As events unfold, we await revelations. The states of cumulation, conservation, and tension all entail a looking forward to something, a foreshadowing of what is to come.

Both artist and audience remain at least partially in the dark as the aesthetic experience in which each is engaged gradually unfolds. Thus, they both are in a position to anticipate what is coming next. Yet their respective positions differ dramatically. To the audience an art object is a finished product, an accomplishment awaiting scrutiny. To the artist (or performer) it is a work in progress, a project under way, something yet to be accomplished. In a narrative work, for example, the audience is free to guess what will happen next, whereas the artist has prior knowledge. Those differences give rise to corresponding differences in the way anticipation becomes manifest.

After a project is finished, the artist typically awaits the reaction of others to her work. This waiting to hear what others think has no direct parallel in the experience of the audience, though public acceptance of a work, the eagerness to see or hear it, depends in large measure on what others (e.g., critics and reviewers) think of it. Thus, in an extended sense, the audience too awaits the reviews.

The Formal Characteristics of Aesthetic Experience as Analytic Tools

Thus far I have focused on the psychological manifestations of what Dewey refers to as the formal characteristics of an aesthetic experience. I have talked about what it feels like to encounter resistance or to undergo tension. I have spoken of how the accumulation of meaning allows us to follow the plot of a narrative cognitively. I have discussed the way anticipation might be differently undergone by artists and spectators.

We must remember, however, that for Dewey experience does not just go on under the skin or inside the consciousness of the experiencer. It happens within the world at large. It encompasses the total transaction taking place between the organism and its environment. This means that the concepts of cumulation, conservation, tension, and anticipation have physical manifestations as well as psychological ones. They are characteristics of the total experience as it temporally unfolds, and are not confined to what is going on inside the head or the heart of the experiencer. Indeed, only retrospectively (and then solely for the purpose of an analysis of one kind or another) do we identify each characteristic and assign it a location, psychological or otherwise.

When we characterize an aesthetic experience as one in which opposing tensions struggle for dominance or one in which the qualities of anticipation or cumulation become acutely salient, we are saying something about the experience as a whole and not just about the way it registers on the person engaged in it. We must keep this in mind if we are to avoid falling into the trap that Dewey warns us against, which is that of positing a permanent and unbridgeable gap between the inside and the outside of experience, between subjective and objective, self and other, or whatever other historically sanctioned dichotomy we might choose to employ.

Does this mean that art objects themselves conserve meaning or anticipate their own conclusion or undergo a buildup of tension? Yes, in a manner of speaking, it does. We commonly refer to a work that builds up to a climax. We describe it as containing elements that clash with or contradict each other. In the case of works that unfold narratively, we have no trouble referring to the way early sections lay the ground for later ones. Those ways of speaking testify to the fact that Dewey's four essential categories apply as easily to physical objects as to the inner life of the experiencer.

We come finally to the question of how to make use of Dewey's categories. What good does it do to know that all or most aesthetic experiences are marked by the qualities of cumulation, conservation, tension, and anticipation? (In asking that question we must keep in mind Dewey's willingness to have other qualities added to those that he names.) When and how might such terms be employed in either the creation or the consumption of an art object?

The most general answer to that question would seem to be, When we run into difficulties of one kind or another, when we are trying to figure out how to proceed or what went wrong with the situation we are in (or, retrospectively, when we want to know what was so right about it). In short, we employ analytic terms when undertaking an analysis of some kind. The analytic situations in which terms like *cumulation, conservation, tension,* and *anticipation* might play a part are too varied to even begin to enumerate. All we can say about them is that they deal with the unfolding of an experience. When we consider what went wrong in a particular situation—why we lost interest, for example, or why the situation failed to retain the attention of others—our answer can almost always be framed in terms that make use of one or another of Dewey's four categories.

Mentioning that situations run into difficulty helps to underscore another of

Dewey's main points: that the sole reason for reflective thought (i.e., for under-taking an analysis of any kind) is to extricate oneself from a problematic situation. The problems that we face are always part of the situation we are in, though they can contain references to difficulties that we (or others) have encountered in the past and might face again in the future.

We must be careful, however, not to interpret the phrase *problematic situation* too narrowly. As Thomas Alexander, in a trenchant analysis of Dewey's aesthetics, notes, "The model of experience which Dewey presents is not a simple progression from a condition of routine, automatic behavior which is suddenly disorganized by a 'problematic situation' leading to mechanical analy-sis, experimentation, reorganization and reintegration with a consummatory kick closing it off. There are a number of phases or functionally diverse parts operating at each moment."

Alexander further seeks to correct a common misunderstanding that arises from Dewey's effort to be as clear as possible. He says: "It is true that there is a temporal overall structure to *an* experience, and Dewey does tend at times to simplify this structure, so that one might get the impression that every signifi-cant moment of human existence follows the pattern of a motorist driving along, oblivious to the world, having a flat tire, being awakened to the need, fixing the tire, and merrily going on his way with the satisfaction of having gotten out of a jam" (Alexander 1987, 127). The flat-tire model of problem-solving does crudely fit many of life's situations, as Alexander would doubtless acknowledge. It lacks the subtlety, however, that would enable it to mirror with anything approaching accuracy even the degree of complexity involved in fixing a flat tire. Alexander explains how Dewey deals with that subtlety. "Balancing this teleological dimension of experience is Dewey's conception of experience as a total *field* of action which has a complex structure at each and every moment and different degrees of focus, clarity, obscurity, and organiza-tion. It is *this* which changes from one moment to the next, not by a jerky series of mechanical actions, but by increasing articulation, illumination, meaning, and apprehension. To summarize: one must keep vividly in mind that experi-ence for Dewey is *both* process and field—a "field-process" if you will. Structure is temporally *dynamic;* activity is *ordered*" (Alexander 1987, 128).

The concepts of cumulation, conservation, tension, and anticipation refer to the dynamics of experience. They aid our understanding of what goes on between the onset of *an* experience and its fulfilling conclusion. The complex-ities introduced by each of the four concepts help to avert the oversimplification entailed in the flat-tire conception of problem solving.

The Place of Perception in an Art-Centered Experience

Beyond exemplifying experience in its integrity, an art-centered experience brings increased clarity to what it means to perceive something. Indeed, in Dewey's view, it does little else, for, as he sees it, "an aesthetic experience, the work of art in its actuality, is *perception*" (LW10, 167). The role that Dewey sees perception as playing in such experiences serves to highlight the importance of perception in human affairs in general.

Perceiving versus recognizing. We first need to distinguish between perceiving, on the one hand, and the more mundane sensory experiences of sight, sound, smell, taste, and touch, on the other. To perceive an object is not simply to see, hear, smell, taste, or touch it. It is to make sense of what one senses, to partake of its meaning. Dewey puts it succinctly when he says, "*What* is perceived are meanings, rather than just events or existences" (LW1, 248).

Yet perceiving in the fullest sense, in the sense in which we find perception operating within the confines of an art-centered experience, involves far more than attaching a name to things. "To see, to perceive," Dewey tells us, "is more than to recognize." What more? Why is recognition a deficient form of perception? It is so, Dewey explains, because "mere recognitions occur only when we are occupied with something else than the object or person recognized. It marks either an interruption or else an intent to use what is recognized as a means for something else" (LW10, 30).

In that fuller form of perception that we associate with the arts the object is looked on not as something to be used for some other purpose but as something worthy of attention in its own right, an entity or event of intrinsic value. To perceive in this fullest sense is not to "identify something present in terms of a past disconnected from it" (LW10, 30), which is what we do when we go about attaching labels to things, identifying them as belonging to this or that category or (in the case of art products) as having been produced by this or that artist. Instead, the way we link past and present in perception is by carrying into the present a past that will serve to expand and deepen the meaningfulness of the perceived object.

The temporal nature of perception. The kind of full-blown perception to which Dewey refers does not occur instantaneously. Far from it. Unlike recognition, it takes time. It develops. It unfolds. Dewey says: "In no case can there be *perception of an object* except in a process developing in time. Mere excitations, yes; but not an object as perceived, instead of just recognized as one of a familiar kind" (LW10, 179).

One of the interesting aspects of the unfolding or developing of our perception of many, if not most, art objects is that the process need not be continuous. We may interrupt our perceiving of the object and return to it at a later time. Indeed, from the standpoint of the artist this is the norm. Few, if any, works of substantial scope and size are produced in a single sitting. The artist must temporarily abandon the work and return to it on numerous occasions spread over a considerable period of time, often months or even years. Audiences, too, may interrupt their intake of meaning from a work—as is common in the reading of a novel, for example—or they may have their perception of the work interrupted for them, as happens with intermissions in the theater or with works serialized on television or in magazines.

Many works of art are also perceived as a whole on more than one occasion by artists and audiences alike. Musical works, paintings, and poems, for example, are typically heard, read, and seen many times over by the same listeners, readers, and viewers. Whole novels are often reread, and theatrical productions rewitnessed. Each successive rewitnessing or rereading is never exactly the same as the preceding one, for the perceiver has changed personally in the interim (at times profoundly, we might suppose, particularly when the interlude between perceptions has been exceptionally long). The object of perception may have undergone significant change as well. But the similarities between successive encounters are usually sufficient for the later event to be looked on as a repetition of the earlier one rather than as something entirely new.

In seeking to understand how perception operates, what makes repetitious encounters interesting is the fact that earlier opinions and beliefs concerning the object may be modified or become unsettled by later ones. With repeated exposure a work of art may grow stale and tiresome, or, conversely, it may become increasingly enriched through the acquisition of new meanings. All such changes testify to the dynamic nature of perception, to its changing yet conservative character.

Even when direct perception ceases, opinions and beliefs about the perceived object, including thoughts as to its ultimate meaning, frequently continue to form. Indeed, it is often the case that so-called final opinions about a book, a play, or a movie do not become firmly established until sometime after the book has been closed or the theatrical event has become only a memory. Even then the opinions may turn out not to be as final as we initially thought them to be. The poet who wrote, "The music in my heart I bore, / Long after it was heard no more," gave utterance to an experience known to us all (Wordsworth 1984, 320).

The relational character of perception. Dewey stresses the relational character of perception. To perceive, he insists, is to perceive relations, to take note of how one thing relates to another. The most fundamental of those relations has to do with what a person does and what happens in response, that is, what is then undergone as a consequence of the doing. That pairing of doing and undergoing and our noting of how one relates to the other not only sets the conditions of learning but also gives shape and significance to experience. What counts is our noting that relation, for, as Dewey points out, "an experience has pattern and structure because it is not just doing and undergoing in alternation, but consists of them in relationship. . . . The action and its consequence must be joined in perception. This relationship is what gives meaning; to grasp it is the objective of all intelligence. The scope and content of the relations measure the significant content of an experience" (LW10, 50).

The relations that we perceive become the qualities of the objects or events that we focus on. They are immediate. In the arts, they inhere in the very substance of the work being created or appreciated. When we pause to think about those qualities—especially when we seek to convey our thoughts to others—they take the form of ideas. Two important points for Dewey are, first, that without our perception of how things are related, there can be no such thing as an experience and, second, that "the *basic* condition is *felt* relationship between doing and undergoing as the organism and environment interact" (LW10, 217, emphasis added).

Beyond the fundamental conjunction of doing and undergoing there lie all kinds of other relations that make up the totality of our perceptual field. Among the most important of these are the interminglings of the senses working in harmony—the coordination of eye and hand, of sight and sound, of taste and touch, and so forth. "Seeing, hearing, tasting," Dewey tells us, "become esthetic when relation to a distinct manner of activity qualifies what is perceived" (LW10, 55). In other words, it is how we see and how we hear and taste that determine when and whether an object or a total experience is looked on as esthetic. "Nothing," says Dewey, "is perceived except when different senses work in relation to one another. . . . Unless these various sensory-motor energies are coordinated with one another there is no perceived scene or object. But equally there is none when—by a condition impossible to fulfill in fact—a single sense alone is operative" (LW10, 179).

The combinations of sensory conditions that yield perceptual awareness do not register solely as mental events. In psychological terms, they are as much felt as thought. The way we take them, whether as thought or as emotion, will depend on the circumstances. As Dewey puts it: "Immediately, every perceptual awareness may be termed indifferently emotion, sensation, thought, desire; not that it *is* immediately any of those things or all of them combined, but that when it is taken in some *reference,* to conditions or to consequences or to both, it has, in that contextual reference, the distinctive properties of emotion, sensation, thought or desire" (LW1, 230). To illustrate the cogency of Dewey's point, consider how we query friends about their reactions to books read or performances attended. "How was it?" we ask, leaving plenty of room for the inclusion of all sorts commentary, classifiable under any and all of Dewey's rubrics.

Perception and object (or event) as correlative. The uniqueness of each perception, its specificity with respect to a particular object or event, is another of its properties that Dewey makes much of in his theorizing. Object (or event) and perception are correlative. The two are coterminus in their particularity. Here is Dewey's version of that overlap: "We speak of perception *and* its object. But perception and *its* object are built up and completed in one and the same continuing operation. What is called *the* object, *the* cloud, river, garment, has imputed to it an existence independent of an actual experience; still more is this true of *the* carbon molecule, *the* hydrogen ion, the entities of science generally. But the object of—or better *in*—perception is not one of a kind in general, a sample of a cloud or river, but is *this* individual thing existing here and now with all the unrepeatable particularities that accompany and mark such existences" (LW10, 181).

In ordinary affairs, we often do not attend to the individuality of the perceptual object. Instead, we but recognize it. We see it as belonging to a particular class of objects, not as a singular being but as one of many. Our perceptual apparatus commonly stalls at that point. Dewey describes this state of affairs and contrasts it with what happens under the more favorable circumstances that characterize an aesthetic experience. "Now under the pressure of external circumstances or because of internal laxity, objects of most of our *ordinary* perception lack completeness. They are cut short when there is recognition; that is to say when the object is identified as one of a kind, or of a species within the kind. For such recognition suffices to enable us to employ the object for customary purposes. . . . Esthetic perception, on the other hand, is a name for a full perception and its correlative, an object or event" (LW10, 181–182).

The two most important consequences of what Dewey refers to here as full perception lie, first, in what it does to the immediate quality of experience and, second, in what it does to the enduring value of the object perceived. The two are closely related, as Dewey notes. When the quality of an experience is at its height or is most intense, so too is the value that we place on the object that stands at its center. We can only love, in other words, what we fully perceive. Nor need love be the end of it. "Under some conditions," Dewey points out, "the completeness of the object enjoyed gives the experience a quality so intense that it is justly termed religious. Peace and harmony suffuse the entire universe gathered up into the situation having a particular focus and pattern" (LW4, 188).

Perception as redemptive. The redemptive potency of the kind of experience just described reaches its height when a work of art stands at its center. In the following quotation, which, though lengthy, defies effective summary, Dewey explains why.

> A work of art elicits and accentuates this quality of being a whole and of belonging to the larger, all-inclusive, whole which is the universe in which we live. This fact, I think, is the explanation of that feeling of exquisite intelligibility and clarity we have in the presence of an object that is experienced with esthetic intensity. It explains also the religious feeling that accompanies intense esthetic perception. We are, as it were, introduced into a world beyond this world which is nevertheless the deeper reality of the world in which we live in our ordinary experiences. We are carried out beyond ourselves to find ourselves. I can see no psychological ground for such properties of an experience save that, somehow, the work of art operates to deepen and to raise to great clarity, that sense of an enveloping undefined whole that accompanies every normal experience. This whole is then felt as an expansion of ourselves. . . . [W]e are citizens of this vast world beyond ourselves, and any intense realization of its presence with and in us brings a peculiarly satisfying sense of unity in itself and with ourselves. (LW10, 199)

To avoid interjecting more meaning than Dewey intends into that passage, we would do well to note that the world beyond this world to which he pictures art introducing us is nothing like Plato's world of forms, nor is it anything like the other world or the hereafter of many religious believers. For Dewey, the world beyond is figurative. It is but the deeper reality of the world in which we live daily, the world of our ordinary experience. Art, in Dewey's view, does not transport us from the workaday world into another realm of being. It but reveals the potentiality of the world in which we live.

An example. To concretize much that has been said in this section on perception, let us imagine what might be involved in something as seemingly simple as my perception of an apple. I would begin by pointing out that, strictly speaking, I never perceive *an* apple, at least not as Dewey wants to employ the concept of perceiving. The indefinite article *an* does not fit the conditions of perception. What I perceive instead is *this* apple, this *particular* object. To perceive it fully, as opposed to recognizing it to be an apple, is to perceive it in its particularity, to take note of its weight, its color, its shape, its texture, its odor, its taste, even its blemishes and irregularities. Moreover, it is to take note of these qualities not serially, one by one, but relationally and to some extent simultaneously. I hold the apple in my hand as I examine its color and texture. I bite into it, and the separate sensations of taste, smell, touch, sight, and even sound (the crunch as I bite down) are practically indistinguishable.

Though my perception of the apple inevitably takes time (there being no such thing as instantaneous perception), it does not normally begin with a feeling of uncertainty and move toward certainty. I do not start by seeing a blob of red, then smell a particular odor, then touch a certain waxy surface, and so on, until I finally put those separate sensations together to form an idea of an apple or to come to the conclusion that what I am holding is an apple. There could be special circumstances under which I might come close to proceeding that way, however. I might do so, for example, if I were strolling through a foreign market and came upon a display of objects that looked like apples but were not clearly so. ("Are they what I think they are? Hmmmm. Let's see.") Most of the time, however, when I come upon an apple, what I witness is not just something that looks vaguely familiar, like an object that I have seen before. What I see at once is simply an apple. I recognize it immediately. My doing so points to the role of what Dewey calls *funded knowledge* in an act of perception. I recognize the object to be an apple because I have cognized apples before. I already know what they look like. But note once again that recognition is only the first phase of full perception.

How do I know when my perception of the apple is complete? I never do, says Dewey, at least not absolutely. As applied to perception, the notion of fullness, or completion, is only relative. Perception is always open-ended. There is always more to see, or hear, or touch, or smell, or think about. Yet no object or event lasts forever, nor does an encounter with it. Sooner or later the perceiver turns to something else, even though a particular object or event offers more to be perceived.

From an educational perspective a far more interesting question than when to stop perceiving something concerns when and how to begin the process. Dewey makes the point that when we are bent on getting something done or on reaching a goal of some kind (which is most of the time), we customarily treat objects and events solely in terms of their instrumental value. We recognize them and make use of them, but we do not actually perceive them, at least not in the appreciative manner that Dewey describes. Our customary way of not perceiving our surroundings, of being blind to their subtleties, may become so habitual that we seldom, if ever, cast a truly appreciative eye on anything. So the question becomes, What makes us pause long enough to see things truly and well? What triggers appreciative perception? Dewey's answer, though partial, is "cultivated taste." Here is how he puts it: "Cultivated taste alone is capable of prolonged appreciation of the same object; and it is capable of it because it has been trained to a discriminating procedure which constantly uncovers in the object new meanings to be perceived and enjoyed" (LW1, 299). And how do tastes become cultivated? Through the arts is one way. Dewey explains:

> In one of its meanings, appreciation is opposed to depreciation. It denotes an enlarged, an *intensified* prizing, not merely a prizing, much less—like deprecia-tion—a lowered and degraded prizing. This enhancement of the qualities which make any ordinary experience appealing, appropriable—capable of full assimila-tion and enjoyable, constitutes the prime function of literature, music, drawing, painting, etc., in education. They are not the exclusive agencies of appreciation in the most general sense of that word; but they are the chief agencies of an intensified, enhanced appreciation. As such, they are not only intrinsically and directly enjoy-able, but they serve a purpose beyond themselves. They have the office, in increased degree, of all appreciation in fixing taste, in forming standards for the worth of later experiences. (MW9, 246)

More will be said about this office of the arts in the Chapters 3 and 4.

The experiential extension of direct perception. Art-centered experiences com-monly do not begin and end in the physical presence of, or with the enactment of, the art object. At the front end of such experiences artist and audience alike typically do a considerable amount of planning or preparing before the art object comes into being or is witnessed as a finished product. This preparatory phase is not simply ideational or imaginative. It is not just a matter of thinking about what is to happen, though thinking and imagining may play a large role in the process. On the part of the artist, materials must be obtained, instru-ments readied, sketches drawn, and so forth. On the part of the audience, calls must be made, tickets purchased, reviews read, travel undertaken, and more. Throughout this process expectations are being formed (accumulated and conserved, as we would now say) and a state of readiness engendered. We look forward to our encounter with the object or event with an ever increasing degree of anticipation and eagerness. How long that preparatory stage may last will vary from one art-centered experience to another. It may also differ signifi-cantly for artists and audiences. An artist, for example, might begin to envision a work years before its execution, whereas for audiences the preparatory period is usually much briefer.

At the far end of such experiences, beyond the creation and appreciation of the art object itself, lie the afterthoughts and imaginings that it occasions. These, too, occur routinely for artist and audience alike, though again, there may be important differences in how the work continues to resonate for each group. There may also be differences from one art form to another. For audiences of the performing arts it is often not until the curtain has fallen and the houselights go on that the evaluation of the performance begins in earnest. That process may take a lot of time for some, requiring them to see and hear the performance more than once; for others, their response may all be sorted out on the way home.

More than the evaluation of the object or event extends beyond our direct perception of it. We continue to think about the work and to recall it imaginatively in other ways as well. We discuss it with others, we daydream about it, we remain cheered by it or upset by it long after it has ceased to exist as an immediate event. We use it as a standard against which to judge other works, past and future. Dewey says: "The work, in the sense of working, of an object of art does not cease when the direct act of perception stops. It continues to operate in indirect channels." That the work of the artwork indirectly continues leads Dewey to conclude that "there is no final term in appreciation of a work of art" (LW10, 144). Its effect "presses forward in future experiences, even if only subconsciously" (LW10, 142).

The contribution of perception to meaning. Direct perceptions come and go. They are, says Dewey, "intermittent and discrete, like a series of signal flashes, or telegraphic clicks." "Yet," he goes on, "they involve a continuum of *meaning* in process of formation" (LW1, 233). Though discrete, they contribute to a cumulative state of affairs. That continuum of meaning deals with potential consequences in which the present and the future are inextricably linked. "To *perceive*," says Dewey, "is to acknowledge unattained possibilities; it is to refer the present to consequences, apparition to issue, and thereby to behave in deference to the *connections* of events." The potential consequences known to us through perception engender an attitude that Dewey describes as "predictive expectancy, wariness." That attitude alerts us to what could come into being (i.e., become consequent) if the object or event is acted upon in certain ways. It also alerts us to what will happen, whether or not anyone acts to intervene in its occurrence. Those consequences "also *mark* the thing itself, and form its nature; the event thus marked becomes an object of contemplation; as meaning, future consequences already belong to the thing" (LW1, 143–144).

The notion of an event being marked by its future consequences establishes the objectivity of meaning. It says that meaning resides in objects and events as definitively as it does in the mind or the eye of the beholder. Rain may not always pour from a threatening sky, but the threat of its doing so belongs as much to the sky as it does to the consciousness on which that awareness registers. This is not to say that all perceptions are true. We may see the sky as threatening even when it is not, even perhaps when the sun is brightly shining. (Someone whose judgment veers that far from the norm we would probably call demented or at least suspect that he or she is speaking a language different from our own.) What makes the sky truly threatening is the empirically established connection between clouds of a certain form and color and certain kinds of ensuing weather. We may subject our perceptions to empirical test and come to place ever greater trust in them, but as perceptions, they are what they are, independent of what we may subsequently come to believe about them. Dewey sums up the existential status of perceptions in this way: "Empirically, however, the characteristic thing about perceptions in their natural estate, apart from subjection to an art of knowing, is their irrelevance to both truth and error; they exist for the most part in another dimension, whose nature may be suggested by reference to imagination, fancy, reverie, affection, love and hate, desire, happiness and misery" (LW1, 235). In short, perceptions must be tested (i.e., subjected to the art of knowing) before we can attest to their truth or falsity beyond the perceptual field of the person experiencing them. Yet as perceptions, they have a meaning that remains incontrovertible, whether or not they turn out to be verifiable in other terms.

Perception for its own sake versus perception put to use. When we are not trying to fathom the meaning of an object or event but only responding with delight to whatever we witness or hear—the beauty of a sunset, let us say, or the antics of a kitten with a ball of yarn, or a story told by a friend or a familiar tune—we might be said to be engaged in *perception for its own sake.* The first two examples—those involving the sunset and the kitten—pertain to what we earlier called aesthetic experience in general. The latter two—those referring to the story and the tune—refer to that subset of aesthetic experiences that we have been calling art centered.

Perception for its own sake, whether for experience in general or art-centered experience, differs from the kind of perceiving that goes on when we are engaged in the solution of a problem, as when we are trying to make our way somewhere and have to read the signs that will lead us there. The latter form of perceiving we will call *perception put to use.* Efficacy, rather than intrinsic enjoyment, is its natural culmination.

A distinction akin to this one is often introduced when trying to decide the class or status of an object or event as a work of art. If all we do is enjoy looking at it or listening to it, so the rule goes, we call it fine art. If we enjoy its immediate presence but also put it to use, it is practical art. And if we gain no immediate enjoyment from it but simply put it to use more or less inattentively, it is not art at all.

As rules of thumb, those distinctions have their uses. In some situations they work quite well. They also, however, tempt us to overlook a number of other distinctions that also prove helpful and must be kept in mind. Dewey pointed repeatedly to the limited usefulness of the fine art–practical art distinction.

> It is tempting to make a distinction and say that a thing belongs to the sphere of use when perception of its meaning is incidental to something else; and that a thing belongs to fine art when its other uses are subordinate to its use in perception. The distinction has a rough practical value but cannot be pressed too far. For in produc-tion of a painting or a poem, as well as in making a vase or a temple, a perception is also employed as means for something beyond itself. Moreover, the perceptions of urns, pots and pans as commodities may be intrinsically enjoyable, although these things are primarily perceived with reference to some use to which they are put. (LW1, 283)

Both of Dewey's points stand in need of elaboration. When he says that in the production of a work of art (whether fine or practical) perception is "em-ployed as means for something beyond itself," he alludes to the fact that every art object must be designed and executed as a physical object (even "found" art objects must be removed from their original context, readied for display, and so on). Design and execution entail perceiving in the service of a goal that lies beyond itself, that is, beyond sheer perceiving. The artist may or may not enjoy what she is doing at each moment while producing the work, but whatever her immediate reaction, she must also be caught up in perceiving a wide range of relations that have to do with what goes with what, with how this fits with that, with how the work hangs together as a whole.

What is true for the artist is true for the object's spectators or audience. They, too, must often labor to see or to understand what an art object means or why it has its particular form or content. In the throes of that labor they may be forced to interrupt their immediate enjoyment of the object and adopt a more perception-put-to-use than perception-for-its-own-sake point of view. It may be that the work's puzzling qualities are themselves enjoyable. The puzzling elements may even have been designed and put there on purpose, a possibility already mentioned in my discussion of the role of tension in an art-centered experience.

By pointing out that useful objects—like a teaspoon—may also be intrinsically enjoyable, Dewey reminds us that perception for its own sake (attention to the immediacy of experience) is always an option. We are always free to take in the aesthetic dimension of an experience, to see objects and events not solely in terms of where they lead or how they might serve us but also as centers of attention in their own right. Our failure to partake of life's richness, to enjoy its qualitative immediacy, leaves us divorced from the here and now, vainly directing our thoughts and aspirations toward an imagined future that never arrives. That condition, Dewey would say, is to be avoided at all costs. Works of art help to instruct us in the how and the why of avoiding it.

Chapter 2 The Spirituality of Art-Centered Experiences

In Chapter 1, I laid out the bare bones of Dewey's ideas about what the arts contribute to human affairs; in Chapters 3 and 4 we will look at what it might mean to put those ideas into practice. This chapter serves as a bridge. The need for a bridge arises in part from things that Dewey leaves unsaid in his account. For example, though he goes to great lengths in explaining how art-centered experiences may teach us something about how to make more of our experience artlike in quality, he has relatively little to say about other potential lessons that the arts might teach. Once we have mastered the lessons that Dewey sees the arts as teaching, what is left for them to do? Dewey addresses that question by indirection when he says: "In an imperfect society— and no society will ever be perfect—fine art will be to some extent an escape from, or an adventitious decoration of, the main activities of living. But in a better-ordered society than that in which we live, an infinitely greater happiness than is now the case would attend all modes of production" (LW10, 87).

I find that statement somewhat misleading. It suggests that Dewey believes there will always be a place in our lives for the fine arts as a form of entertainment and as adventitious decoration but that our need for them on a more vital level will diminish as the artfulness of ordinary experience increases and becomes more widespread. Dewey, I suspect, would have been uncomfortable with that summary, yet it does come close to capturing what he said. It also gives voice to a view that several others have put forward over the years, both in the distant past and in recent times. Such views have been harshly criticized both then and now. In this chapter I will examine the pros and cons of the view through the eyes of both its defenders and its critics. Though Dewey will drop out of sight for a time, his ideas will reappear long before the chapter comes to a close.

The first question to be explored is this: Might it be an office of the arts, either wholly or in part, to wean us from our historical attachment to artistic objects and performances, to usher in an age in which the arts as we have known them for centuries no longer have a place or at least no longer function as they once did? That radical (some would say outrageous) possibility is thoughtfully examined by George J. Leonard in a book entitled *Into the Light of Things: The Art of the Commonplace from Wordsworth to John Cage* (1994). After tracing the history of what he calls the second art world, which began, in his telling, near the turn of the eighteenth century and was marked by "a change in what certain artists intended to accomplish," Leonard concludes that although the arts have definitely not outlived their usefulness, as several prominent figures had predicted would happen—among them Wordsworth, Emerson, Carlyle, and Ruskin—they have indeed only recently emerged from a phase of their history during which their future was seriously called into question. As a consequence of the arts having passed through that period of questioning, Leonard tells us, today's artists and their audiences stand on the threshold of a new era, "a new art world," and perhaps, he adds, "a final, permanent [one]." Far from believing that art is over, Leonard himself insists that insofar as the future of the arts is concerned, "there has been no moment this fresh since the late 1790s when Wordsworth wrote *Lyrical Ballads*." His work closes on the following note of optimism: "Goethe, at the beginning of the last art world, wrote that the people born after such a time are like those who walk in the reaped field picking up the gleanings. After living so long in the gleaning-time of the second aesthetic, the fresh time has come around to us again" (Leonard 1994, 192).

Leonard draws inspiration for his view from Arthur C. Danto, whose writings are by now familiar to all who take a serious interest in the arts. In his book *The Transfiguration of the Commonplace* (1981), which contains the fullest account of his position, Danto argues that, beginning in the late 1880s, painters throughout Europe and America began to break away from pure representation and became increasingly absorbed with the question of what constitutes a work of art. Their preoccupation with that question, which Danto looks on as being philosophical in its expression, culminated in the art of the 1960s and 1970s, when, as Danto more recently put it, art for the first time "achieved a philosophical sense of its own identity" (1994, 324). With that achievement, Danto concludes, the predominant narrative that gave shape and direction to the arts for more than a hundred years finally came to an end.

Like Leonard, Danto speaks of art's future in positive terms. His matching words of hope come as he describes the plethora of possibilities facing artists from the late sixties forward. "Once art had ended you could be an abstractionist, a realist, an allegorist. . . . Everything was permitted, since nothing was historically mandated. I call this the Post-Historical Period of Art, and there is no reason for it ever to come to an end. Art can be externally dictated to, in terms of either fashion or of politics, but internal dictation by the pulse of its own history is now a thing of the past" (Danto 1992, 9).

Though Leonard and Danto share the belief that a vital phase of art's history has come to an end, and though both speak optimistically about what lies ahead, there remain crucial differences between them. What Leonard sees as having reached its logical fulfillment (though not perhaps its termination) is a particular use of the arts, a way of employing them in the service of a goal that lies outside the arts themselves. That goal, Leonard tells us, is to awaken us or, more accurately, to reawaken us to the delights of the commonplace, to the wonder and beauty that reside in ordinary objects and everyday scenes. To Leonard, that goal is fundamentally religious in its orientation.

What Danto sees as having ended is a guiding narrative—an inner logic, one might say—that had given a sense of direction, first, to representational art and, later, to modern art. The search for an inner logic to art, Danto believes, had by the mid- to late-sixties been taken as far as artists could take it. From that point forward it was up to philosophers (like Danto himself, presumably) to complete the task or at least to pursue it further.

In putting forth their separate arguments both Leonard and Danto ascribe landmark status to particular works of art. Each focuses on a single work that epitomizes the termination of the historical process that he describes. For Leonard, the culminating work was John Cage's *4' 33"*, first performed in Maverick Concert Hall in Woodstock, New York, on August 29, 1952; for Danto, the work of equivalent significance was Andy Warhol's *Brillo Box*, first displayed in Manhattan's Stable Gallery in the spring of 1964. Each brings to a head, or so it is claimed, the underlying issues whose development provides the backbone of one or the other's account. Each work is described as having been revelatory, even epiphanic, for many in the audience. In the case of Warhol's *Brillo Box,* Danto testifies to having shared in the epiphany. Leonard appears not to have witnessed a live performance of Cage's *4' 33",* but he does report the experience of someone who was present and was so affected. He also describes a similar experience of his own, brought on, apparently, by being immersed in the cultural climate of the fifties and sixties, when works by artists like Cage and Warhol were a common topic of discussion among New York intellectuals.

Of the two theses just summarized, Leonard's is by far the more paradoxical. The notion of painters trying to penetrate to the very heart of art through the medium of their own works excites the imagination, to be sure, as it clearly did Danto's in 1964 when he hit upon that conception while gazing at Warhol's *Brillo Box.* But the excitement that it generates lacks the puzzling aspect, not to say the humor, implicit in the idea of art being consciously employed as an instrument of its own undoing. The arts have certainly been criticized many times in the past by those who look on them as idle pastimes or even as a source of corruption. They have also been viewed by Hegel and others as transitory, as elements of an intermediary stage on the way to a universalized consciousness. But for artists themselves to join in the attack, for them be among art's detractors, sounds not just contradictory but downright odd.

Even though efforts to make use of the arts in this perverse way seem not to have worked—at least not for most of art's public—we still may profitably ask, as Leonard has done, Why was the idea attractive in the first place, and why does it remain so today for some people? We also need to ask, however, whether the idea may be flawed in ways that initially went unnoticed. Was it, in other words, a bad idea from the start, or did it just happen to go wrong somewhere along the way?

Unfortunately, Leonard does not consider either possibility as fully as it deserves, although the idea of using the arts to awaken us to the folly of finding comfort in the arts seems worthy of close examination in itself and leads to a host of other questions about how the arts can and do relate to common experience. Should we, for example, conceive of the arts as being in competition with ordinary experience, forcing us to choose between the two of them at crucial points? Or might the relation between life and art be more complementary than opposed?

John Dewey insightfully explored such questions in *Art as Experience.* Arthur Danto and a host of others continue to probe them today. To participate in that exploration, using Leonard's thesis as a starting place, I must summarize his argument in sufficient detail to reveal its structure and underlying premises. I shall then turn to the work that he deems exemplary: John Cage's *4' 33"*. After examining what Leonard and others have to say about that work, I will move to the broader issue of the relationship between art and ordinary experience.

GEORGE LEONARD'S ARGUMENT

Leonard's thesis boils down to this: Throughout the past two hundred years there has been a move afoot to denigrate the importance of the arts and to replace them, as a source of human gratification, with a deepened and refreshened appreciation of the beauty to be found in nature and in the ordinary affairs of life. This back-to-nature thesis has been put forward by many others over the years. More recently, M. H. Abrams (1971) and Harold Bloom (1971) have offered a similar story about the phase of art's history that began in the mid to late eighteenth century. Leonard's telling of that now familiar tale gives it a fresh twist, however. He adds a note of stridency lacking in prior accounts. He does so by focusing on several of the more extreme statements made by advocates of what Leonard speaks of as the anti-art position. These individuals argued that life itself contains a sufficiency of beauty, making the arts not only unnecessary but actually distracting. In the past, Leonard claims, historians have either dismissed such statements out of hand or have overlooked them entirely. To have done so, he believes, was a big mistake.

According to Leonard, the anti-art movement began with the onset of Romantic thought in the late eighteenth century. Its English version was spearheaded by the young William Wordsworth, who gave poetic voice to a vision of the future in his "Prospectus," a fragment of verse that first appeared at the end of his poem "Home at Grasmere." The latter was later reprinted as an introduction to a longer and more ambitious work entitled "The Recluse."

In the section of "Prospectus" to which Leonard attends, Wordsworth asks why it is that Paradise and Elysian groves and the lost continent of Atlantis should be only "departed things" and "mere fiction of what never was." Why can't we create equivalent glories here on earth? he wants to know. We can and will, is his answer. All we need to do is change the way we relate to the world. We need to look upon it with increased love and affection. On the happy day when that new way of looking has been realized, the Elysian groves and Paradise itself will lie before us.

For the discerning intellect of Man
When wedded to this goodly universe
In love and passion, shall find these [fabled vistas]
A simple produce of the common day. (Wordsworth 1983, 537)

What is the role of the artist, particularly the poet, in effecting that glorious state of affairs? How can he or she help bring about that ultimate wedding of Man's intellect and the goodly universe? And what will happen to the arts when that glorious day arrives? Wordsworth answers with a metaphor. The poet's job, he informs us, is like that of a minister rehearsing the marriage vows. "Long before the blissful hour arrives," I "would chant, in lonely peace, the spousal verse of this great consummation."

Leonard sums up the implications of Wordsworth's position in "Prospectus": "Those who would teach people to find paradise in the 'simple produce of the common day' had to have been necessarily ill at ease with the very concept of an art object, of an elite object superior to the commonplace whose exaltation was their very goal." Such visionaries, Leonard asserts, must necessarily be "anti-art, or at least anti-art object" (Leonard 1994, 24).

Wordsworth's anti-art sentiments turn out to be relatively mild compared with others that Leonard cites. Sharper commentary comes from Emerson, Carlyle, and Ruskin. All three, in one way or another, advocate abandoning the arts entirely once they have performed their function as a means of enlightenment. Emerson's views are typical. In his essay, "Art," Emerson points out that "it has been the office of art to educate the perception of beauty" (Emerson 1983, 432). Painting and sculpture "are gymnastics of the eye, its training to the niceties and curiosities of its function" (434). Yet art's office, particularly as it has been performed by painting and sculpture, "seems to be merely initial" (433). Emerson spells out the meaning of what it means to be initial in no uncertain terms. "Painting seems to be to the eye what dancing is to the limbs. When that has educated the frame to self-possession, to nimbleness, to grace, the steps of the dancing-master are better forgotten" (434).

Sculpture comes off even worse than painting in Emerson's treatment of it. "The art of sculpture is long ago perished to any real effect," he casually remarks. "It was originally a useful art, a mode of writing, a savage's record of gratitude or devotion" (437). But no longer. Nowadays, to him, the following pair of experiences are typical. "Under an oak tree loaded with leaves and nuts, under a sky full of eternal eyes, I stand in a thoroughfare; but in the works of our plastic arts, and especially of sculpture, creation is driven into a corner. I cannot hide from myself that there is a certain appearance of paltriness, as of toys, and the trumpery of a theater in sculpture" (438). And so: "Away with your nonsense of oil and easels, of marble and chisels, except to open your eyes to the masteries of eternal art, they are hypocritical rubbish" (434).

Nor does music escape Emerson's criticism. "The sweetest music," he tells us, "is not in the oratorio but in the human voice when it speaks from its instant life tones of tenderness, truth, or courage" (438). Human conversation, the soft murmurs of lovers, the orator's declaration, the call to arms—these are sounds that provide a true balm to the human spirit, more so than do the harmonious tones that issue from the concert hall.

When he turns to the writing of prose and poetry, Emerson becomes far less dismissive than when discussing the visual or aural arts. Indeed, his stance toward literature can only be called eulogistic, to employ one of Dewey's favorite phrases. "The use of literature," he informs, "is to afford us a platform whence we may command a view of our present life, a purchase by which we may move it" (408). And the poet "is representative. He stands among partial men for the complete man, and apprises us not of his wealth, but of the commonwealth" (448). Nor is that all. The poet "unlocks our chains and admits us to a new scene" (463). "He announces that which no man foretold. He is the true and only doctor; he knows and tells; he is the only teller of news, for he was present and privy to the appearance which he describes. He is a beholder of ideas, and an utterer of the necessary and causal" (450). Here is Emerson's testament to what the poet does for him personally: "He smites and arouses me with his shrill tones, breaks up my whole chain of habits, and I open my eye on my new possibilities. He claps wings to the sides of all the solid old lumber of the world, and I am capable once more of choosing a straight path in theory and practice" (409). Poets, Emerson concludes, "are thus liberating gods" (462). This lavish praise on behalf of poetry raises the question of whether all the arts introduce us to the beauties of nature and the wonders of human invention or only some.

Carlyle and Ruskin, Leonard tells us, harbor anti-art sentiments akin to those expressed by Emerson. He quotes Carlyle as saying, "May the Devil fly away with the Fine Arts!" (Leonard 1994, 90). Ruskin flatly declares, "I believe any sensible person would change his pictures, however good, for windows." Leonard also quotes Ruskin as saying things that allow for art's value yet do so in ways that deprecate its standing. Thus, "You will never love art well till you love what she mirrors better" and "The love of art involves the greater love of nature" (Leonard 1994, 99).

Leonard notes that both Ruskin and Emerson express self-contradictory sentiments with respect to the place of art in human affairs, whereas Carlyle remains consistent in his vituperative rejection of art. "He despises art objects," Leonard concludes (101). Yet Carlyle, like Emerson, treats literature much more diffidently than he does the visual arts. He lauds his fellow countrymen Robert Burns and Sir Walter Scott, and he has the highest of praise for Dante and Shakespeare. So it is not the arts in toto that Carlyle rejects. As with Emerson, it is principally the visual arts that suffer the brunt of his scorn.

Using quotations such as these, Leonard comes to the following conclusion. Starting with Wordsworth, individuals of a certain religious orientation began to employ the arts for an essentially religious purpose, one that had little or nothing to do with art itself. Although these individuals made use of the arts for religious ends, they were never really comfortable doing so, for their basic goal was to turn their audience's attention away from art objects and toward the natural world. The goal of pulling away from the arts entirely was finally reached, Leonard claims, in the last half of this century. Its attainment is epitomized in the career of John Cage and becomes most starkly manifest in his work *4′33″*. Speaking of those who shared in Cage's goal and who worked toward its accomplishment, Leonard observes, "Once these people were able to teach their lessons without art's dangerous, competing objects, they did so, with loud self-congratulation." He further notes, "When we think of the joy with which they finally abandoned art objects, we realize having this religious orientation actually made people necessarily anti-art, or at least anti-art *object*" (Leonard 1994, 24). That, in a nutshell, is Leonard's account.

The religious orientation to which Leonard refers carries the label Natural Supernaturalism, a term coined by Thomas Carlyle in the early 1830s and subsequently adopted by the critics M. H. Abrams and Harold Bloom, who use it to characterize a broad set of beliefs having to do with the loss of faith in traditional religion and the wish to replace that loss with a deepened appreciation of the natural world. As Abrams describes it, "The general tendency was, in diverse degrees and ways, to naturalize the supernatural and to humanize the divine" (Abrams 1971, 68). Though the term itself comes from Carlyle, a Scotsman, Bloom finds in Natural Supernaturalism a variant of what he calls the American religion. Speaking of the form that it took within English Romantic poetry, Bloom says, "Though it is a displaced Protestantism, or a Protestantism astonishingly transformed by different kinds of humanism or naturalism, the poetry of the English Romantics is a kind of religious poetry, and the religion is in the Protestant line, though Calvin or Luther would have been horrified to contemplate it" (Bloom 1971, xvii). Its American variant "frequently is the actual substance of what we confront in what at first seem secular phenomena in the United States." As Bloom sees it, "The central fact about American life, as we enter the final decade of the twentieth century, is that our religiosity is everywhere" (Bloom 1992, 38–39).

Leonard takes Abrams and Bloom to task for assuming "that because we first encountered variants of Natural Supernaturalism in the artworld it must have something intrinsically to do with the artworld" (Leonard 1994, 22). He calls that assumption erroneous. If we are to believe Leonard, not only does Natural Supernaturalism have nothing intrinsically to do with the artworld, it doesn't even belong there. On the contrary, he pictures it as having struggled for nearly two centuries to escape art's embrace.

Abrams's and Bloom's error, Leonard believes, lies in their failure to take seriously those statements by Emerson, Wordsworth, and others that express "stunning hostility," if not outright contempt, for various kinds of art objects (23). If we take such statements to heart and connect them with events taking place in the artworld of the 1960s, we see in a flash—Leonard reports it as having been, for him, an "aha" experience—that art and Natural Supernaturalism constitute a sorry mismatch, a shotgun marriage whose future happiness was doomed from the start.

But is that so? Must one see the mismatch in a flash? Is the conjoining of the arts and Natural Supernaturalism, or whatever one wishes to call the religious orientation that Leonard speaks of, as ill-fated a union as he makes out? The quotations that he cites on behalf of his thesis certainly pack a punch. That such opinions were expressed not by a few obscure cranks and eccentrics but by major literary figures cannot help but make us sit up and take notice. Their rhetorical power aside, the statements remain unsettling. They make us wonder why critics as astute as Abrams and Bloom overlooked the significance of such telling remarks when they undertook their earlier surveys. Was it, as Leonard suggests, because of an erroneous assumption concerning the intrinsic linkage between Natural Supernaturalism and the artworld? Or could there be some other explanation? Might there be a connection of some kind between a religious orientation, on the one hand, and various kinds of artistic endeavors, on the other, without it being one for all to see? And might not the complexity or subtlety of such a connection partially explain some of the contradictions and inconsistencies apparent in the writings of Emerson and Ruskin? Could it be that Emerson and Ruskin, when launched on one of their periodic outbursts against one or more of the arts, were often so overcome by the strength of their conviction that they failed to think things through as carefully as they might otherwise have done?

Probing a little more deeply than we have yet have done into Leonard's aha experience—occasioned by suddenly seeing the relation between the anti-art sentiments of Wordsworth and others and the end-of-art arguments of the 1960s—we encounter more puzzles. Leonard finds it "extraordinary" that no one yet has drawn the linkage between Wordsworth's talk of "the simple produce of the common day" and Danto's transfiguration of the commonplace (Leonard 1994, 23). To remark upon the absence of such a discussion and to call it "extraordinary," however, implies that the relation between the two is clear and unequivocal. But is that so? Are Danto and Wordsworth talking about the same thing? There are similarities between them, true enough. They both highlight the relation between art and common things. They both speak of a time when certain functions of art may become obsolete. But to imply, as Leonard does, that they are thereby referring to the same set of circumstances, that today's artists who paint Brillo boxes or who compose musical events that feature no intentional sound are somehow adrift in "Wordsworth's current," stretches surface resemblances to the limit (216).

We have come to a huge gap in Leonard's argument, one that he acknowledges but does little to repair. What I find missing is a sustained account of what was going on in the arts between the time of Wordsworth and the arrival of modernists like John Cage. For the most part, Leonard leaves his readers guessing about what took place between Wordsworth's declaration of purpose in his "Prospectus" of 1814 and John Cage's $4'33''$, first performed in 1952. He clearly wants us to believe that the former somehow prefigured the latter. But he does not provide the missing links of historical influence. Nor does he draw the connections rationally.

Because Leonard jumps from Wordsworth to Cage in a single bound, we must do so as well, for our purpose is not to fill the gap so much as it is to consider the merit of the overarching argument; that is, we seek to understand what may be right or wrong about the goal of using the arts to undo the arts. The fact that Wordsworth and Cage (among others) may have pursued that common goal for reasons having little to do with each other and therefore without the continuity of purpose that Leonard ascribes to them does not detract from the fact that both argued on behalf of such a goal. To probe beneath that surface similarity I need to offer an extended account of Cage's

4′ 33″, a work lauded as "a cultural landmark for our times" and "the pivotal composition of this century" (Revill 1992, 166). Cage himself describes it as "perhaps my own best piece, at least the one I like most" (Kostelanetz 1988, 65). My reason for telling the story of Cage's work at some length (aside from its intrinsic interest) is that it illustrates so well what it means for a single art-centered experience to insinuate itself into the fabric of a person's life. The detailed account also allows for connections to be drawn to Dewey's work.

CAGE'S *4′ 33″*

Cage reports that he conceived of composing a piece like *4′ 33″* in the late 1940s, though it was not until 1952 that the work premiered (Kostelanetz 1988, 66). His initial idea, which he described in a lecture given at Vassar College in 1948, was "to compose a piece of uninterrupted silence and sell it to Muzak Co." The piece was going to have these features: "It will be 3 or 4½ minutes long—those being the standard lengths of 'canned' music—and its title will be *Silent Prayer*. It will open with a single idea which I will attempt to make as seductive as the color and shape and fragrance of a flower. The ending will approach imperceptibility" (Kostelanetz 1993, 43). The question of how to deliver on his conception occupied Cage's thoughts for some time. "In fact," he says, "I probably worked longer on my 'silent' piece than I worked on any other. I worked four years" (Kostelanetz 1988, 67).

What took him so long? Fear, we are told: "I was afraid that my making a piece that had no sounds in it would appear as if I were making a joke" (Kostelanetz 1988, 67). But fear of being misunderstood provides only a partial explanation. Other influences were at work. Between 1948 and 1952 Cage became keenly interested in Zen Buddhism and attended lectures on that subject given by Daisetsu Teitaro Suzuki at Columbia University. Those lectures left their mark. As David Revill, one of Cage's biographers, puts it, "Engagement with Zen brought to fruition various aspects of his aesthetic, such as impersonalism, and the belief that modern music could help reconcile listeners with modern life; it urged on the working through of his ascetic tendencies. It clarified his understanding of what constituted beauty, what constituted art, and what its function was" (Revill 1992, 118). Less philosophical aspects of Cage's encounters with Suzuki may have left their mark as well. For example, Cage reports that "Suzuki never spoke loudly. When the weather was good, the windows were open, and the airplanes leaving La Guardia flew directly overhead from time to time, drowning out whatever he had to say. He never repeated what was said during the passage of the airplane" (Revill 1992, 109).

As important as Cage's studies of Zen may have been in strengthening his determination to present a silent composition, another key influence was at work, too: the work of a friend, the artist Robert Rauschenberg. Rauschenberg's influence turned out to be decisive. As a fellow student at Black Mountain College, Rauschenberg had painted a set of canvases that were entirely white. (When exhibited in 1953 they were appropriately titled *White Paintings*.) These became, in Cage's words, "airports for particles of dust and shadows that are in the environment" (Kostelanetz 1988, 188). Inspired by his friend's artistic breakthrough, Cage yearned to do something equivalent for the sounds of the environment. "When I saw those [Rauschenberg's white canvases],' I said, 'Oh yes, I must; otherwise I'm lagging, otherwise music is lagging'" (Kostelanetz 1988, 67). His response to Rauschenberg's challenge was the piece *4′33″*.

In Cage's own listing of his musical compositions, the following entry appears: "*4′33″* (1952), tacet [a musical term meaning, literally, 'be silent'], any instrument or combination of instruments: This is a piece in three movements during all three of which no sounds are intentionally produced. The lengths of time were determined by chance operations but could be any others" (Kostelanetz 1993, 52). In the program of the premier performance, the three movements of *4′33″* were listed as 30″, 2′23″, and 1′40″, designations referring to the length of each section in minutes and seconds. The total came to four minutes and thirty-three seconds, as the work's title indicates. Though Cage states that any instrument or combination of instruments may be used in performances of *4′33″*, the sole instrument used to date has been the piano.

Performances

The premiere of *4′33″* in Woodstock in 1952 was on the occasion of a benefit concert on behalf of the Artists Welfare Fund. Cage's work was the last piece on the program. Here is Leonard's description of what took place. "In the premiere, the pianist David Tudor walked out to a piano in . . . [an] auditorium which opened onto some woods. At a signal he opened the keyboard as any pianist would do who was about to play. A hush fell; and then he sat for 4′33″, though he did close the keyboard cover three times to signify the work's three 'movements,'" Leonard remarks that the first performance was "incredibly lucky" because at its beginning a brief summer storm passed overhead. The storm's phases (distant thunder, then rain, then clearing) coincided almost perfectly with the three movements of the piece (Leonard 1994, 170).

The second performance, which occurred in Carl Fisher Concert Hall in New York City on April 14, 1954, lacked the incidental sounds of a summer storm but, inevitably, had an aural background of its own. Allan Kaprow, who was in the audience that day, offered this recollection some years later.

> It was in the summertime [Kaprow's memory is incorrect: the month was April] and the windows were open, either in the hall or in the hallway outside. We heard the traffic sounds. David Tudor . . . came out and sat at the piano, and I believe he had a somewhat formal outfit on, as befitting a performer. He adjusted, in the usual manner, his seat—I remember this very vividly—because he made a pointed activity out of it. He kept pushing it up and pushing it down. He had a stopwatch, which was the usual way of John's things—being timed. And he opened up the piano lid and put his hands on the keys as if he was going to play some music. What we expected. We were waiting. And nothing happened. Pretty soon you began to hear chairs creaking, people coughing, rustling of clothes, then giggles. And then a police car came by with its siren running, down below. Then I began to hear the elevator in the building. Then the air conditioning going through the ducts. (Leonard 1994, 188–189)

Audience Reactions

Cage recalls that during the premiere "people began whispering to one another, and some people began to walk out. They didn't laugh—they were irritated when they realized nothing was going to happen." He adds somewhat wistfully, "They haven't forgotten it 30 years later; they're still angry" (Kostelanetz 1988, 65–66). One witness reported that during the heated discussion that followed the evening's recital, a local artist stood up and "with languid vehemence" made a suggestion. "Good people of Woodstock, let's drive these people out of town" (Revill 1992, 166).

Allan Kaprow, whose description of the New York performance I have just presented, had this to add as he recalled watching David Tudor sitting motionless before the piano. Kaprow gradually realized that nothing else was going to happen. "One by one all of us, every one of that audience there—and I think they must have been all of our kind [presumably artists or New York intellectuals]—began to say, 'Oh. We get it. Ain't no such *thing* as silence. If you just listen, you'll hear a lot'" (Leonard 1994, 189). Though not everyone present may have agreed with him, Kaprow was probably not alone in coming to his proud conclusion. His reaction comes close to what Cage had hoped for. Commenting on those who walked out of the Woodstock performance, Cage remarks, "They missed the point. There's no such thing as silence. What they thought was silence, because they didn't know how to listen, was full of accidental sounds" (Kostelanetz 1988, 65).

Other Interpretations

In an interview in 1982 Cage suggests that his "point" in presenting *4'33"* was not simply to demonstrate that there is no such thing as silence but also to suggest that the sounds occurring naturally "constitute a music which is more interesting than the music which they would hear if they went into a concert hall" (Kostelanetz 1988, 65). Others have come to a similar conclusion. Daniel Herwitz, a philosopher who studies modern art, has rephrased Cage's point: "Cage might appear to be saying merely that old fogies should open up their ears so that a world of contemporary sounds can strike them with interest—a kind of irresistible plea for openness in hearing. However, he is emphatically stating something much stronger. He is saying that any concatenation of sounds is music." (Herwitz 1993, 146). Cage's stronger statement does away with so many of the criteria by which music (or any of the other arts) is normally judged that it comes close to eliminating judgment altogether. Re-marking on our customary unwillingness to apply the term *music* to sounds in general, Herwitz says, "The criteria we rely on in deciding not to call these various sound concatenations *music* is that they lack either the kind of overall coherence, development, closure, and elaboration characteristic of works of music or the element of human intention—the compositional hand—that distinguishes art from nature or from the purely fortuitous" (145).

Herwitz reads Cage as delivering two competing messages: one radical, the other less so. The more radical one, which Herwitz calls a form of philosophical skepticism, or, alternatively, "utopian transcendence," "attempts to break through form or to dispense with it so as to allow us to get down to the business of an unmediated reception of the world." Cage's practice "is to get one's ears to hear from scratch. Only Cage does not aim to construct a new way of hearing but to so totally destroy the old that our ears will be reborn" (142). This form of rebirth cannot occur, however, according to Herwitz, for it posits the possibility of "transforming the world into the condition of completely natural hearing" (161), a condition that Herwitz finds unimaginable.

The less radical message Herwitz ascribes to Cage's enduring interest in Zen Buddhism. "In his Zen voice Cage offers *4'33"* not as an image of transcendence but as a way of musically posing Zen questions in the context of Zen training." He explains that "Cage's Zen artistry in *4'33"* is to have invented a performance which flouts the possibility of being a musical piece, for there is nothing to squeeze out of its score. . . . [It seeks] to put a full stop to the urge to make sense of sound. . . . In this sense, 4′33″ is meant to confound the musician and the philosopher [alike]" (163). Herwitz's talk of utopian transcendence and of audiences being reborn as listeners comes across as strongly evangelical, even though it contains no reference to the Christian Gospels. It brings to mind Leonard's emphasis on the religious orientation of Natural Supernaturalism and all that he sees following from it. The same is true of Herwitz's depiction of Cage's Zen artistry. Like Christianity, Zen holds out the promise of a life transformed or reborn.

Richard Kostelanetz, who has written extensively on Cage, has coined a special term to refer to works like 4′33″. He calls them inferential art, which he defines as "a particular kind of creative work, which, though negligible in itself, manages to imply (and thus to have inferred from it) a challenge to conventional rationales." Kostelanetz acknowledges that all art "embodies implications," but, he insists, "only certain rare works successfully express far more inference than artistry" (Kostelanetz 1991, 106). Cage's 4′33″, in his opinion, was such a rare work, making it a quintessential example of inferential art.

Kostelanetz draws four inferences from 4′33″. First, its "'music' consisted of all the accidental noises in the room" (107). Second, "in all performed pieces, what is written as a silent passage is actually filled with extraneous sound (noise), because pure silence is physically impossible." (Third, "no musical piece can twice give us exactly the same aural experience." And fourth, "accidental noise and humanly produced music have equal status within a listening experience" (108).

The Interpretations Interpreted

Herwitz, Kostelanetz, and Leonard are but three of the many commentators who have written on Cage and his works over the years. Of those that I have read, almost everyone mentions 4′33″. It is, after all, Cage's most publicized work and the one he himself liked best. However, none that I have read adds substantially to the remarks of the three mentioned. Consequently, I shall restrict my comments to what those three have said.

The most obvious generalization to make about 4′33″—one on which the three commentators seem to agree—is that the work readily lends itself to more than one interpretation. In Kostelanetz's terms, a number of "inferences" can reasonably be derived from the work. Kostelanetz believes that works like 4′33″ are designed to keep their audiences guessing about their meaning and to stimulate a wide range of interpretations, almost as though the artist doesn't want to be pinned down interpretively. Whether or not that is so (and the generalization is easy to doubt), it is certainly true that sensitive interpreters, like those whose commentary we have been reading, ascribe multiple meanings to the work. Thus when a spectator like Kaprow inwardly shouts "Eureka!" a short way through the performance and prides himself on having understood the point almost at once, we may be reasonably sure that whatever he understood was not all there is to understand. The same is true, though less obviously so, of those who stamped out of the auditorium in anger, even as Kaprow was congratulating himself. They, too, or at least some of them, may have come to a partial understanding of what the piece was about. Some may even have reached the same conclusion as Kaprow did, the difference between them being that whatever the leavers understood they didn't like.

A second point of agreement, at least between Leonard and Herwitz, is that the work has something to do with a religious attitude or, as Leonard prefers, a "religious orientation," though what that something is remains unclear. There seem to be three possibilities. In thinking about them one should keep in mind that when Cage initially contemplated the design of such a piece he planned to call the piece *Silent Prayer*.

One possibility, which, following Leonard, we will call the Natural Supernaturalist alternative, is to look on *4′33″* as a device for calling the listener's attention to the music of the natural world—the sounds of wind, rain, birdsong. The reason for calling such an outlook religious is presumably that the sounds of nature are God given, rather than humanmade, which makes listening to them with that thought in mind akin to an act of piety: the silent prayer that Cage initially imagined.

A second possibility, the "Zen" alternative (I borrow the term from Herwitz), is to look on *4′33″* as a device for awakening the listener to the music that resides in all the sounds that surround us, whether natural or artificial. The reason for calling this outlook religious is that an all-embracing acceptance of whatever sounds are produced in the environment is more pious in its orientation than one that urges us to concentrate on the sounds of nature. The all-embracing view comes closer to the Zen attitude of ascetic passivity.

Although Cage's intentions appear to have been much closer to the Zen alternative than to the Natural Supernaturalistic one, the judgment as to which one provides the best fit depends at least in part on which of the two performances of *4′33″* the critic attended or later selected as being most representative:

the one in Woodstock in 1952 or its repetition in New York City two years later. At the Woodstock performance the period of silence coincided with the passage of a brief thunderstorm overhead. Listeners were treated first to the sound of thunder, next to the patter of rain, and finally, we might imagine, to the distant call of birds, celebrating the storm's passage. Leonard deemed the coincidence lucky, thereby revealing his own acceptance of a Natural Supernaturalist interpretation of the piece. We can easily understand why he might have come to that conclusion (even though he was not present at the performance). In the idyllic setting of Woodstock's Maverick Concert Hall and under the unusual circumstances of a perfectly timed thunderstorm, it would not have been hard to conclude that the heavens were putting on a better show than the one going on indoors. Though the attentive listeners on that rainy day may also have had to contend with the sounds of some people leaving and perhaps even with the snorts of stifled laughter, they could, if they wished, choose to ignore such crude breaches of concertgoing etiquette.

The second performance of *4′33″* offered a different set of circumstances. No sounds of nature filled the acoustical void created by David Tudor's nonplaying. Instead, according to Allan Kaprow, there were only the wail of a police siren, the hum of an air conditioner, the muffled sound of the elevator moving up and down in its shaft, and, even closer at hand, the creaking of chairs and the rustling and giggling of discomfited members of the audience. In short, the demands on the listener, both aurally and cognitively, were of a very different order from those the Woodstock listeners had to deal with. The message in New York could not possibly have been that nature's sounds are superior to conventional music. Instead, Cage's piece constituted a declaration that any sound, even the hum of an air conditioner or a scornful guffaw, offers a music of its own. This is why Leonard has to be wrong (at least from Cage's point of view) in calling the Woodstock thunderstorm a lucky event. The storm, following the Zen interpretation, actually subverted Cage's intention.

A third possible interpretation of *4′33″* also links it to a religious outlook, though I suspect that doing so would make Cage uncomfortable. It relates to the radical skepticism that Herwitz sees lurking within Cage's piece and possibly within his project as a whole. What *4′33″* invites us to do, according to Herwitz, is "to hear sounds as what Kant would call *things in themselves,* things apart from any projection of our categories—here, our modes of imputing to sounds structure and anthropomorphism" (Herwitz 1993, 151). Hearing sounds this way, Herwitz argues, is utterly incapable of human attainment. We cannot divest our surroundings of their accrued meaning and begin afresh. Thus, Herwitz tells us, the radical skepticism latent in Cage's work is doomed. We are left with Cage's milder admonishment to expand the category of music to include the ordinary sounds of the ordinary world.

I, too, discern a form of skepticism buried deep within *4' 33"*, though not the classic philosophical version that Herwitz entertains. What I see thrown into doubt by the piece is not the question of whether we can ever hear sounds pristinely, stripped of their associative meanings but, rather, the more disturbing question of whether anything is worth listening to at all. This doubt finds expression in the attitude of indifference that governs (more accurately, fails to govern) the work's core of silence. It is tempting to conclude that Cage's work has as much to do with the physical antics of Tudor as he sits before the piano as it does with the random sounds that fill the acoustical void.

Mark C. Taylor, a theologian deeply interested in the arts, remarks on a tendency among both modern and postmodern visual artists to deform and deface images, thereby destroying their conventional beauty. Taylor calls this total process "disfiguring." He uses the concept of disfiguring to order a vast number of artistic innovations over the past several decades. One form of disfiguring that Taylor discusses (perhaps its most extreme form) he calls unfiguring. More specifically, he describes it as "an unfiguring that (impossibly) 'figures' the unfigurable" (Taylor 1992, 8). Its chief method is negation. It speaks of absence. As Taylor points out, "The language of absence is silence, which is the absence of language. The process of dis-figuring . . . erases signifiers in order to reveal the transcendental signified that is believed to be the Real. Within this ascetic economy, various strategies of negation are penultimate, for they always point to a surpassing affirmation" (141–142). Perhaps Taylor should have said. "They *almost* always point to a surpassing affirmation," for, as he goes on to say, "as abstraction approaches its end, however, an ominous possibility emerges: perhaps what negation affirms is negation itself. To affirm negation, and nothing but negation, is to affirm nothing. If the negation of signifiers ends by affirming that the transcendental signified is nothing, signs are not significant but are left to float freely in a world without security" (142). Does Cage's work point toward such a meaningless and insecure world? Does the negation of its central silence affirm negation itself, as Taylor fears may happen when one diddles with nothingness? Or does his work manage to escape that ominous possibility and thereby remain a symbol of surpassing affirmation? I have no doubt how Cage would have answered those questions in 1952. He would have pressed for a positive and affirmative reading of *4'33"*, rather than one that focused on the negating hush at its core. I side with that kinder interpretation myself, yet I must acknowledge that Taylor's darker view remains a possibility.

We began with Leonard's claim that there are anti-art sentiments embedded in the Natural Supernaturalist tradition. Leonard thought that when the arts are employed in support of a religious orientation, especially one that celebrates the ordinary and the commonplace, they inevitably cast a negative light on art itself, urging its abandonment. Here, once again, is the way he puts it. The person being spoken of is Wordsworth, but the statement fits all who followed in that tradition. "Those who would teach people to find paradise in the 'simple produce of the common day' *had to have been necessarily* ill at ease with the very concept of an art object, of an elite object superior to the commonplace whose exaltation was their very goal" (Leonard 1994, 24, emphasis added). Is Leonard correct? Must an artist who uses her art to encourage others to seek beauty in nature be necessarily ill at ease with the very concept of an art object? Why so? The thought that art and nature must compete is based on the assumption that we only have so much "free" time available, and if we spend it looking at or listening to a work of art, we can't spend it reveling in the beauty to be found in the simple produce of the common day. But most of us spend little time doing either. During the bulk of our waking hours we are neither contemplating works of art nor enjoying the wonders of nature. Instead, we go about "getting and spending," as Wordsworth says, attuned chiefly to the demands of the immediate situation. That being so, the problem becomes one of finding a time and place for both kinds of aesthetic pursuit. One need not compete with the other.

It remains true, as Leonard so convincingly shows, that each of the central figures whom we have been discussing—Wordsworth, Emerson, Ruskin, Carlyle, and even Cage—is on record as having said some nasty things about one or more of the arts. Emerson criticizes sculpture. Ruskin wants to throw out painting. Cage tells us that street noises are more musical than the sounds issuing from concert halls. Though such anti-art statements may come as a shock, they do not seem to be entailed in the position that each man took toward art's instructional role. In other words, they come across as a form of posturing rather than as serious argument. As Leonard himself points out, the actual behavior of each of those men—their lifelong involvement with the arts and with artists—belies the sincerity of their words. I am not inclined to take such statements too seriously—certainly not as seriously as Leonard recommends.

At the same time, I do find them curious. They bring to mind the many exclusionary manifestos and doctrines that have heralded revolutionary turns in the arts throughout this century and earlier. Indeed, Wordsworth's preface to his *Lyrical Ballads* was just such a manifesto. Typically, the authors of such documents not only set forth a reasoned program of their own but also seek to banish the competition. And they do not always fight fair. Reflecting on all of this, I am brought to wonder whether there might not be something about our experiences with the arts that actually encourages or even engenders the kind of dogmatic enthusiasm and prejudicial blindness contained in such extreme statements. I will return to that possibility in due course. For now, however, I invite a return to Dewey's prime question, which has to do with the kinds of experiences that works of art are prone to engender.

THE TOTALITY OF ART'S IMPACT

The commentary of critics like Herwitz and Kostelanetz makes it seem as though the sole task for the audience in coming to grips with a piece like *4′33″* involves trying to figure out what its author was trying to say. That task is central—of that there can be no doubt. But there is more to the experience of encountering the work. What such an intellectual approach leaves out is the totality of our response to the work: how it makes us feel and how it ties to our memory of other works and to our broader knowledge of the world. Most important, it leaves unexamined the question of how we might be changed as humans as a result of our encounter with the work. This fuller set of considerations covers what I would term the totality of the individual's transactions with the work. Kostelanetz hints at the breadth of that totality when he observes that "in addition to serving a polemical function in an aesthetic argument, [some of] these works . . . , once understood, *induce an experience that includes, but transcends, aesthetic apprehension* as it is traditionally conceived" (Kostelanetz 1991, 106, emphasis added).

Many, if not all, who witnessed Cage's *4′33″* came away from the experience changed in one way or another. Some were angry and remained so for some time. Others were amused. Still others were dumbfounded. A few, like Allan Kaprow, looked on the experience as eye-opening, even mind-boggling. Kaprow reports, "I was very struck by *4′33″*. I intuited that it was his most philosophically and radically *instrumental* piece. 'Instrumental' in the sense that it made available to a number of us not just the sounds in the world but all phenomena. Then the question is, now that everything's available, what do you do?" (Leonard 1994, 188–189).

Kaprow's report may not be the best example of how a single art-centered experience may continue to reverberate within the life of the individual long after the physical encounter is past, but it will suffice to introduce that important topic. What makes the topic important within the present context is not only that such experiences are life-altering events. It is also that they connect to what Dewey refers to when he speaks of an experience whose quality is "so intense that it is justly termed religious" (LW4, 188), one in which "we are carried out beyond ourselves to find ourselves" (LW10, 199). I want to examine three examples of such experiences, each involving an encounter with a single work of art.

The first has already been mentioned. It deals with Arthur C. Danto's reaction to Andy Warhol's *Brillo Box*, which Danto first observed on exhibition in 1964. He speaks of it as "my revelatory moment in art" (Danto 1994, 6). He reports having been immensely excited—"knocked off my horse" is the way he puts it—by certain works of Warhol, works, he tells us, "that others found blank or meretricious or cynical or silly" (237).

What excited Danto about *Brillo Box* in particular was the question to which it gave rise, which was, Why should this object be seen as a work of art while something altogether like it (i.e., an ordinary carton designed to hold Brillo pads) should not? That question, Danto saw at once, was profoundly philosophical. It was, as he put it, "the deep question in ontology of how something could be a work of art while other things which resembled it to the point where at least their photographs were indiscernible, were not" (384).

What made the object even more remarkable in Danto's eyes was its ordinariness, the fact "that it was drawn from a kind of underground of familiar imagery so seemingly distant from the aesthetic preoccupations of those nominally interested in art that it came as a shock to see it in an art gallery, while at the same time it was clear that there was nothing in the prevailing conception of art to rule it out" (Danto 1992, 40).

Besides raising an interesting philosophical question and being shockingly out of place, *Brillo Box*, as Danto came to see it, stood for "a total conceptual upheaval" in art, "a kind of revolutionary reversal" whose effect was enduring and profound (Danto 1990, 7, 292). Danto describes himself as having been in a state of "philosophical intoxication" after his visit to the exhibit. Within months he had written an article for a philosophical journal based on his experience and on the philosophical musings that it had engendered. He soon was also describing his infatuation with Warhol's work before audiences of artists (who were for the most part unfriendly [Danto 1986, x]). His book *The*

Transfiguration of the Commonplace came out in 1981, and soon after that he began to write on art in art journals. Subsequently he became the art critic for *The Nation* and one of the most highly respected critics in the country.

Danto's initial exposure to Pop Art, an early form of what later became known as postmodernism, was by no means limited to the works of Warhol. About the same time as Warhol's show at the Stable Gallery, Danto also became interested in the works of Robert Rauschenberg, Jasper Johns, and Roy Lichtenstein, among others, each of whom was exhibiting works composed of common objects that had been in some way transformed into works of art. The cumulative impact of those works made an indelible impression on Danto, leading him, years later, to declare that "Pop [Art] redeemed the world in an intoxicating way." He also had a curious experience, one that had nothing to do with art per se but was obviously triggered by his intense absorption with artworks of the type described. Here is his report.

> I have the most vivid recollection of standing at an intersection in some American city waiting to be picked up. There were used-car lots on two corners, with swags of plastic pennants fluttering in the breeze and brash signs proclaiming unbeatable deals, crazy prices, insane bargains. There was a huge self-service gas station on a third corner, and a supermarket on the fourth, with signs in the window announcing sales of Del Monte, Cheerios, Land o Lakes butter. Long Island ducklings, Velveeta, Sealtest, Chicken of the Sea. . . . Heavy trucks roared past, with logos on their sides. Lights were flashing. The sound of raucous music flashed out of the windows of automobiles. I was educated to hate all this. I would have found it intolerably crass and tacky when I was growing up an aesthete. . . . But I thought, Good heavens. This is just remarkable! (Danto 1992, 139–140)

What *I* find remarkable about Danto's report are not only the suddenness with which his changed outlook came about and the dramatic reversal of feeling that accompanied it but also the temporal gap between his sidewalk epiphany and his exposure to the works of Pop Art. One might expect such a change to occur immediately upon leaving the Warhol exhibit at the Stable Gallery, let's say, or soon thereafter, rather than days or weeks later (or could it have been months or years?).

Leonard, in his book *Into the Light of Things*, testifies to having had a similar experience, also stimulated, it would seem, by his exposure to the intellectual and artistic climate of New York in the 1960s. "I looked up from a meal in a New York luncheonette one day and saw beauty so overwhelming that I, like Danto, can never forget the moment. The late afternoon summer sun was pouring through the plate glass window onto the candy counter's tiered display, igniting hundreds of rolls of Lifesavers into bars of living color. 'Anything I say, do, or think, is art,' Allan Kaprow was proclaiming in those days. Even those of us not in the artworld savored that new power" (Leonard 1994, 173).

I also wonder how long Danto's, or Leonard's, altered perception endured. Not very long, would be my guess. Neither man reports the change to have been permanent, and I would think that he would have done so if such had been the case. Yet we can be sure that the memory of the event was enduring, including a number of its visual details. Later we will explore how such memories form a part of what Dewey refers to as *an* experience.

Over the years Danto has continued to think and to write about the Warhol work and the exhibition in which he first encountered it. "Some years later," he reports, "I began to attach a different philosophical significance to the exhibition. First of all, I came to feel that with the *Brillo Box,* the true character of the philosophical question of the nature of art had been attained" (Danto 1992, 6). He continues to recall with pleasure (twenty-five years after the event) the atmosphere of the Stable Gallery on that April evening in 1964. "I have the most vivid recollection of that show, and of the feeling of lightheartedness and delight people evinced as they marveled at the piles of boxes, laughing as they bought a few and carried them out in clear plastic bags" (Danto 1990, 290).

My goal in presenting this brief account of Danto's experience with Warhol's *Brillo Box* has not been to take a stand for or against his estimation of the work's significance. Instead, I want to make some general observations about art-centered experiences. Before doing so, let me introduce two further examples, each of which stands as powerful testament to the transformative power of individual works of art.

The first is a report on an art critic's encounter with a display of works by the sculptor Carl Andre: eight arrangements of ordinary bricks, of the kind used in the building trade. They were displayed on the floor of the Tibor de Nagy Gallery in Manhattan. The critic Peter Schjeldahl offers this account of coming upon them.

> The lightning of the movement called minimalism—in retrospect, the dominant aesthetic of the last two decades and one of the most important renovations of the art idea in modern history—struck me in March 1966, when I entered the Tibor de Nagy Gallery and saw some bricks on the floor: eight neat low-lying arrangements of them. Construction in progress, I thought, and I turned to leave. Then another thought halted me: what if it's art? Scarcely daring to hope for anything so wonderful (I may have held my breath), I asked a person in the gallery and was assured that, yes,

this was a show of sculpture by Carl Andre. I was ecstatic. I perused the bricks with a feeling of triumph.

Why?

I could not have explained at the time. It seems to me now that my response to Andre's bricks, like the appearance of the work itself, had been long and well prepared, partaking in one of those moments of zeitgeist when unruly threads of history are suddenly, tightly knotted. What elates then is the illumination, in a flash, of much that has been inchoate and strange in the world and, most of all, in one's own sensibility. An instinct for the radical, a hunger for irreducible fact, a disgust with cultural piety, an aesthetic alertness to the commonplace—all these predispositions were galvanized for me, in a form that embodied and extended them. At the root of such an epiphany is the youthful need to be acknowledged, to know that one is not utterly negligible or crazy, and here was an art (was it art?) that existed in relation to me and that I, in a sense, created.

. . . With [the brick works] at my feet as I walked around the gallery, accumulating views, I felt my awkward self-consciousness, physical and psychological, being valorized, being made the focus and even the point of an experience. I had had intimations of this from artists other than Duchamp, mainly Johns and Warhol. By contrast, though, Johns's moody emblems seemed "too personal" and Warhol's iconizations of mass culture "too social." Here, at last, was the purely and cleanly existing heart of the matter. (Wilson 1991, 204–205)

The striking similarities between Danto's and Schjeldahl's accounts—the lightninglike speed of the shift in perception, the memorable singularity of the perception, the sense of heady excitement that accompanied it, the feeling of having penetrated to the heart of something—hardly require emphasis. The chief difference between the accounts lies in fact that Schjeldahl restricts his report (at least in the account that I have read) to the single occasion of his first encounter with the work of Carl Andre, whereas Danto reports on his Warhol experience again and again and has been doing so for decades.

An additional set of differences between their accounts deserves mention. These have to do with how the particular work functioned within the psychological makeup of each person. For Danto, the main effect of his encounter with *Brillo Box* seems to have been a bringing-together of his philosophical and his aesthetic interests. His insight into the significance of that work enabled him to apply his expertise as a philosopher to a range of questions that had long interested him but had not been at the center of his professional life (Danto was a painter before he became a philosopher). He saw Warhol and others like him as having gone as far in the role of philosophical investigators as the arts would ever take them. From that point forward, Danto believed, it was up to philosophers like himself to press on in identifying the criteria that distinguished artworks from ordinary objects. Like a relay runner at the ready, Danto figuratively seized the baton that Warhol held out to him. To say that he ran with it would be a gross understatement.

Schjeldahl, too, speaks of a drawing-together of at least four disparate elements of his "sensibility"—his instinct for the radical, his hunger for irreducible fact, his disgust for cultural piety, and his aesthetic alertness to the commonplace. All of these, he tells us, became galvanized as he suddenly realized that the odd arrangements of bricks on the floor before him were not just bits of leftover masonry but works of art. He also reports a feeling of vindication in the presence of Andre's works, almost as though they proved him to have been right all along despite the opinion of others. He admits that such a feeling sprang from a youthful need to be acknowledged and also perhaps from a wish to be a contributor to the enterprise of art.

Schjeldahl's reactions strike me as being more developmental or perhaps even adolescent than Danto's. That is to say, they sound as though they contributed to his psychological development, making him feel a bit more grown up. Danto, on the other hand, seems to have been rejuvenated professionally, rather than propelled developmentally, by his encounter with the Warhol exhibit. Both men, however, seem to have benefited psychologically. The differences in those benefits were ostensibly more closely related to where each man stood in his career and his personal life than to any other aspect of their encounters.

A third example of an art-centered experience of epiphanic dimensions is offered by Mark C. Taylor, the theologian whose views on disfiguring in the arts have already been mentioned. Taylor reports on his encounter with an earthwork by Michael Heizer entitled *Double Negative*. The work, which is located about eighty miles northeast of Las Vegas in the Nevada desert, consists of two cuts in the earth. The two excavations, which measure fifty feet deep and thirty feet wide, are on opposite sides of a deep indentation on the eroding edge of Mormon Mesa, making them look like all that remains of a single cut whose center has been obliterated by erosion. From its starting point the floor of each cut pitches down at a forty-five-degree angle. Their combined length is fifteen hundred feet. Two hundred and forty thousand tons of sandstone were removed to form them. The displaced stone fans out in spills that cascade down the cliff side of each excavation.

Taylor reports on two visits to *Double Negative,* taken two days apart. One was made by helicopter, the other by car to the edge of the mesa and then by foot along the sloping floor of one of the cuts. In the accounts he graphically describes the excavation and its desert setting from the air and from ground level, respectively. Both accounts convey Taylor's utter fascination with the work and all that he sees it as symbolizing. The report of his journey by foot contains the fullest description of what the experience meant to him. To capture its richness, I quote from it at length.

> Neither a sculptural nor an architectural object but something else—something other—*Double Negative* is a tear that beckons to approach, indeed, to enter. This work of art cannot be appreciated from without but must be viewed from within. To enter the tear, I had to descend the steep and uneven slope of the rent earth. Only beneath ground level did the stunning proportions of this extraordinary work clearly emerge. . . . From the bottom of the cut, the precision of the lines, surfaces, and planes dissolves. The work is eroding. Its walls crumbling and floor littered with refuse and debris from ancient eons, the *Negative* is a constantly changing ruin. This work of art was not constructed to escape time but to embed us in it ever more deeply. As I passed below the surface, I realized the profound truth of what I had long suspected: to dig down is to go back . . . back through layers and layers of space and time to an *archē* that is, perhaps, "older" than the beginning of our world, the world, any world.
>
> The walls of tear display vast murals, rich collages, assemblages, and combines of unspeakable beauty. Colors and shapes, forms and figures too intricate and complex to have been crafted by any human hand suggest a haunting anonymity, a terrifying impersonality, an inhuman intelligence. Enduring yet fragile sediments release a disturbing fossilized murmur. At the edge of the work, the ground grows even more insecure. Loose sand and gravel fell from beneath my feet, adding to the ever-changing shape of the spoil. The work of art continues.
>
> The late afternoon light of the gray winter day created a somber mood. In the distance, the Virgin River wound its way along the base of the Arizona mountains. Gazing across the canyon to the far side, the cleavage seemed to separate as much as unite. At this edge, on this margin, the void was truly unavoidable. As I turned from the unsettling emptiness of space to the expansive corridors of time, silence unexpectedly rushed toward me. Not just any silence but an overwhelming silence that pressed palpably on my ears, creating a pressure that was almost unbearable. But I did not flee; rather, I paused to linger with the *Negative* in the faint hope that I might become more silent than the silence around me. At this moment silence became visible. *Nothing appeared.* (Taylor 1992, 272)

Taylor ends his account by referring to a silence that became visible—a Cagean silence, one might say. Is that a coincidence? Could it be that the stillness that pressed palpably upon Taylor's ears bore some resemblance to the absence of anticipated sound that caused members of Cage's audience to flee Woodstock's Maverick Concert Hall on that showery evening in 1952? I think not. To equate the two is tempting, but altogether too neat. Cage's silence was filled with sound; Taylor's was not. Cage, the citydweller, reveled in the abundance of life; Taylor, high in the desert, found himself face to face with nothingness.

All such differences notwithstanding, there remain important similarities between Cage's and Heizer's projects. Both created works that arouse thoughts of metaphysical extremes—for example, emptiness-fullness, absence-presence. Each radically challenges conventional practice. Cage, the composer, sought to get rid of conventional music. Heizer, the visual artist, constructed works that were difficult to locate and all but impossible to see. Each relates to his audience in a manner that might be called indifferent or even contemptuous.

What is of interest within the present context is less the relation between the works of Cage and Heizer than the similarities and differences between the experiences of Danto, Schjeldahl, and Taylor. Their accounts tell us a great deal about what it is like to undergo an extreme form of art-centered experience, one having as its outcome a sudden burst of insight or an otherwise dramatic change in the experiencer's perception or conduct. They reveal such experiences to be rare in occurrence and idiosyncratic in character. They also shed light on the power and the complexity of the emotions involved. They show how such experiences reverberate in the lives of those who undergo them long after the artwork is no longer physically present. Not only do the experiences remain alive as experiences; they even seem to expand over time, continually accruing fresh layers of meaning.

On the topic of their rarity, it is hard to say how often in a lifetime one might encounter a work of art that induces an epiphanic experience. Once or twice perhaps? Certainly not often. Danto reminds us that the probability of such an event depends in part on the frequency and intensity of one's exposure to art. "My sense is that anyone who has had any sustained intercourse with art must at some time have undergone some such experience" (Danto 1994, 236). He may be right. Who knows? In any event, the key to the question lies in his phrase "sustained intercourse with art," for just being in the physical presence of art, the way museum guards are, for instance, would hardly suffice to bring about the kind of transformative experience that he has in mind.

In addition to being rare, such experiences are also unpredictable in their effects. The two qualities are not the same. Even rare experiences do not always knock us off our horse, the way Danto's encounter with Warhol's *Brillo Box* did to him. Some might even flee in the presence of such a work, as many in Cage's audience did. The effective potency of such works remains unpredictable.

What is unique about each work has to do with the fit between the experiencer and the work itself. The accounts of Danto, Schjeldahl, and Taylor accentuate the idiosyncratic nature of that relation. Danto, for instance, reports having attended the Warhol exhibit on a night when most of those in attendance readily accepted *Brillo Box* as a work of art and, in a spirit of urbane sophistication, were eagerly purchasing units from the work to take home with them. (From his description it might have been opening night.) Had he attended later in the week, when those in attendance, according to Leonard, were much less appreciative of Warhol's genius, would he still have been struck by the realization that Warhol had pushed the question of art's criteria to its physical limit? Perhaps so, but the probability of that happening would surely have lessened. Imagine Schjeldahl (rather than Taylor) visiting *Double Negative*. Imagine him doing so after a night on the town in Las Vegas. Would he, too, feel as though he was treading the expansive corridors of time? At the end of his walk, would he, too, have come face to face with nothingness? Not likely. No more than would Taylor, adrift in Manhattan and wandering into the Tibor de Nagy Gallery, have become ecstatic over stumbling upon Carl Andre's bricks. In short, such experiences reveal almost as much about the experiencer as they do about the artwork. They weave together the strands of a life history, the peculiarities of the situation, and features of the work itself.

Given the unpredictability and idiosyncracy of such experiences, they hold out little promise of being used systematically to extend art's influence. Teachers of the arts are hereby forewarned. It seems fruitless to expose students to art objects or to have them construct such objects in the simple hope that doing so will dramatically change their lives. Sustained intercourse with the arts is certainly a way of increasing the chances of such life-transforming experiences. It is, however, no guarantee that they will take place.

Danto, Schjeldahl, and Taylor all describe emotions in their reports. Each man was visibly shaken by his experience, each in a different way. The reported feelings include surprise, elation, ecstasy, puzzlement, confusion, delight, dizziness, a sense of intoxication, and, in the case of Taylor, a mixture of awe and fear. For Danto and Schjeldahl the dominant emotion was excitement or exhilaration.

In each instance the source of the emotion did not reside in the physical features of the work (although the setting and the scale of Heizer's *Double Negative* may be sufficient to induce a feeling of awe in most people). Rather, the emotion appeared to arise in response to the situation as a whole, which included the work, its setting, and the sensibility of the observer. What seems to have happened to both Danto and Schjeldahl was that each was first struck by a feeling of puzzlement or confusion. Then, as time wore on, that sense of disorientation disappeared and was replaced by a succession of feelings, some more sharply articulated than others. Taylor, by way of contrast, seems not to have been puzzled at the start. His report does not reveal what his initial feelings were, though how he wound up feeling is clear enough. His report closes with an expression of religious awe tinged with fear.

The avowed spirituality of Taylor's response to *Double Negative* prompts our asking whether either or both of the other accounts might reasonably be called spiritual in character. Neither appears so at first glance, but Danto has written elsewhere that art exists for the sake of moving "the souls of men and women" (Danto 1994, 242), a phrase whose spiritual overtones are blatant. Schjeldahl, describing his feelings about his first encounter with Andre's bricks (some years after the fact), declares that "precisely a sense of beginning—a new world, a tabula rasa—fueled my afflatus" (Schjeldahl 1994, 207). *Afflatus,* according to Webster, refers to some kind of divine inspiration. Thus, both men incline toward a spiritual interpretation of what happened to them.

I conclude, therefore, that those art-centered experiences that make a pro-found difference in our lives deserve being called spiritual—though perhaps not religious in the conventional sense—insofar as they involve feelings and thoughts of a transcendental nature. What is transcended in such situations are the boundaries of custom. The experiencer undergoes an altered sensibility, achieves a novel way of looking at things.

ELIZABETH BISHOP'S "THE FISH"

My four examples of transformative experiences associated with the arts have dealt exclusively with the reactions of spectators. Each person came upon a particular art object and was subsequently changed as a result of having en-countered it. I turn now to the question of what goes on when the spectator is also the work's creator. The art object to be considered here is a poem by Elizabeth Bishop entitled "The Fish." A close look at that poem and then at the way it became integrated into the fabric of Bishop's life should prove helpful in two ways. It should deepen our understanding of transformative experiences in general by providing us with an artistic rendering of one such experience. It should also provide yet another example of how such an experience retains its magnetism for years, exerting something akin to a gravitational pull within the life of the experiencer.

Bishop's poem first appeared in *The Partisan Review* in 1940. It later was published in Bishop's first volume of collected poems, *North and South,* which came out in 1946. Since that time it has grown to be one of her most popular and most celebrated works. In brief, the poem tells a story, a fish story, one might say, though vastly different than the usual tale that bears that name. The latter traditionally tells of a fisherman whose catch got away. Its dominant emotions are of loss and lament. The fish being lost causes the fisherman to lament.

Bishop's fish story features a different set of emotions. It is a celebratory tale. Though it starts with a hooked fish being drawn close to a boat, just the way the conventional tale begins, it ends in victory rather than defeat, victory, paradoxically, for both the fish and the fisher-poet, whom I take to be the poem's author in real life. The tale gets underway straightforwardly enough. "I caught a tremendous fish," Bishop begins, "and held him beside the boat / half out of water, with my hook / fast in the corner of his mouth." The fish, oddly enough, seems not to have resisted his captor. "He hadn't fought at all," the poet says. Pulled halfway out of water, he simply hangs there, "a grunting weight." There then begins a process of close inspection, a looking to see what kind of creature this fish might be. That process takes up almost the entire poem.

The fish at first sight is ugly: "battered, and venerable / and homely." It is also old. Its skin is hanging in tatters, like strips of "ancient wallpaper." It is "speckled with barnacles," that are "infested / with tiny white sea-lice." It has "two or three rags of green weed" hanging from its underside. And yet, beneath this stupefying ugliness there lurks a strange beauty, which the poet slowly grows to appreciate. The hanging pieces of skin that look like strips of wallpaper turn out to be patterned with "shapes like full-blown roses." The barnacles on the fish's side form "fine rosettes of lime." Even "the frightening gills" that agonizingly open and close to take in "the terrible oxygen" are "fresh and crisp with blood."

As though mesmerized by this strange object that at once attracts and repels, the poet allows her fancy to take flight. She begins to imagine what the fish's insides look like. There, too, she pictures a combination of ugliness and beauty, "coarse white flesh / packed in like feathers," "the dramatic reds and blacks / of his shiny entrails," "the pink swim-bladder / like a big peony." Returning her gaze to the visible surface of the fish, she next looks into its eyes and finds there a clouded luster—yellowed "irises backed and packed / with tarnished tinfoil / seen through the lenses / of old scratched isinglass." The eyes are larger, though shallower, than her own. They shift a little as she looks at them, but not to return her stare. What seems like movement is the flickering reflection of an object tilted toward the light.

Finally, the poet's gaze moves to the fish's mouth and "the mechanism of his jaw." What comes into sight at this point is truly spellbinding. For there, "from his lower lip,"

> —if you could call it a lip—
> grim, wet, and weaponlike,
> hung five old pieces of fish-line
> or four and a wire leader
> with the swivel still attached,
> with all their five big hooks
> grown firmly in his mouth.
> A green line, frayed at the end
> where he broke it, two heavier lines,
> and a fine black thread
> still crimped from the strain and snap
> when it broke and he got away.
> Like medals with their ribbons
> frayed and wavering,
> a five-haired beard of wisdom
> trailing from his aching jaw.

The poet is transfixed by this incredible sight. "I stared and stared," she says. And then, when she tears her eyes from the fish and lifts her head to look around, something miraculous happens:

> victory filled up
> the little rented boat
> from the pool of bilge
> where oil had spread a rainbow
> around the rusted engine
> to the bailer rusted orange,
> the sun-cracked thwarts,
> the oarlocks on their strings,
> the gunnels—until everything
> was rainbow, rainbow, rainbow!

The poem's ending is inevitable, given all that has led up to it. "And I let the fish go." A fitting conclusion, one must say, to a most unusual fish story.

Because Bishop's poem depicts an ordinary experience in the process of becoming transformative, it invites us to reflect upon that process, asking how it comes about and what might be done to increase the likelihood of such an occurrence. It first reminds us that such experiences may have as their starting place the most ordinary of events, which may occur when we least expect them. In at least this sense, Danto's and Schjeldahl's experiences resemble what happened to Bishop's angler. They, too, were doing something that, for them, was quite ordinary (i.e., visiting an art gallery). They, too, were caught by surprise. The fact that the setting for each of them was an art gallery does, however, alter things a bit, art galleries being places where one might go in search of a mind-boggling experience. Bishop's poem serves to remind us that transformative events may be undergone in the most unlikely of settings, even when we are not fishing for them.

Bishop's tale intimates that such experiences usually require a break in the ongoing flow of events. The act of fishing, in this instance, was interfered with while the fisher-poet inspected her strange catch. Had she quickly netted or gaffed the fish and hauled him aboard, the way most fishers would likely have done, she may have had no story to tell. To be transported, in the sense in which we are using the term here, requires taking leave of one activity in order to pursue another.

Bishop's power as an observer stands out in her poem. Hers is a very special kind of visual acuity. It is not just the ability to look closely and see details, although that is a part of it. It is also the power to see what is not there physically but is there imaginatively. This capacity to view the world figuratively, through simile and metaphor, allows us to see things as something else, to see what they stand for as well as what they are. The brown skin of Bishop's fish did not just hang in strips; it hung there "like ancient wallpaper." The barnacles that speckled his sides were "fine rosettes of lime." His coarse white flesh is thought to be "packed in like feathers," and his pink swim bladder is imagined to look like "a big peony." The irises of the fish's eyes are "backed and packed with tarnished tinfoil seen through the lenses of old scratched isinglass." Such descriptions are more than detailed; they are inventive and fresh. They enable the poem's readers to see freshly as well.

Bishop's capacity to see beneath the surface of things (epitomized in her imaginative probes into the fish's interior) reaches its effective culmination as she gazes upon the fish's jaw and discovers the "five big hooks" firmly embedded there. To Bishop, those hooks become "like medals." That insight triggers the flood of feeling that marks the apex of Bishop's transformation, the final stage in the release of emotional energy that has been building throughout the poem. She looks up to find a rainbowed world. "Victory" had filled her "little rented boat," making the oil slick on the pool of bilge, the rusty bailer, thwarts, oarlocks, gunnels, shimmer with a halo of color. What really filled, we might imagine, were Bishop's eyes, brimming with tears. As seen through those teary lenses, everything in her world would indeed have been "rainbow, rainbow, rainbow!" One critic even speaks of that exultant cry as signaling a "tear-streaked epiphany" (Travisano 1988, 117). Small wonder that she let the fish go. I picture her cutting the line rather than trying to remove the hook, thus leaving the hero's last medal in place, pinned there by a now awestruck admirer.

How long did the fisher-poet's tear-streaked epiphany endure? Was it only until she wiped her eyes dry with the back of her hand? Or are we to believe that the experience ushered in a new way of looking at the world, a way of seeing it radiant with promise and hope, with virtues, such as courage and the pride engendered by stoic suffering, belonging not to humans alone but being broadly shared by creatures very unlike us? That possibility is implied by the burst of emotion at the poem's end.

Considerations such as these take us beyond the poem itself. They point in the direction of biography, leading us to wonder what place the poem had in Bishop's life. Before addressing that question, however, we need to look more closely at the symbolic and the formal aspects of the poem. Doing so should help us to relate the poem to some things that Dewey tells us about how the arts work.

We turn first to what to what might be called the poem's message. Commentators seem agreed that the poem is best read as a moral tale. Its story is one of victory—the victory that filled the little rented boat at the poem's close. The poem presents us with a double triumph, one involving the fish, which successfully eludes capture for at least the sixth time, the other involving the fisher-poet, who succeeds in coming to see the fish as an object worthy of respect and compassion and, when she does so, is rewarded by a beatific vision. One critic, Willard Spiegelman, speaks of the fisher-poet as exemplifying a kind of "natural heroism," which entails "not the elimination, or conquest, of the enemy, but the embracing, subsuming, and internalizing of him." He continues: "In the largest sense, separateness is denied, and victory is earned: another word for her heroism is love" (Spiegelman 1983, 171).

A second critic, Thomas Travisano, sees the fisher-poet's coming to terms with the fish as a kind of "spiritual achievement." He explains: "As far back as Virgil, pastoral has been a genre that calls for moral understanding of things overlooked and undervalued. Here, the potential to overlook lies with the observer and (implicitly) with the audience. The observer has so controlled egotism, in particular the arrogant tendency to see blindly and judge super-ficially, that elation ennobles the oily bilge at the bottom of the boat until one sees *its* overlooked beauty, which is analogous to the overlooked beauty of the fish. . . . For Bishop, observation is a moral act, since whether it is done carelessly or scrupulously bears moral fruit" (Travisano 1988, 67).

Travisano also describes Bishop's method as dramatizing "an observer un-consciously defeating the sin of pride." He further explains: "Instead of exult-ing in the victory of catching a tremendous fish, as most of us would do, the observer overcomes this kind of egotism, and the subtler egotism that would see the fish only in human terms, and thus achieves greater victories: she achieves self-knowledge and the knowledge of something other, finding outside the self an unforeseen courage, persistence, and beauty" (71).

Yet a third commentator, Richard Moore, sees the moral of "The Fish" in a slightly different way. Though he, too, stresses the importance of Bishop's way of looking at things, especially her use of careful observation, he points out that the value of such painstaking scrutiny lies not so much in its capacity to uncover overlooked beauty, as Travisano suggests, as in its power to objectify, to see things as they are rather than as one wants them to be. Here is the way Moore puts it: "It is because the poet is able to see the fish coldly and dispassionately as a thing in itself and not something exclusively hers, not something edible, fearful, or sentimental (for sentimentality is another form of devouring things), that she can discover what it really is, and is to her" (Moore 1956, 258).

According to Moore, Bishop's special way of looking does not stop there. It goes beyond objectivity. By relating what she sees to her own experience (largely through the use of similes), the fisher-poet manages to give the fish character. And that, Moore argues, contributes to its becoming real. "Perhaps the appre-hension of a character in things is an essential part of seeing them as real at all" (Moore 1956, 254). The process, in Moore's view, operates reciprocally. As the object (in this case, the fish) becomes real, so, too, does the observer. Moore explains: "To know its character, one must relate it to what one remembers of houses, roses, feathers—anything. In doing this, one makes it part of one's experience: it remains part of oneself, but one becomes more real because one has made the fish more real" (258–259). The final portion of Moore's explana-tion is a bit obscure, for it is not at once clear why the fisher-poet should become more real by making the fish more real. What I think he means by that is that any effort to view the world objectively—that is, to see its objects as being of value in their own right, as existing independent of one's own wishes and desires—results in a heightened awareness of the separation between self and world, which contributes in turn to a clearer definition of the self. By coming to see the fish as an object with unique properties, possessing the right to an existence of its own, the observer's natural inclination to see herself and her own right to existence in the same light is thereby strengthened. In that sense, therefore, she becomes more real, as the fish does.

These various interpretations of the moral message to be found in Bishop's poem return us to the question of the connection between art and spirituality. Here again we are dealing with an art object whose implicit meaning points in a spiritual direction. As in the case of Warhol's Brillo boxes and Andre's bricks, the work's subject matter is once again a common object (a fish) that undergoes a transfiguration, changing from something ordinary to something extraordinary, and doing so, in this instance, almost before our very eyes. Few readers of "The Fish" may be fortunate enough to undergo the kind of transformative experience that the poem's narrator seems to have undergone or that Danto and Schjeldahl report. What does that tell us about art's spiritual function? How does it relate to Leonard's thesis with which this chapter began?

The poem certainly does not suggest, as Leonard does, that the function of art is to turn our attention toward the beauties of the natural world, thereby making art less necessary than it might otherwise be. In offering the poem to her public, Bishop is not recommending that we should go out and spend more time looking at fish and less time reading poems. She may be indirectly inviting us to look more intently at everything (poems included) than we normally do, and it may appear to follow from that invitation that the more time we spend looking at nonpoems of whatever sort, the less time we will have available for poetry (and other arts, presumably). But that apparent conclusion turns out to be false, as I have already tried to point out. It is false because for most of us the bulk of our life is not spent looking or listening intently at or to anything at all. Instead, we typically see and hear only what serves us at the moment. There is no reason, therefore, why the time spent in inspecting a common object—a venerable old fish, say—needs to be taken from the time we might spend in reading and studying a poem about a fish or anything else. In short, for most of us the competition between time spent on art and time spent in appreciative contemplation of objects within the world need not constitute a zero-sum game. We have more time to do either than most of us realize, provided that we are willing to give up other things. It is in getting and spending that we chiefly lay waste our powers. Looking and listening in an artful manner make up but a small fraction of our doings.

Bishop's poem is, then, most readily understood as a lesson in looking. That lesson is so clearly stated, so physical, that it hardly seems worthy of further comment. As Moore puts it, "One feels that something has been so completely discovered in the particulars that any statements or conceits about what has been discovered would be superfluous and mar the effect" (Moore 1956, 253). Yet, as Moore himself proceeds to show, that lesson generalizes beyond the actions portrayed. Treating the poem as a whole, as Bishop does the fish, we find within it things to admire. A good portion of what we find turns out to be expressive or symbolic in character. Indeed, as we proceed with our own close looking, the poem itself, like the fish that it describes, takes on a character of its own. It becomes real in the sense that Moore intends. This, we might add, is not solely Bishop's lesson, nor even poetry's lesson. It is taught by all of the arts, though seldom as explicitly as here.

To view "The Fish" as a composition is to ask questions about its inner working, about rhythm, rhyme, and meter. It is to ask how those formal properties contribute to (or hinder) the poem's overall effect. It is to note, for example, how Bishop's habit of repeating words a few lines apart and sometimes within the same line (e.g., the repetitions of "wallpaper," "gills," "bones," "lip," "line," "jaw," "stared") stitch the poem together. It is to appreciate how those tiny repetitions ready the reader for the triple repeat of "rainbow" at the end. It is to note how the poem's seventy-six lines of predominately trimetered verse, unrelieved by stanzaic division, resemble the elongated shape of the fish being described.

It is also to ask questions about the resources that the poet has drawn upon, about external influences that may account for some of the poem's features. Did Bishop catch the fish that she describes, or is the poem a fictional account? Short of asking her, which is now impossible, who can say? The poem's power as a work of art has little to do with truth or fiction in the conventional sense. Yet the question of how the arts might transform an already extraordinary experience into an even more extraordinary one does bear upon all that has been said. Let us therefore toy with the question of Bishop's real-life experience.

The description of the aged fish makes us believe that Bishop must have looked at such a creature sometime in her life. Yet the artfulness with which those details are revealed make it very unlikely that the description is a factual, chronological report. Instead of being last, for example, the fish's jaw would have been the very first part of its anatomy to have come to her attention. "Fine rosettes of lime" and "tiny white sea lice" would have come to her attention much later on. So even if the poem's story is grossly factual, the poem offers an artful reconstruction of experience rather than a step by step or minute by minute account of what happened.

The artfulness of the presentation raises an interesting question: What if the real-life fisher had not been as artful in inspecting the fish as the fisher-poet had? Would he or she still have undergone the transformative shock that the poem describes? For example, what if the fish's jaw with its five embedded hooks had been the first part of the anatomy to come into focus rather than the last? Would that sight still have had the numbing effect that it has in the poem? Possibly. But for the experience to work for others, the events of the experience almost have to be arranged artfully. And if the artful arrangement works for its audience, why not for the poet as well? Could it be, in short, that even extraordinary experiences must be made into art if they are to become transformative for those who undergo them?

An intriguing set of comments about the inner workings of the poem and their relation to the psychology of the poet comes from David Kalstone, one of Bishop's biographers. Kalstone (1989, 86–87) suggests that Bishop may have been reaching into her own past for the images of "stained wallpaper," "scratched isinglass," and "tarnished tinfoil" that she uses to construct the similes that poetically "capture" the fish. He calls those images "flawed instruments of vision"—in part, presumably, because of their "scratched," "stained," and "tarnished" quality. He suggests that they may have been "painfully" glimpsed by Bishop. The poem as a whole, he declares, is "filled with the strain of seeing."

What makes Kalstone's suggestions intriguing is the hint of there being a kind of isomorphism between the activity of the person aboard the boat and the work of the poet. Both are engaged in bringing something to the surface, hauling it up, one from the water, the other from memory. As Kalstone puts it, "On some readings, the poem has the air of summoning up a creature from the speaker's own inner depth—the surviving nonhuman resources of an earlier creation" (Kalstone 1989, 87). The prize, in both instances, bears the traces of having survived the ravages of time.

The parallel between the two activities—fishing and writing a poem—may be too fanciful for some. "After all," someone might complain, "doesn't every product of the creative imagination require a certain amount of 'fishing around'?" "It surely does," has to be the answer. But the fishing metaphor mirrors the poem's subject matter, which is probably why it surfaced for Kalstone. Did Bishop think of herself as fishing around in her own inner depth while writing the poem? Who knows? Probably not, would be my guess. But she was doing so all the same, Kalstone insists, no matter whether the metaphor, by extension, applies to every instance of artistic endeavor.

The resources drawn on and the influences brought to bear include the poet's grasp of poetry, which means not only the poems that the poet may have read and memorized over the years but also his or her understanding of what poetry stands for, how it should be written, and so forth. In the case of Bishop's "The Fish," Travisano tells us, three sources of influence stand out. The first is Bishop's friend and mentor, Marianne Moore, who taught the aspiring poet the value and the moral necessity of close observation. The second is Edgar Allan Poe, from whom, through extensive study, Bishop absorbed the lesson of withholding the punch of her poem until its very end. And the third is Gerard Manley Hopkins, whose poetry underscored for her the virtue of presenting a record of the mind at work, of offering a developmental history of how understanding comes to be. All three of those influences, Travisano insists, are at work in "The Fish." Each contributes to making it a poetic gem.

We turn finally to the creation of the poem as ongoing experience, to what it must have been like to have written "The Fish." Lacking testimonial evidence, we are left to our imagination. A few of the poem's compositional features, plus knowledge of Bishop's work habits, give us at least an inkling of some of the questions and considerations that must have been on her mind during the compositional process. We can be reasonably sure, for example, that the poem was not dashed off in the course of an afternoon. Though the idea for it may have been born aboard the little rented boat (if there ever was such a conveyance), its details surely did not take final form until long after the fishing journey was over and the boat reached shore. Bishop's biographers describe her as having been a meticulous poet. This leads me to suspect that the process of writing "The Fish" extended over weeks and possibly months—perhaps even longer. In an ode written in her honor, Robert Lowell jestingly asks,

> Do
> you still hang your words in air, ten years
> unfinished, glued to your notice board, with gaps
> or empties for the unimaginable phrase—
> unerring Muse who makes the casual perfect? (Lowell 1973, 198)

What does it mean for a poet to struggle with a single poem for that length of time? It doesn't mean that he or she spent every waking hour at the task. Bishop's writing of "The Fish" was more than likely an off-and-on affair, interrupted not only by daily routines but laid aside for spells of time.

The high probability of such interruptions having occurred forces us to acknowledge that experiences, even *an* experience, need not proceed smoothly from beginning to end; an experience may be a totality whose elements are temporally discontinuous. This may seem odd at first, for many ordinary experiences—having a meal, going to the dentist, taking a walk in the woods—occur without break. However, it takes only a moment's reflection to come up with contrary instances. The experience of reading a book often takes many hours, parceled out in sessions of varying lengths. An even more attenuated form of discontinuity characterizes the experience of a friendship, which may extend over a lifetime yet contain long periods during which there is little or no contact between the two parties. Most experiences that involve the construction of something meant to endure, which would include all artistic endeavors, likely are discontinuous in this way.

When there is a product of some kind, as with the preparation of a meal, let us say, or the writing of a poem, the product's completion would seem to bring the experience to an end. Not necessarily so, however. In many such instances (perhaps in most of them) the experience neither begins with the physical production of the object nor ends with its completion. In short, production is but a phase of the more extended experience in which the product remains central. Before the work begins, there is often a period of planning and of preparing for its execution (recall Cage's stewing around with the idea for *4′33″* for four years or more before it was actually performed). After the work is complete, it is shared with others, maybe peddled, explanatory comments are offered about its meaning or about the conditions of its construction, and sometimes it is protected from abuse by others and even from the meddling of the well-intentioned. Bishop's correspondence about "The Fish" contains much that is instructive about the postproduction phase of experience.

On February 5, 1940, Bishop wrote to Marianne Moore from her residence in Key West, Florida. She enclosed a copy of "The Fish" and explained in her letter, "I am sending you a real 'trifle.' I'm afraid it is very bad" (Bishop 1994, 87). Two weeks later she again wrote to Moore. After thanking her for her "very helpful" comments on "The Fish," Bishop continues: "I did as you suggested about everything except 'breathing in' (if you can remember that), which I decided to leave as it was. 'Lousy' is now 'infested' and 'gunwales' (which I had meant to be pronounced 'gunn'ls') is 'gunnels,' which is also correct according to the dictionary, and makes it plainer. I left off the outline of capitals [for the first word of each line], too, and feel very ADVANCED" (89). Close to a month later, on March 14, 1940, Bishop wrote Moore to announce that *Partisan Review* was printing the poem that month.

The next mention of "The Fish" in Bishop's letters refers to a weekend festival of poetry held at Bard College in the fall of 1948. Apparently Bishop had agreed to participate in a panel discussion of poetry but had not anticipated that she would be asked to read a poem of her own. When it came time to do so, "I said I was too tired, so Cal [Robert Lowell] read for me, 'The Fish'" (174).

On February 27, 1970, almost thirty years after "The Fish" appeared in print, Bishop wrote to Lowell, thanking him for dedicating three poems to her. She also remarks on his "capacity for re-doing things" and, in that connection, has this to say about her own work: "I think I'll try to turn that damned 'Fish' into a sonnet, or something very short and quite different. (I seem to get requests for it every day for anthologies with titles like *Reading as Experience,* or *Experience as Reading,* each anthologizer insisting that he is doing something completely different from every other anthologizer. But I'm sure that is an old story to you.)" (515).

The final mention of "The Fish" in Bishop's letters occurred on October 6, 1979, the day she died. On that date she wrote to John Fredrick Nims, the editor of *Poetry* magazine, who wanted to reprint the poem in a college textbook that he was editing. Nims wanted to attach some footnotes to the poem. Bishop objected.

> I'm going to take issue with you—rather violently—about the idea of footnotes. With one or two exceptions (I'll mention them later) I don't think there should be ANY footnotes. You say the book is for college students, and I think anyone who gets as far as college should be able to use a dictionary. If a poem catches a student's interest at all, he or she should damned well be able to look up an unfamiliar word in the dictionary. (I know they don't—or most of them don't—but they should be made to somehow. The older poems you are using of course may require some help—but mine certainly don't!) "Isinglass" is in the dictionary; so is "gunnel" (see "gunwale"); so is "thwarts." (638)

Thus, for thirty-nine years Bishop's experience with "The Fish" was intermittently revived and extended. The poem remained a presence in her life as long as she lived. The emotional character of the experience seems to have undergone several modulations over the years, from dismissive and self-deprecating ("a real 'trifle'"; "I'm afraid it's very bad") to prideful ("published this month") to playfully contemptuous ("damned 'Fish'"), with a nurturing and protective motherliness occurring now and again (e.g., her disagreements with

Moore and Nims). Bishop's emotional attachment to the poem remains evident, providing a continuity that runs through the more transient ups and downs of her feeling about it.

Even as brief a glimpse of the artist's experience as Bishop's letters afford should be enough to sustain the general point that the composing of a poem (or any work of art) is but a single phase or segment of the artist's transactions with the work. The totality of those transactions have as their common focus a singular object in one or more of its historical manifestations—as an idea yet to be realized, as a work in progress, as a finished object infused with meaning, as an object of recollection, as the subject of discussion or debate, and so forth. Each of these ways of relating to the work makes up a portion of the artist's experience with it. Each may extend over a long or short period of time. Each may be subdivided, depending on one's reasons for wanting to do so and on the circumstances of the individual case.

Looking on these extensions of experience that include both the before and after of aesthetic production allows us to better understand the power of art to be transformative for both the artist and the audience. It helps to reveal how an art object continues to exert its influence long after the artist has declared it finished. The artist's work with the object is not complete at that point. What lives on is not solely the artist's memory of making the work. There remains an emotional residue as well, evinced in the artist's attachment to the work. Over time, that attachment and the extended experience in which it becomes manifest result in the work's becoming so intertwined into the fabric of the artist's life that its many ramifications are no longer individually distinguishable.

FOUR PERSPECTIVES ON THE SPIRITUALITY OF ART

It is time now to ask what our five examples of epiphanic art-centered experiences tell us about art-centered experiences in general and about Dewey's theory of the arts in particular.

What they make evident, first of all, is something we all know, which is that such experiences are rare events. They occur infrequently and unexpectedly. They may be occasioned by artworks of almost any kind. Our examples made use only of contemporary works, but they were extremely varied in style and content: Cage's *4′ 33″*, Warhols's *Brillo Box*, Andre's *Equivalent VIII*, Heizer's *Double Negative*, and Elizabeth Bishop's "The Fish." A broader selection could easily have included works from the past and from other areas of art. The crucial point is that there is no telling where, when, or whence such an experience might occur.

An obvious corollary to the rarity of such experiences is that the same art object may strike different people differently. Not everyone is moved to epiphanic heights by the same object. Some may never have such an experience. As Danto points out, "[Epiphanic experiences] are unpredictable. They are contingent on some antecedent state of mind, and the same work will not affect different people in the same way or even the same person the same way on different occasions" (Danto 1997, 178).

As our examples illustrate, such experiences are invariably memorable. Indeed, they not only live on in memory but powerfully influence what people do and say. They affect choices and plans. They alter lives. Danto's testimony may not be typical, but it serves to make the point: "Few works have meant as much to me as Warhol's *Brillo Box,* and I have spent a fair portion of my waking time in working out the implications of my experience of it" (Danto 1997, 178).

There is yet another observation to make about our five examples. Considering what it adds to our understanding of Dewey, this observation may be the most important of all. The diversity exhibited by the examples suggests that epiphanic art-centered experiences may be occasioned by almost any kind of art, but it also reveals a crucial difference. This difference shows up most clearly in the contrast between what the Bishop poem and what the other four examples ask of their audiences.

The poem invites the kind of reflection epitomized in the story that it tells. It asks to be read slowly and carefully, much the way the poem's narrator examines her catch. As an art object, "The Fish" calls for close examination. Only then does its internal beauty become evident. Only then do we, as readers, begin to appreciate its complexity.

The Cage, Warhol, Andre, and Heizer works, on the other hand, confront their viewers with a very different set of demands. Each work asks to be understood, true enough, much as does the Bishop poem, but not by means of a gradual process of coming to appreciate the intricacies of its internal structure. Each has its say in a very different manner, making a more or less abrupt impact and being almost defiant in its assertiveness. Both the Warhol and the Andre works prompt viewers to stare but not to look, at least not in the slow and controlled manner that Bishop's narrator adopts. The inactivity of the pianist in Cage's 4′33″ presumably comes as a surprise to most of its audience. One may listen to the natural sounds that fill the work's silence, but not in the way one follows the structural harmonics and melodies of a conventional piece of music.

Heizer's *Double Negative* may trigger a feeling of awe and may invite contemplation, as it did for Taylor, but it does not call for a close inspection of its various parts. The two gashes in the earth separated by a natural outcropping of the mesa's surface do indeed cohere to form a whole, made explicit in the work's title, but a view from the air above is required to make that coherence visible. Taylor does inspect the surface of the work on his walking tour of it, but he does not do so to better appreciate how its parts cohere.

These differences between the analytic demands of the Bishop poem, on the one hand, and those made by the remaining four works, on the other, are not to be confused with differences in the media—between written and visual works, that is. A different set of examples might easily have reversed the comparison. Nor is the difference essentially historical, although the Bishop poem was written well before the other works were completed, and I can hardly imagine any of the latter having been undertaken much before the date when it actually appeared. Instead, the difference grows out of alternative, and perhaps even opposing, conceptions of what art is for and how it is to be appreciated.

On the one side is the view that the arts present us with objects whose self-contained beauty is to be studied and admired (much like Bishop's fish). On the other side is the view that the arts exist chiefly to shake us up intellectually and emotionally, to convey a message about the essence of art or to shock us into a heightened self-awareness or to bring before us as boldly as possible some hitherto neglected aspect of the human condition. Such works may indeed be appreciated aesthetically—they may have an emotional appeal as well as an intellectual one (as the commentary of Danto, Schjeldahl, and Taylor attests)—but they are not to be lovingly examined or carefully read or listened to attentively, as is necessary when we seek to appreciate a work's internal structure.

With this set of distinctions in mind, let us turn to what such differences have to do with Dewey's view of the arts. Dewey, as we have seen, placed a lot of emphasis on the holistic character of *an* experience. In so doing he also emphasized the feelings of fulfillment and satisfaction that accompanied such experiences. Those feelings, Dewey insisted, recurred throughout the course of the experience's unfolding. His four concepts of cumulation, conservation, tension, and anticipation relate to the dynamics of such experiences and to the mounting pleasure that they bring.

At the same time Dewey's analysis leaves plenty of room for the continued enrichment of such experiences through the acquisition of new knowledge (via keener perception, for the most part), leading to a deepened appreciation of the art object's qualities and a heightened sense of its intrinsic worth. Another way of describing such changes makes use of the concept of meaning. As meaning accrues, according to Dewey, experience grows with it. Indeed, experiential growth is but the expansion of meaning.

Within Dewey's theorizing, both conceptions of art's function seem to be in operation, one in which the internal dynamics of the piece being examined or worked on are paramount, the other in which external considerations, such as what the piece says about other works or how it relates to tangential aspects of the artist's or the spectator's world, come to the fore. Can Dewey have it both ways? Can his theory accommodate works as disparate in form, content, and purpose as Bishop's "The Fish" and Warhol's *Brillo Box?* I believe it can, though to see how it might do so requires that we keep in mind that Dewey's theory focuses on experience and not on art objects per se. Art objects are of importance to Dewey principally as they operate within experience, giving it structure and becoming carriers of meaning.

As conditioners of experience, artworks function in a variety of ways. Some call for close inspection of the work itself, requiring attentive listening or careful examination of the physical object. Others make heavy demands on our capacity to read the work symbolically, to think about what it stands for and why it does so. The same is true of the emotional temper engendered by various works. Some works calm the human spirit, others arouse it. Some comfort, others annoy. The only thing that Dewey insists on is that every work as a physical object call for some form of sensory inspection. Every work conveys some expressive meaning; that meaning is embedded in the work, and grasping it depends on the prior experience of artist or audience. And every work, when properly attended, occasions an emotional response of some kind whose affect permeates the experience as a whole.

As far as Dewey is concerned, all works of art have these features. What varies for him are their ratios. Every historical period of art tends to elevate one or more of the features over the others. Defenders of the status quo or of the avant-garde often go so far as to deny the status of art to objects that fail to comply with whatever is *à la mode.* Dewey calls for an end to such squabbles. As he points out, "A catholic philosophy based on understanding of the constant relations of self and world amid variations in their actual contents would render enjoyment wider and more sympathetic" (LW10, 256).

Dewey strives to attain that understanding through his philosophy. He does not legislate the subject matter of art. Nor does he prescribe its form. His philosophy easily accommodates, therefore, the kinds of differences that we have been discussing. What he argues against are those conceptions of art that deny the interactive nature of experience—including theories that divorce art from common experience, placing it on a pedestal or in a world of its own.

Realizing this accommodation takes us a good way toward understanding the catholicity of Dewey's views as they relate to different kinds of art. We are left wondering, however, what to do with his emphasis on the holistic nature of art-centered experiences when the art object in question fails to exhibit well-roundedness in any obvious way or when its contents explicitly deny that norm. We are also left wondering about the pertinence of such criteria as anticipation and consummation when the work of art lacks narrative structure and does not in any other way contribute to the smooth unfolding of an experience. How do such notions apply, for example, to developing an appreciation for Warhol's *Brillo Box?* One way of answering the question would be to acknowledge that they don't apply to the art object but to the experience in which that object is central. The trouble with that answer is that it begs the question, for we then must ask how the same notions apply to the experience as a whole. The answer to the latter question is evident in some instances but not in others.

I conclude, therefore, that some of what Dewey called the "generic traits" of *an* experience turn out not to be quite as generic as he made them out to be. It is surely the case that many art-centered experiences unfold in exactly the way that Dewey describes—moving steadily and inexorably toward a satisfying and fulfilling culmination. But it seems equally clear that not all do. Moreover— and this is the key point—to observe that such qualities are noticeably absent from certain art-centered experiences is not necessarily to say something negative or critical about the work itself.

Which of Dewey's generic traits have the broadest range of applicability when used as conceptual tools to enlighten us about what goes on within art-centered experiences? The two that seem the most general have to do with the *expansion of meaning* and the *attainment of a full perception*. These notions apply as readily when the object of the experience is Warhol's *Brillo Box* as when it is a Bishop's "The Fish." Indeed, if we follow Dewey's reasoning, there can be no art-centered experience worthy of the name in which the two notions of expanded meaning and full perception do not come into play. What changes throughout the course of an art-centered experience is precisely the relation among its elements; that is, what changes is the object's meaning. To speak of meaning *and* perception turns out to be misleading, for they, as we have already seen, are inextricably intertwined. To perceive is to perceive meaning. The term affords no other reference.

The centrality of perception in Dewey's theorizing about the arts, and about experience in general, can hardly be overemphasized. Not only must we perceive art objects in order to appreciate their worth, but doing so is at least one means by which we come to better perceive other objects and events, including ourselves and others. Thus coming to perceive art objects with ever increasing clarity and depth has moral consequences. Dewey explains them this way: "The moral function of art itself is to remove prejudice, do away with the scales that keep the eye from seeing, tear away the veils due to wont and custom, perfect the power to perceive" (LW10, 328).

In Dewey's assertion that a moral function of the arts is to perfect the power to perceive, some readers may hear echoes of Leonard's worry about the arts being used to undo the arts, about the arts being subverted to serve what Leonard calls religious ends, or at least ends that are far more general and expansive than art's own. There are hints of such an outlook here and there in Dewey's writings, as we have seen, but when examined carefully, their similarity to Leonard's thesis quickly vanishes. In *Art as Experience,* for example, in a statement quoted at the start of this chapter, Dewey says, "In an imperfect society—and no society will ever be perfect—fine art will be to some extent an escape from, or an adventitious decoration of, the main activities of living. But in a better-ordered society than that in which we live, an infinitely greater happiness than is now the case would attend all modes of production." This might be taken to imply that as society improves—a condition brought about in part by the exemplary nature of the arts—the arts themselves, particularly the so-called fine arts, will become less needed, save as an escape or adventitious decoration of the main activities of living. Such a reading of Dewey's statement would be deficient, however. It overlooks the linkage of the arts to a conception of the ideal.

By now it should be clear that what we are calling art-centered experiences have built within them, so to speak, a telos, a directionality, a tendency to be an idealization of experience. Occasionally, if we are fortunate, we come upon a work, or are involved in making one, that brings us about as close as we are liable to get to that ideal condition within the framework of the experience itself. When that happens, as Dewey points out, the experience is often felt to have a religious or spiritual character. Such were the fortunate experiences that we have been looking at. Under such conditions, self and object become momentarily indistinguishable, as if we were, in Dewey's description, "introduced into a world beyond this world which is nevertheless the deeper reality of the world in which we live our ordinary experiences. We are carried out beyond

ourselves to find ourselves" (LW10, 199). Even under less fortunate circumstances, that is, when ideal conditions are a long way off, our encounters with
art objects of all kinds may at least be said to point in such a direction. The art
objects stand for the promise of attaining the best under current circumstances.

Arthur Danto comes close to echoing Dewey's views on this point, particularly as it applies to the ambitions of many contemporary artists. Yet he also
differs from Dewey in a way that proves to be instructive. He beings by saying,
"I think it is the possibility of such experiences [those of an epiphanic nature]
that justifies the production, the maintenance, the exhibition of art, even if the
possibility, for whatever reason, is unactualized for most persons" (Danto 1997,
178). He later says that the kind of experience that he is speaking of "belongs to
philosophy and to religion, to the vehicles through which the meaning of life is
transmitted to people in their dimension as human beings" (188). But between
those remarks he says this: "There is one feature of contemporary art that
distinguishes it from perhaps all art made since 1400, which is that its primary
ambitions are not aesthetic. Its primary mode of relationship is not to viewers as
viewers, but to other aspects of the persons to whom the art is addressed" (183).
In other words, Danto seems to be saying that unless the primary relation of a
visual art object is to the visual senses, that is, to the viewer as viewer, it cannot
be considered aesthetic.

As if to reinforce that judgment, Danto, at an earlier time, had this to say
about the aesthetic merits of Warhol's *Brillo Box:* "There would be a kind of
aesthetic pathology . . . in saying 'I'll take *Brillo Box*' when offered a choice
between it and one of Cézanne's *compotiers* or some irises of Van Gogh" (Danto
1990, 4). At the same time, Danto insists that what we all search for today in the
arts is meaning, the kind of meaning that religion was capable of providing, or
philosophy. In this view, much of modern art is the embodiment of a search for
something ideal and absolute, a search for an art that is pure and foundational.
This is the art that Mark Taylor writes about and journeys to see. It is also the art
of abstract expressionism, which Meyer Schapiro vigorously championed from
the 1930s on. The paintings of the abstract expressionists, Schapiro writes,
"induce an attitude of communion and contemplation. They offer to many an
equivalent of what is regarded as part of religious life: a sincere and humble
submission to a spiritual object, an experience which is not given automatically,
but requires preparation and purity of spirit" (Shapiro 1982, 224).

Donald Kuspit, yet another critic who has much to say about the spirituality
of much of modern art, distinguishes between two kinds of modern works:
those that employ what he calls "total abstraction" and those that make use of

"total realism." Both, he believes, give expression to the spiritual and the mystical but do so in different ways. Art that makes use of abstraction is what Kuspit calls "silent art," silent in the sense of containing little or no reference to the world of meaningful objects that we normally deal with. Art that relies on total realism he refers to as "alchemical art," since its goal is to transmute worldly objects into unworldly ones, using them to generate a spiritual atmosphere. In his words: "In both total abstraction and total realism the diverting outer has been eliminated, generating a sense of inner necessity. [Both] . . . involve the same process of reducing the 'artistic' to a minimum. Art that seems to be 'pure' in its being results; it no longer represents, but 'presents,' as a subjective indication of inner necessity and as radical 'objectivity'" (Kuspit 1986, 314). He explains that "both silence and alchemy are spiritual in import, but where silence is an articulation of the immaterial, alchemy is a demonstration of the unity of the immaterial and the material" (315).

Kuspit's category of silent art calls to mind Mark Taylor's confrontation with silence during his visit to Heizer's *Double Negative* in the Nevada desert. Taylor left no doubt that his experience was quasi-mystical. Kuspit explains why that might have been so. "The silent painting [and, by inference, other forms of abstract art], contemplated in a more than casual way, has a numinous effect simply by reason of its radical concreteness, its unconditional immediacy. This . . . is functionally mystical—that is, it is not the vehicle of communication of religious dogma but of a certain kind of irreducible, nondiscursive experience." He adds, "The question of religious belief is separate from the question of spiritual experience, which is what silent painting engages" (Kuspit 1986, 319).

Kuspit's phrase "contemplated in a more than casual way" constitutes a crucial element in his explanation of how abstract art, silent painting, comes to have a spiritual effect. It suggests that the spectator must be prepared for such an outcome and may even have to work hard to achieve it.

Yet a third view of the spirituality associated with art-centered experiences comes from the eminent art historian Meyer Schapiro, mentioned above. It relates to Dewey's views more closely than do the other two. Like Danto and Schjeldahl, Schapiro looks on modern art, particularly abstract expressionism, as being especially concerned with the expression of spiritual values. Such paintings, he says, "induce an attitude of communion and contemplation. They offer to many an equivalent of what is regarded as part of religious life: a sincere and humble submission to a spiritual object, an experience which is not given automatically, but requires preparation and purity of spirit" (Schapiro 1982, 224). But such an experience is not available to all, Schapiro cautions.

"Only a mind open to the qualities of things, with a habit of discrimination, sensitized by experience and responsive to new forms and ideas, will be prepared for the enjoyment of this art" (223). Those unprepared for the enjoyment of modern art are not thereby deprived of undergoing a similar experience in the presence of quite different kinds of works. This is so because every successful work of art, under appropriate conditions, may contribute to an experience that has spiritual overtones. Its potential to do so, Schapiro asserts, depends on the experiencer's perception of the work's unity of form and content. Yet that unity is not itself a unitary concept.

Schapiro distinguishes between two forms of unity that the form and content may exhibit. The first is inevitable; the second is not. The inevitable kind of unity, which Schapiro speaks of as the "indivisible oneness of form and content," refers to the undeniable fact that every work of art, no matter how good or bad, has to have a form of some kind, and it has to have content—it has to refer to something or be about something. Even works that are nonrepresentational have form and content. In such works, "the relations and qualities of the forms, their expressive nature, in the context of the work's function, are the content or meaning of the work" (42). In other words, where there is no representational content, form becomes content.

Schapiro's second kind of unity rests on judgment. It entails, as he puts it, "a criterion of value," and refers to "an accord of specifiable forms and meanings . . . [that] *appear* comprehensive enough to induce the *conviction* that everything in the work is stamped with this *satisfying* accord which is a ground of its beauty" (42, emphasis added). Judgment of this kind of unity, however, can seldom be made with certainty. It always depends in part of the viewer's vantage point. It has, therefore, the status of a hypothesis, something to be continually tested and refined in the light of further personal observations and the observations of others. What makes unity especially contentious under certain circumstances is that both form and content may be variously identified and described. In other words, the artwork is open to competing definitions of its form and content. "In attributing a unity of form and content to a work we are free to abstract the aspect of forms and meanings that might coincide. It is not *the* form and *the* content that appear to us as one, but an aspect or part of each that we bring together because of analogy or expressive correspondence. Content and form are plural concepts that comprise many regions and many orders within the same work" (42–43).

Schapiro introduces the connections between the work's unity and the concept of spirituality in this way: "Both concepts of unity—the perfect correspon-

dence of separable forms and meanings and the concept of their indis-
tinguishability—rest on an ideal of perception which may be compared with a
mystic's experience of the oneness of the world or of God, a feeling of the
pervasiveness of a single spiritual note or of an absolute consistency in diverse
things" (48). To this explanation Schapiro adds a cautionary note. He warns
against using the attainment of such a perceptual "high" as a signal to cease
exploring the work. "I do not believe that this attitude [of perceived oneness],
with its sincere conviction of value, is favorable to the fullest experience of a
work of art." Why not? Because, he explains, "it characterizes a moment or
aspect, not the work as disclosed through attentive contemplation, which may
also terminate in ecstasy. To see the work as it is one must be able to shift one's
attitude in passing from part to part, from one aspect to another, and to enrich
the whole progressively in successive perceptions" (48). The fullest experience
of a work of art, and seeing the work as it is—these remain, for Schapiro, the
proper goals of aesthetic scrutiny. Moments of perceptual delight, even ones
approaching ecstasy, may occur along the way, true enough, and we should
certainly be grateful when they do. But the more enduring rewards for the
experiencer, Schapiro gives us to believe, lie in the fullness of the experience
with the work, which is an outgrowth of what Schapiro calls critical seeing.
"Critical seeing, aware of the incompleteness of perception, is explorative and
dwells on details as well as on the large aspects that we call the whole. It takes
into account others' seeing; it is a collective and cooperative seeing and wel-
comes comparison of different perceptions and judgments. It also knows moments of sudden revelation and intense experience of unity and completeness
which are shared in others' scrutiny" (49).

We are now in a position to bring together what Danto, Kuspit, and Schapiro have to say about the spirituality of art. My goal in doing so is to show how
their points of view relate to what we already know about Dewey's outlook. At
the same time I will use the comparison to prepare the way for an extended look
at how some of Dewey's ideas might be put into practice.

All three of the critics look on visual art (principally painting) as being
peculiarly concerned with spiritual matters. Leaving aside art whose content is
explicitly religious, this is more true of modern art, it would seem, than of art
before the twentieth century. All also agree that the viewer's capacity to appreciate what modern art is up to and, more significantly, to sense its spirituality
directly requires a special kind of sensitivity.

Danto says that art-centered experiences are contingent upon some antecedent state of mind. Thus individual art objects will not produce the same

response in different people. He says that art (presumably any kind of art) can mean very little for someone who has so far been blind and numb to art. One needs knowledge to have such experiences, he insists, yet not the kind of knowledge that one is likely to acquire through formal instruction. Apparently the kind of knowledge to which he refers comes about through continued exposure to the arts, provided, of course, that such exposure involves more than simply being in art's presence. Kuspit, too, acknowledges that an appreciation of abstract art has to be cultivated in a more than casual way. But in the writings that I have read he does not spell out how to cultivate that appreciation.

Of the three, Schapiro has the most to say about how one comes to perceive the spiritual dimension of a work of art. His discussion of the subject remains fragmentary, however, and its various elements do not cohere as much as one might like. As we have seen, Schapiro calls for preparation and purity of spirit as necessary for the appreciation of modern art. He also calls for a habit of discrimination, sensitized by experience and responsive to new forms and ideas. Schapiro says little about how such spirit and habit might be attained.

For appreciating art in general and for distinguishing, in particular, between spiritual satisfaction and the fullest experience of a work of art, what Schapiro has to say is more illuminating. He points out that the source of greatest pleasure derives from one's perception of an accord, a judged unity, between form and content. He makes clear that there is no single way of looking at either form or content. Both may be viewed in several different ways. This means that every work of art is open to multiple interpretations.

He insists that the fullest experience of a work goes beyond one's perception of its unity, however much the latter might momentarily delight and inspire. A fuller and more enduringly appreciative perception requires critical seeing, a dwelling on details, an careful examination of parts, a comparison of what one sees with what others have said about the work, and so on. Critical seeing does not rule out the perception of unity. Even the cautious and well-versed artist or art viewer may delight in what is perceived. Presumably, however, the delight of perceiving unity will be enriched or deepened by the care taken in arriving at a fuller perception.

What would Dewey say to all this? I believe he would find much to agree with in the three accounts. He would approve of the centrality that Danto gives to the notion of embedded meaning. He would acknowledge the usefulness of Kuspit's efforts to distinguish between the purposes served by abstract and realistic art. And he would certainly applaud Schapiro's talk of the unity of form and content.

At the same time I believe that he would be made uneasy by elements in each of the presentations. I think Dewey would be uncomfortable with Danto's use of the term *aesthetic*. Danto speaks as though van Gogh's painting of irises, for example, is to be looked on as aesthetic, whereas Warhol's *Brillo Box* is not. I think Dewey would disagree. He would point out that it is the experience that either deserves or does not deserve the adjective *aesthetic* and not the art object. Dewey, I believe, would want to call Danto's experience in the presence of the Warhol work aesthetic, no matter what Danto might want to call it. The adjective refers to the experience as a whole, he would say, and not to the object per se. The fullness and immediacy of one's participation with an object is what constitutes the aesthetic quality of the experience.

As for Kuspit's commentary, Dewey would have no difficulty in acceding to the value of distinguishing between abstract and realistic art, but he would probably feel uncomfortable with the terms *silent* and *alchemical*. All of art, Dewey would say, is silent in some ways (it does not declare what it is about) and alchemical in others (it magically transforms the ordinary, turning material into media). Both kinds of art (the abstract and the realistic), when well executed and appropriately witnessed and reflected on, have the capacity to generate experiences that deserve to be called spiritual.

Dewey would be least troubled, I would guess, by Schapiro's account of how the arts work, but he might still feel constrained by Shapiro's concentration on the work itself, rather than on the broader experience in which the work is central. Schapiro allows for there being many different ways in which the form and content of a work may be identified and interpreted. There are thus many corresponding ways in which the unity of the two, their accord, may be achieved. At the same time, the diversity implicit in Schapiro's account is not nearly as inclusive as the references that one comes across in comparable statements by Dewey, of which the following (which I have quoted before) is typical: "In art as an experience, actuality and possibility or ideality, the new and the old, objective material and personal response, the individual and the universal, surface and depth, sense and meaning, are integrated in an experience in which they are all transfigured from the significance that belongs to them when isolated in reflection" (LW10, 301). Can Schapiro's key notions of form and content be expanded to include all that Dewey refers to here? It is not clear to me they can, at least not without diluting the meaning of the terms to the point that they are unrecognizable.

What all four commentators, including Dewey, agree on is that the unification that marks a successful art-centered experience—one that moves in the direction of spirituality—does not occur automatically. It does not happen to those who just happen to be in the physical presence of art. It may not be willed into happening, sad to say, not even by those who fervently yearn to have an epiphany. Yet neither does it need be left to chance. On this point our commentators agree. We can ready ourselves for an art-centered experience in a variety of different ways, thereby increasing the likelihood of its occurrence. What are some of those ways? That is the question to which we now turn.

Chapter 3 Experience as Artifice: Putting Dewey's Theory to Work

This exploration of Dewey's theory of experience, to prove worth-while, should make a difference in one's life. It should affect in one way or another how one looks at things, which in turn ought to affect what one does and says. Should it fail that test, if all this discussion leaves behind is the fading memory of what has been read, the time spent at the task will have been wasted. That judgment has the backing of many pragmatic thinkers. William James, for one, long ago proclaimed, "The whole function of philosophy ought to be to find out what definite difference it will make to you and me, at definite instants of our life, if this world-formula or that world-formula be true" (James 1907, 45). Dewey affirmed James's judgment a few years after it was made, but he qualified it: "The chief function of philosophy is not to find out what difference ready-made formulae make, *if true,* but to arrive at and to clarify their *meaning as programs of behavior for modifying the existent world*" (MW4, 104).

In Dewey's view the reader of philosophy has a larger role to play than that of figuring out what difference it would make if the philosopher's formulae are true. The reader actively contributes to the philosopher's project by trying to put personally derived conclusions into practice. In so doing, the reader helps to clarify the meaning of the project as a whole. That is the challenge to be faced in this third chapter of *John Dewey and the Lessons of Art*.

Because Dewey cast a broad net in his intellectual undertaking, because his theory purports to cover all of experience and not just a portion of it, the difference that it makes in one's life ought to be correspondingly broad. This means, for example, that those of us who are educators should not only benefit professionally from an understanding of Dewey, which is the conventional reason for turning to him, but personally as well. We should come to feel the impact of his thought in our daily lives as much as in our professional dealings with colleagues and students. The same holds true for all other readers.

This being so, I have chosen to separate the personal and the professional aspects of applying Dewey's theory, allowing for some inevitable overlap in the treatment of each. Chapter 3 focuses principally on what Dewey's teachings appear to be telling his readers about how to live their lives in general. Chapter 4 deals with the implications of his theory for the conduct of teaching. I must warn far in advance, however, that Chapter 4 offers nothing like a full-scale treatment of Dewey's educational thought, which would be a major undertaking in and of itself. Instead, it focuses on the excesses of child-centered and subject-centered teaching to highlight the benefits of trying to make use of Dewey's thinking about the arts. Paradoxically, one thought that readers will glean from that final chapter is that Dewey himself might have benefited as much as anyone from a wholehearted effort to put his theory into practice.

THE CRAFTING OF *AN* EXPERIENCE

More than one reader of *Art as Experience* has come to regard Dewey as someone who cares more about experience than about art. Harold B. Dunkel, for example, who edited a special issue of *The School Review* on the centennial of Dewey's birth, notes that "from reading Dewey one does not get the impression of an avid gallery-walker, an incessant concert-goer, or an omnivorous reader of literature. It does not seem that any of the arts ever 'spoke' to him very directly" (Dunkel 1959, 236). Dunkel's assessment, harsh though it may sound, strikes me as just.

Dunkel goes on: "In *Art as Experience* one often gets the impression of the philosopher rather than the art-lover at work. That is, Dewey has the air of a man who, having developed a general philosophic theory, feels he must test its adequacy by applying it to the traditional philosophic fields, one of which was aesthetics" (236). That impression, too, I agree with in the main, though it seems to me that Dewey did not turn to the arts simply as a way of testing the adequacy of his theory in yet another philosophical domain. He did so, I would say, chiefly because his thoughts had been moving in that direction for quite some time. In his exploration of the arts Dewey reached the source of a number of the key ideas that had been guiding his vision for years. He found there the embodiment of what it means to undergo *an* experience. The idealization of experience that the other arts embody, Dewey called "the greatest intellectual achievement in the history of humanity" (LW10, 31).

But though humanity's discovery of the arts may constitute the greatest of achievements, its chief value, for Dewey, lies in what it portends for the transformation of all human experiencing. Recognizing that to be so, Dunkel recommends, only half in jest, that we reverse the words in the title of Dewey's book, calling it *Experience as Art*. As he explains, "We would not be surprised, then, if Dewey should seem ultimately to turn the concept of artistic recreation toward the totality [of experience] itself and should see experience of the finest quality as one which is created, experience which is itself a work of art" (Dunkel 1959, 237).

In 1983 Joseph Kupfer seemingly acted on Dunkel's suggestion. He wrote a book entitled *Experience as Art*. In it he seeks to show "the basic importance and pervasiveness of the aesthetic in various spheres of life, not just in the obviously aesthetic" (2). Sexual activity, sports, and classroom learning are three of the major spheres of life to which Kupfer devotes attention. Others include "an aesthetic of contemporary violence," "the drama of decision-making," and the individual's confrontation with death (v).

Though broadly sympathetic with the reasoning behind Dunkel's suggested inversion of the words in the title of Dewey's book and though agreeing with Kupfer's point about the pervasiveness of the aesthetic, I have chosen to use the expression "experience as artifice" rather than "experience as art" to stand for the essence of what Dewey recommends. While I agree with Dunkel that Dewey looked on created experience as being of the finest quality, I am not sure that it helps to apply the term *art* to experience writ large. What seems to me crucial, and what I take Dewey to have been insisting on all along, is the notion that all of experience can be treated in an artful manner, not just those portions that are confined to specific spheres of life—which is why I can't quite go along with Kupfer's choice of particular domains of application. Even the most trifling of experiences, in Dewey's view, has plastic properties. We can, therefore, within limits fashion almost any segment of our lives to become superior in experiential terms to what it would have been without our effort. As Dewey says, "Art is a quality of doing and of what is done. Only outwardly, then, can it be designated by a noun substantive. Since it adheres to the manner and content of doing, it is adjectival in nature" (LW10, 218).

To look on experience as *artifice,* to see it as a contrivance, as something that is partially constructed (and partially not), is not the same as calling it art. Rather, it is to emphasize the malleability of experience without at the same time insisting that the concept of art be extended to cover everything we do. Dewey's implicit claim, in other words, is that even the most mundane and routine of our doings could become more infused with significance and there-fore more meaningful to us if crafted in a manner that roughly parallels the making of an art object. Our capacity to shape experience in this way cannot create miracles. It cannot not transform sow's ears into silk purses. It can, however, add value to our lives. That alone makes such efforts worthy of study.

To summarize much that has been already said, the arts, above all, teach us something about what it means to undergo *an* experience. Successful encoun-ters with art objects and performances offer a set of standards by which to judge ordinary experiences. Such art-centered experiences are distinguished by their unity and wholeness. They are consummatory. They are accompanied by feelings of fulfillment and satisfaction. They are self-sufficient and meaningful. They do not point beyond themselves. Lesser forms of experiencing, by way of contrast, contain but fragments, mere shards, of what Dewey would call *an* experience.

Experience as Artifice

To call *an* experience artificial is not to deny its reality. As experience, it remains real enough, yet the unity and wholeness that we ascribe to it are in some sense contrived—crafted, as it were—both in their initial occurrence and in our subsequent recollection of what took place. Dewey's two principles of continu-ity and interaction—the one emphasizing the way in which past, present, and future are in constant interplay within the confines of our experiences and the other highlighting the constancy of the physical transaction between organism and environment—are themselves sufficient to make clear that there is no experience without a past and none without a future. Likewise, there is neither organism nor environment (no sustaining field of forces) without some kind of an exchange going on and without a background against which the partic-ularities of *an* experience become evident. What this means above all is that the beginnings and endings of experiences, or what we call their beginnings and endings, are almost always arbitrary, at least to some extent. They commonly are arrangements rather than naturalistic occurrences. The performing arts show this to be so, as do most of the literary arts, especially those that rely on narrative structure. Novels and poems do not just start and finish in mid-phrase. They begin and end in a contrived manner. So do theatrical productions. The care taken in trying to be sure that the viewing audience or the reading public is prepared for those beginnings and feels satisfied with those endings is, of course, a large part of the artist's labor. Her success in that regard is often taken as a measure of her artistic talent.

Were we to take this art lesson seriously, we would spend more time than we usually do, I suppose, trying to *frame* portions of our experience, seeing to it that beginnings and endings stand out as such, instead of drifting aimlessly from one segment of experiencing to another or being explosively catapulted from one to the next. The various ways that framing may occur are without number. Even the briefest survey reveals a host of framing conditions: rituals, ceremonies, preludes, preambles, introductions, finales, farewells. Were we to try to make portions of our ordinary experience more artlike, the difference between old and new practices would lie not so much in our doing something utterly novel, something that we had never seen happening in any other context. Rather, it would reside in our applying in this about-to-be-revitalized situation or class of situations a degree of attentiveness and formality that we heretofore had applied or had seen applied in quite different contexts.

At the risk of trivializing matters, consider how someone might go about framing a segment of ordinary experience. Imagine a person who usually grabs a bite of lunch on the run, and who does so almost unthinkingly, wanting to transform that daily habit into something that at least on most days begins to resemble *an* experience. First, that person would set aside more time for lunch. No more five-minute stops at the nearby lunch counter. No more eating on the job. Perhaps the event would also change from a solitary occasion to a social one. A companion might be sought. Greetings and goodbyes would enter the picture. So might plans and prior arrangements—getting to lunch and going from lunch. The cost might change. Even the way one dresses for the occasion may be affected. For the person undertaking such a renovation of old habits, the midday meal would soon cease to be just plain old lunch. It would become something special.

Each imagined change in our hypothetical example adds to our appreciation of what Dewey means when he speaks of art as being a quality of doing and of what is done rather than a noun substantive. The art of our transformed lunch hour will seldom, if ever, qualify as a noun substantive, no matter how careful its preparation or how classy the restaurant in which the meal is taken. Yet the proposed changes should make evident the increased artfulness of the experience.

The crafting of our new and improved lunch hour need not and indeed cannot stop with the gross changes already named. More refined adjustments are called for. For example, it would hardly count as *an* experience to have lunch in a restaurant with a friend if, during the whole time, one's thoughts were elsewhere. The sheer fact of attendance at such an event presupposes making an honest effort to keep one's attention focused on what is going on while being a fruitful contributor to the conversation. To become distracted or to get into an unexpected argument with the luncheon partner would mar the event, making it unlikely that either participant would consider the hour to have constituted *an* experience in Dewey's terms.

Let's suppose everything comes off as planned. The expanded time, the upscale setting, and the social nature of the experience leave our crafter-of-a-lunch-hour now feeling satisfied and fulfilled. Has the increased satisfaction been worth the effort? Can the changes be sustained? Dewey's theory does not answer those questions. Only the person engaged in the activity and making the effort can do that. Yet the emphasis that Dewey places on *an* experience, plus his insistence that we look to the arts for guidance on how to fashion such events, do strongly imply that most of us would be better off than we now are if a larger segment of our lives was transformed in a manner analogous to the one described. Dewey would also insist that whatever changes we might make in our daily habits, narrow though their focus may be, would have repercussions in other domains of our life.

It may not be our lunch hour that we focus on in our efforts at self-reform. We might choose instead the time spent between dinner and retiring or a morning ritual that involves physical activity of some kind. Perhaps we decide not to concentrate on any specific segment of the day but, instead, undertake a new outdoor project that may take weeks or months to accomplish—the repair of a fence, let us say, or the redesign of a garden. Whatever the undertaking, the problem that we face remains essentially the same: How shall we treat this activity or this segment of our life so that its integrity as *an* experience becomes manifest? The answer will vary from one activity or segment of our life to the next, yet some of its properties will be fairly common across many different kinds of situations.

As we have seen with our example of the modified lunch hour, in many or most situations that we might wish to transform into something resembling *an* experience, our attempts entail giving special attention to beginnings and endings. We attend to the way the activity gets under way and to the way it culminates. At the front end, this heightened attention usually means spending time on planning and preparation. Getting ready to undertake the activity may involve physical activity, such as assembling materials or making arrangements, but it often includes becoming emotionally ready as well—savoring the anticipation, working up the nerve to begin, and so forth.

The culmination of the activity, in many ways, also involves forethought. The ending of the activity is to be anticipated and, under the best of circumstances, planned for. Here, too, there may be physical tasks of one kind or another: the business of tidying up, the rituals of taking leave, of bringing things to a close. There are also emotional components to such closures, and they often extend beyond the culminating feelings of fulfillment and satisfaction. The experiences commonly leave us with things to think about, fond memories and lingering afterthoughts. These, too, take time, and they may often involve communicating with others, sharing opinions and comparing notes, affirming and sometimes contradicting someone else's impressions of what had taken place.

In the lunch-hour example I noted that if the person dining with someone was unable to concentrate on both the meal and the conversation, the unity of the experience would be jeopardized and its status as *an* experience would be correspondingly diminished. This implies that having *an* experience requires nothing less than the experiencer's absorption in the task or situation at hand. That may be the case ideally. However, in actuality the criterion of total concentration seems altogether too stringent a requirement, save in those activities, such as mountain climbing or heart surgery, where a momentary lapse of attention could easily prove disastrous. In less hazardous undertakings, some amount of divided attention is probably the norm. This is doubtless so even in places like concert halls and theaters, where concentration is expected and where devices such as the lowering of houselights and prohibitions against late entry help to sustain the audience's focus of attention. Leonard Meyer, a music theorist and art historian, acknowledges the near impossibility of fully concentrating on a musical event: "Actually, it is unlikely that many listeners attend at a maximal level of vigilance at all times. Fully sustained listening is probably 'more honored in the breach than the observance'" (Meyer 1994, 321).

The difficulty of sustaining the quality of attention that *an* experience demands (even with the help of devices aimed at making the task easier) adds to the effort of transforming a segment of ordinary experience into an activity that is at once artfully undertaken and appreciatively consumed. That transformation, as our lunch-hour example made clear, takes both time and energy. It costs something to accomplish, and the costs must be weighed against whatever benefits might ensue. Nor are all the costs contained within the experience itself, not even if we add to the sum the expenses associated with preparation and planning of the experience and with the reflection and reverie that come afterward. There are also the costs of benefits forgone, of what we might have done with the time spent working on this segment of experience rather than that one. Those invisible costs are inestimable in reality. Who can precisely reckon the value of what might have been? Yet the inestimable costs are often felt to be genuine, as is the common feeling of having wasted time.

A recognition of the costs associated with the crafting of *an* experience leads to an obvious question: How much of experience can a person afford to craft in this way? How much of life can we live artfully? The answer to both questions lies somewhere between "less than all of it" and "more than is now the case." We cannot afford to treat all of experience artfully, for the simple reason that the press of events and the demands made on us by others will not allow it, at least not without a more dramatic transformation of our lives than most of us are willing to consider. At the same time, we surely must treat more of our lives in this manner if we are to make them fuller and richer.

So the question becomes: Where do we begin? What portion of our lives should we start to treat more artfully than before? The answers will vary considerably, depending on the circumstances that we each face. Kupfer, as we have seen, recommends attending to specific spheres of life. For starters, he suggests the domains of sports, sexual relations, and classroom activity. He adds decision making and the spheres of social and political activity in which frustrated aesthetic desires turn to violence. There is much to be said on behalf of his approach. Compartmentalizing our lives as he suggests is certainly one way to begin. Indeed, we will soon apply a similar approach when turning to the educational implications of Dewey's theory. What interests me here, however, are the broadest connotations of what it means to apply Dewey's theory to our lives. Given that purpose, we must keep in mind that Dewey's criteria of *an* experience apply to all of experiencing and not solely to selected spheres of life.

No matter where we begin, we must remember that all such efforts will prove costly in both time and energy. We must be prepared to pay those costs. We also need to remember that the unity of experience, no matter how defined, will always remain imperfect. There is no such thing as *a* pristine experience. All of experience is flawed in some way. It more or less has to be, given what Dewey brings us to understand about its generic traits and characteristics.

In specific instances we may choose to overlook those flaws. We may thereby declare this or that experience to have been perfect or ideal. I can easily imagine doing so on a balmy spring day or after an exquisite rendering of Beethoven's Fifth. But even if we mean what we say on such occasions, such a declaration implies only that we have somehow managed to cloak or otherwise discount the unwanted elements that, had we allowed them entry into consciousness, would have detracted from the experience being celebrated. Having pushed them into the background, we are left with what we call perfection. That, too, is part of what it means to craft *an* experience.

Tuning In to the Immediate

As I reminded readers in Chapters 1 and 2, what Dewey refers to as *an* experience is not marked solely by its unity or wholeness. Nor does its characteristic of having a fairly clear-cut beginning and ending—a framing, as I have called it here—exhaust its distinctiveness. It is also typified by an immediacy whose properties engross and absorb the perceptual energies of the experiencer. When immersed in *an* experience, the experiencer's outside world is effectively screened off. The experiencer is aware solely, or nearly so, of the object or event on which his attention centers.

Normal experience, Dewey reminds us, is not so focused. We normally give only fleeting and superficial attention to even those aspects of our environment with which we are physically engaged. We bring our morning cup of coffee to our lips, but we barely perceive the cup as an object with unique properties. We overlook its design, its texture, its color, its weight. We remain oblivious to the reflections of light on its surface, its warmth to the touch, and much more. We give no heed to the cup's history—to how it came into being and how we came to possess it—nor do we think about what its future might be.

This inattentiveness hardly calls for a deep explanation. Our focus is elsewhere. We are reading the morning paper or conversing with our breakfast partner or staring into space and thinking of the day ahead. The features of the cup in our hands are furthest from our mind. Nor is it only the cup whose physical immediacy we presently overlook. We doubtless are paying scant attention to its contents. The coffee that we drink may be only dimly tasted.

Dewey's chief worry about this kind of inattentiveness is not that it closes off portions of our perceptual field. Perception always has to be selective. There are always aspects of our surroundings that we overlook at any given moment. Perception requires us to do so. What concerns Dewey and what should concern us all is not overlooking this or that. Rather, it is that the natural tendency to see past the objects and events that we make use of in the here and now may become so habitual that we no longer notice them at all. In time we find it hard to perceive anything fully. Dewey warns that under such conditions "apathy and torpor" build "a shell about objects"—the shell that art seeks to penetrate (LW10, 109). Art, he says, "quickens us from the slackness of routine and enables us to forget ourselves by finding ourselves in the delight of experiencing the world about us in its varied qualities and forms" (LW10, 110).

Is it art alone that refreshes our sensibilities this way? Or might there be other ways of our coming to delight once more in the world about us? Without the help of art could we, for example, teach ourselves to become more perceptive, more attentive to the particularities of things? If that is a possibility, could we do so not just with respect to physical objects like coffee cups and flowers but also with respect to our fellow human beings and even perhaps with respect to the situations that we inevitably inhabit?

While pondering these questions and trying to formulate answers to them, I chanced upon two books that contained material closely related to my ongoing set of interests. Alerted to the possibility of help from sources that I had overlooked, I kept my eye out for other such books. In time I came across a third that reinforced much that was said in the first two. It did so, however, from yet another perspective. Though none of these books even so much as mentions Dewey, each seems distinctively Deweyan in orientation, at least to the extent of addressing the question of how we might learn to perceive the world more fully and attentively than we do at present. The answers that each gives to that key question are Deweyan in some respects but not in others. They are self-help books written for a mass audience, and, in fact, they helped me understand the broad applicability of Dewey's theory. I turn to them now.

JON KABAT-ZINN'S *WHEREVER YOU GO, THERE YOU ARE*

Jon Kabat-Zinn, founder and director of the Stress Reduction Clinic at the University of Massachusetts Medical Center, is an advocate, teacher, and long-time practitioner of what he calls mindfulness meditation, which he describes as "an ancient Buddhist practice" whose goal is to help its practitioners achieve a heightened awareness of the present moment (Kabat-Zinn 1994, 3). His book is a how-to guide to that form of meditation. It includes general advice interspersed with anecdotal accounts of the benefits to be achieved by meditation, along with words of inspiration and encouragement from the likes of Thoreau, Whitman, Lao-tzu, and others. It also offers specific suggestions about how to proceed.

Mindfulness meditation, as expounded by Kabat-Zinn, is chiefly a way of "non-doing," of stepping out of the stream of ongoing activity for intervals ranging from a few seconds to an hour or more during which time one seeks to cultivate and maintain a special kind of inward attentiveness. As he explains, "What we frequently call formal meditation involves purposefully making a time for stopping all outward activity and cultivating stillness, with no agenda other than being fully present in each moment. Not doing anything" (35). This description notwithstanding, Kabat-Zinn does not mean to imply that one's mind becomes an absolute blank. Quite the contrary. What characterizes one's mental state during meditation is a form of concentration that is in many ways far more intense and demanding than are the degrees of attention that we give to ordinary affairs. What he means by not doing anything is no longer purposefully engaging in normal activities, putting business as usual on hold.

What makes this form of concentration more demanding than most is principally its unfamiliarity. We are not used to it. We are unaccustomed to removing ourselves from the demands and pressures of daily life, from thinking about where our actions are taking us and what is to be gained or lost by doing this or that. Consequently, it takes time and a fair amount of practice, we are told, to achieve the degree of detachment from ordinary affairs that Kabat-Zinn's form of meditation calls for. He does suggest that with practice the task becomes easier. He implies that if we stay at it long enough, we should be able to experience a state of mindfulness even while engaged in our ordinary doings. Ultimately, habit takes hold, this way of relating ourselves to the present promises to usher in a new way of life for those who practice it, or so Kabat-Zinn assures us.

Initially, however, mindfulness is a discipline to be mastered, and since one must begin somewhere, Kabat-Zinn recommends sitting in a comfortable position and attending to breathing in and out. As he explains it, "To use your breathing to nurture mindfulness, just tune in to the feeling of it . . . the feeling of the breath coming into your body and the feeling of the breath leaving your body. That's all. Just feeling the breath. Breathing and knowing that you're breathing. This doesn't mean deep breathing or forcing your breathing, or trying to feel something special, or wondering whether you're doing it right. It doesn't mean thinking about your breathing, either. It's just a bare bones awareness of the breath moving in and the breath moving out" (18–19). What the neophyte soon discovers is that attending to one's breathing is no easy task. Most people find it hard to maintain such a focus for more than a few seconds at a time. Stray thoughts soon enter the picture, as do outside interferences of one kind or another. The would-be meditator soon begins to think of other matters or, in an effort to remain focused, starts to think about breathing itself. Either way, attention flags, and the beginner no longer concentrates on breathing at all.

The difficulty that most people encounter when trying to concentrate in this way attests to the firm hold that a quite different outlook and a quite different set of attitudes have upon our collective consciousness. We twentieth-century Westerners are almost constitutionally unable to follow Kabat-Zinn's directions with ease. We are not used to being attentive to something as seemingly inconsequential as ordinary breathing. We all have far more pressing matters to think about, or so we would claim. The effort to become mindful in the way Kabat-Zinn recommends must strike many busy people as out of place in their otherwise crowded lives.

Attending to one's breathing is only the first step in learning to meditate mindfully. It is such a useful way of getting started, however, that Kabat-Zinn recommends it as a kind of opening exercise for everyone, no matter how experienced he or she might be at meditation. Both beginners and experts may also return to this simple exercise whenever their attention begins to wander within a meditative session. Kabat-Zinn calls it an "anchor line" that "tethers" the meditator to the present moment and guides him or her back as required (18).

The purpose of meditation, as Kabat-Zinn presents it, is not to break away from the hubbub of ordinary living and thereby establish a temporary island of repose within a sea of frenetic activity. Nor is it a way to avoid facing up to reality. In fact, Kabat-Zinn specifically warns against using organized meditative "retreats" solely as a means of escape. The title of his book, *Wherever You Go, There You Are,* underscores the futility of such efforts.

What, then, is the goal of developing a state of mindfulness? It is a way of being "truly in touch with where we already are," Kabat-Zinn says (xiii). To have that happen, "we have got to pause in our experience long enough to let the present moment sink in; long enough to actually *feel* the present moment, to see it in its fullness, to hold it in awareness and thereby come to know and understand it better" (xiv). "Only then," he continues, "can we accept the truth of that moment of our life, learn from it, and move on" (xiv). It is also, he claims, the road to self-knowledge. "Meditation is simply about being yourself and knowing something about who that is. It is about coming to realize that you are on a path whether you like it or not, namely, the path that is your life. Meditation may help us see that this path we call our life has direction; that it is always unfolding, moment by moment; and that what happens now, in this moment, influences what happens next" (xvi).

Yet the activity of seeking to achieve mindfulness as Kabat-Zinn defines it involves more than pausing in the midst of whatever we might be doing to let the immediacy of the present moment sink in. It also entails more than coming to realize one's position on this path we call our life. It is, in essence, a method of self-improvement. At its core lies the hope of becoming a better person by discarding old habits (inattentiveness to the present being chief among them) and taking on new ones.

To aid in this process, Kabat-Zinn recommends the cultivation of a set of attitudes or mental qualities that "support meditation practice and provide a rich soil in which the seeds of mindfulness can flourish" (47). These attitudes are to be worked toward gradually. They cannot, Kabat-Zinn tells us, "be imposed, legislated, or decreed" (47). Each is fundamentally ethical in its orientation. The seven qualities to which he gives particular attention are patience, trust, generosity, dignity, letting go, non-judging, and non-harming. For each of these seven he offers a brief explanation of its place in meditative practice and a word or two about its broader significance.

Here, for example, is part of what he has to say about the cultivation of patience: "In taking up meditation, we are cultivating the quality of patience every time we stop and sit and become aware of the flow of our own breathing. And this invitation to ourselves to be more open, more in touch, more patient with our moments naturally extends itself to other times in our lives as well. We know that things unfold according to their own nature. We can remember to let our lives unfold in the same way. We don't have to let our anxieties and our desire for certain results dominate the quality of the moment, even when things are painful" (50).

Here he is on the importance of generosity: "You might experiment with using the cultivation of generosity as a vehicle for deep self-observation and inquiry as well as an exercise in giving. A good place to start is with yourself. See if you can give yourself gifts that may be true blessings, such as self-acceptance, or some time each day with no purpose. Practice feeling deserving enough to accept these gifts without obligation—to simply receive from yourself, and from the universe" (61).

In the cultivation of all seven attitudes the starting point and the basic object of reference is invariably the self. Meditators are advised to begin by trying to be generous, patient, trusting, non-judgmental, and so forth toward themselves and their inner life. The clear implication is that by so doing, habits will develop whose range of application will extend naturally to other persons and to circumstances within the larger environment.

One obvious result of following Kabat-Zinn suggestions would be to slow the pace of one's life. Kabat-Zinn makes that a specific goal. He calls it voluntary simplicity, which he describes as follows: "Voluntary simplicity means going fewer places in one day rather than more, seeing less so I can see more, doing less so I can do more, acquiring less so that I can have more" (69).

Living this less-is-more philosophy is, as Kabat-Zinn points out, "an arduous discipline . . . always in need of retuning, further inquiry, attention" (70). Yet it is ultimately freeing in its effect, he reports, for it makes the practitioner less compulsively responsive to external prompts of one kind or another. The meditative student learns, for example, that telephones can go unanswered from time to time without dire consequences. Newspapers can be left unread without ill effect. Even the opportunity to make money or to gain in some other material way may be forgone without regret. Over time, the practitioner comes to cherish the greater elbowroom and sense of expansiveness that such a way of life engenders.

As well might be imagined, there is much more to Kabat-Zinn's set of recommendations than I have reported here. But this sketch should suffice to give a fair understanding of what he stands for and of the practices that he advocates. We now ask, How does this outlook and how do these practices relate to Dewey's theory of experience? Do the practices themselves constitute an enactment of what it means to be in touch with the immediacy of experience? Would Dewey have endorsed them, or might he have pooh-poohed the idea of formal meditation altogether, along with such specific suggestions as starting out by trying to concentrate on breathing? What would he say about the promise of self-knowledge through meditative practice and about the attitudes of patience, trust, generosity, and so forth, that Kabat-Zinn's form of meditation seeks to advance?

My guess is that Dewey would have been broadly sympathetic with the therapeutic orientation of Kabat-Zinn's book and with the practicality of much of the advice that it offers. At the same time, I believe he would have had serious misgivings about the book's near exclusive focus on the self and on the goal of self-improvement. Dewey by no means belittled the significance of incremental growth in the direction of becoming a more fully functioning person. He believed, however, that such growth was more likely to take place as a by-product of the effort to act on the world and make it better than by turning attention inward and trying to improve the self. As he explains, "It is not in the least implied that change in personal attitudes, in the disposition of the 'subject,' is not of great importance. Such change, on the contrary, is involved in any attempt to modify the conditions of the environment. But there is a radical difference between a change in the self that is cultivated and valued as an end, and one that is a means to alteration, through action, of objective conditions."

The trouble with such contemplative and inward-looking strategies, according to Dewey, was that they were most "congenial to minds that despair of the effort involved in creation of a better world of daily experience" (LW4, 220). For Dewey, that better world can come about only through direct action. It cannot simply be wished for, nor can it be realized solely by the power of the imagination or by mental tricks (e.g., longed-for changes of attitude).

The difference between Kabat-Zinn's advice and the advice that Dewey might offer stands out most starkly in the way each treats the concept of inquiry. Kabat-Zinn introduces the subject with a sentence that might make any follower of Dewey applaud: "The spirit of inquiry is fundamental to living mindfully." But as he continues the issue becomes cloudy: "Inquiry is not just a way to solve problems. It is a way to make sure you are staying in touch with the basic mystery of life itself and of our presence here." A bit further on he says, "Inquiry doesn't mean looking for answers, especially quick answers which come out of superficial thinking. It means asking without expecting answers, just pondering the question, carrying the wondering with you, letting it percolate, bubble, cook, ripen, come in and out of awareness, just as everything else comes in and out of awareness" (233).

I can't imagine Dewey having any difficulty with the idea of inquiry taking time or with the notion that one ought to avoid quick answers and superficial thinking. I do picture him puzzling over the suggestion that inquiry doesn't mean looking for answers or that it does mean asking without expecting answers. To inquire without any hope whatsoever of resolving whatever perplexity led to the inquiry strikes me, as I think it would Dewey, as the ultimate in purposelessness.

In fairness to Kabat-Zinn, I must say that he does not preclude the attainment of answers to the questions raised by inquiry. He does, however, cast those questions so broadly ("Who am I? Where am I going? What is my way? What is my job on the planet with a capital J?") that one wonders whether they have answers, and if they do, how one might proceed to answer them. "Inquiry," he says, "means asking questions, over and over again. Do we have the courage to look at something, whatever it is, and to inquire, what is this? What is going on? It involves looking deeply for a sustained period, questioning, questioning, what is this? What is wrong? What is the root of the problem? What is the evidence? What are the connections? What would a happy solution look like? Questioning, questioning, continually questioning" (234). The implication seems to be that if we just keep asking for a long enough time the answer will be forthcoming. Dewey would surely not agree. For him, the posing of the question is but the first step along the arduous road to a solution, even though it is a step that may have to be taken time and again.

Perhaps the important difference between them is that Kabat-Zinn sees the posing of the question as crucial, whereas Dewey emphasizes the importance of the steps taken toward its solution. But that doesn't capture their main difference, either. What is more telling is that Kabat-Zinn's questions ("Who am I? What is my way? What is my job on the planet with a capital J?") have an adolescent quality about them. They reek of existential angst. They are not genuine questions of the kind that normal adults ordinarily ask unless they were trying to strike a pose of philosophical profundity.

Dewey never poses such questions himself nor urges them upon others. He does not encourage us to ponder who we are or what our job on the planet might be. Instead, he prompts each of us to frame and reframe whatever question or questions we find to be most pressing from moment to moment and from day to day. He insists, however, that all such questions be tied, fore and aft, to genuine existential conditions, that they arise in response to real problems directly felt and that they lead to efforts aimed at the resolution of those problems. A question that springs from nowhere and that leads nowhere doubly fails Dewey's test of genuineness.

Here it is good to keep in mind where and to whom Kabat-Zinn typically dispenses his advice. He is, we are told, the founder and director of a stress reduction clinic located in a university medical center. He is also the author of an earlier book entitled *Full Catastrophe Living*, which he describes as "a navigational chart, intended for people facing physical or emotional pain or reeling from the effects of too much stress" (xvii–xviii). Thus the typical recipient of the advice he offers is someone in dire need of immediate relief from discomfort brought about by living under excessively stressful conditions. Though the more recent of his books is obviously designed to appeal to a much broader audience than was his earlier one, it is still possible and perhaps even likely that many of his examples, which include the kinds of questions that he imagines his readers asking, are drawn chiefly from his daily encounters with patients. For such individuals experiencing existential angst may be normal and not adolescent. But the genuineness of the questions would not vitiate the difference between him and Dewey in the way each handles the concept of inquiry. For Dewey, pace Kabat-Zinn, even such broad questions as Who am I? and What is my job on earth?—assuming them to be genuinely felt and allowing that they may be naturally occasioned by the trauma of loss or suffering—beg to be answered as much as to be asked.

The attention that Kabat-Zinn gives to the act of breathing and to the significance of bodily posture while meditating doubtless derives in large part from his experience as a practitioner of yoga. As every beginning student of that ancient discipline soon learns, how one attends to one's somatic condition while exercising is crucial. On the face of it, learning to pay attention to such matters seems to have little connection with Dewey's conception of how experience operates. Readers familiar with the depersonalized quality of Dewey's prose may find it difficult to imagine him looking kindly upon such an inwardly focused set of practices. So, too, those who know something of his taciturn New England temperament. On that score, however, both would be quite wrong.

Dewey, it turns out, spent several years of his life as the student of a teacher of physical culture who sought to inculcate techniques of self-control and self-scrutiny closely akin to those that Kabat-Zinn recommends. Beginning in 1916 and continuing into the 1930s and possibly beyond, Dewey studied with F. Matthais Alexander, whose technique of self-help, known as the Alexander Technique, became fairly popular and remains of considerable interest even today, especially among actors and musicians. Dewey wrote the introduction to three of Alexander's books, whose titles were: *Man's Supreme Inheritance* (1918), *Constructive Conscious Control of the Individual* (1923), and *The Use of the Self* (1932). Dewey credits Alexander with having helped rid him of bad posture, a stiff neck, a shuffling gait, and eye difficulties (Lamont 1959, 27). There is even some indirect evidence that the benefits extended to the alleviation of psychological discomforts as well as physical ones (Alexander 1923, 189–190).

Without going into detail about how Dewey become connected with Alexander and how Alexander's teachings became a significant source of insight for him, I can summarily report that Dewey was no stranger to the kind of advice that Kabat-Zinn offers. He knew what it was like to focus on the act of breathing and on the posture of his body as a means of breaking old habits and establishing new ones. He also knew how difficult it was to overcome old ways of behaving. As he remarks in his introduction to Alexander's *Constructive Conscious Control of the Individual,* "The hardest thing to attend to is that which is closest to ourselves, that which is most constant and familiar. And this closest 'something' is, precisely, ourselves, our own habits and ways of doing things as agencies in conditioning what is tried or done by us" (MW15, 315).

What Dewey came to understand, partly as a result of his sessions with Alexander, was that even the most ordinary of our habitual actions, such as the way we stand or sit, operates continuously (even when subdued and subordinate) as part of that working interaction of habits to which the name character is given. As he points out, "Were it not for the continued operation of all habits in every act, no such thing as character could exist. There would be simply a bundle, an untied bundle at that, of isolated acts. Character is the interpenetration of habits" (MW14, 29). He saw that "we cannot change habit directly: that notion is magic. But we can change it indirectly by modifying conditions, *by an intelligent selecting and weighting of the objects which engage attention* and which influence the fulfillment of desires" (MW14, 18, emphasis added). These insights, which he acknowledges as having derived in large measure from his work with Alexander, strike me as being commensurate with much of the advice contained in Kabat-Zinn's book, particularly those sections that recommend giving close attention to one's breathing and posture.

With respect to the connection between theory and practice, Dewey reports that "In the study [of the Alexander Technique] I found that things which I had 'known'—in the sense of theoretical belief—in philosophy and psychology, changed into vital experiences which gave a new meaning to knowledge of them" (LW6, 318). What I find especially noteworthy in that brief testimony is, first, that Dewey's theoretical beliefs preceded his understanding of how to put them into action and, second, that the beliefs themselves were insufficient as guides to practice. It seemingly took months and perhaps even years of tutelage at the hands of F. Matthais Alexander to bring the connection to light, thus giving new meaning to what Dewey knew, changing his knowledge into vital experiences. What that says about the ease of putting Dewey's theory to work in everyday life is not entirely clear to me, but it at least suggests that the means of doing so were not immediately evident to the theory's author. That being so, we must surely be patient in our own efforts to make those connections.

The call for patience returns us to what Kabat-Zinn has to say about cultivating those attitudes or mental qualities that promise to "support meditation practice and provide a rich soil in which the seeds of mindfulness can flourish"

(Kabat-Zinn 1994, 47). The specific qualities that he mentions, we will recall, were seven in number. The question is, Can such attitudes be established by following the kind of advice that Kabat-Zinn offers? What would Dewey say of that possibility? Might he find, as he did with the Alexander Technique, that such a welcome state of affairs was not only possible but was fully in keeping with his theoretical beliefs, even though he himself had not initially foreseen such a happy consequence?

I am not sure what to say about the empirical validity of Kabat-Zinn's claims. Whether one can become more generous, trustful, and so forth, by following the guidelines that he lays down is an empirical question that can probably be answered only by putting such practices to the test. I am somewhat more confident, however, in my beliefs about how Dewey would respond. I believe that he would be sympathetic to the suggestion that fundamental attitudes might be established or at least strengthened in this way, though I suspect that he, too, would want to see that possibility put to the test.

One of my reasons for thinking that Dewey would not turn up his nose at Kabat-Zinn's suggestion is to be found in Dewey's introduction to Alexander's *Use of the Self.* There he speaks not only of "the tremendous difficulty" that he encountered in following Alexander's advice but also of "*the great change in moral and mental attitude* that takes place as proper coordinations are established" (LW6, 318, emphasis added). Thus, he seems to have personally undergone a transformation akin to those that Kabat-Zinn seeks to engender through his regimen of mindfulness.

Another reason for predicting a favorable reaction from Dewey has more to do with his theoretical position than with his personal experience. For Dewey, personal dispositions, such as generosity or trustfulness, are basically habits. They are propensities to act in certain ways under certain circumstances. They are also feeling states, which means that there is a qualitatively immediate dimension to our experience of them. The person who acts generously or trustfully also feels generous or trustful in the process, even though such feelings may not always rise to consciousness. As Dewey explains, "Immediate, seemingly instinctive, feeling of the direction and end of various lines of behavior is in reality the feeling of habits working below direct consciousness" (MW14, 26).

What Kabat-Zinn seems to be trying to do is to encourage his readers (or his patients) to generate such feelings, to bring them into awareness while meditating, or, at the very least, to become conscious of their absence when they resist arousal. Whether that can be done and what the consequences might be for other aspects of our lives seem to me, once again, to be empirical questions. It is quite possible that such practices might be successful for some but not for all.

The important point remains, however, that for Dewey there would be nothing wrong with trying to engender such feelings and then proceeding to see what happens. This said, he would certainly insist that all such efforts terminate in action. It is not enough, in his view, to feel generous; one must also act generously. The same would apply to the other virtues and their related emotions. In his emphasis on the feelings that must accompany virtuous behavior Dewey echoes Aristotle's reasoning as presented in his *Nicomachean Ethics*.

Kabat-Zinn starts out on the same foot. He, too, recommends action. In the case of generosity, he suggests that one begin by acting generously toward oneself—by spending a part of each day in a state of relaxation and meditation, for example. "Fair enough," I think Dewey would say, for his account of his experience with Alexander reveals him to have been willing to treat himself in like manner. I also picture him worrying somewhat, however, about the possibility of such efforts becoming too narrowly focused on the self. The move from treating oneself generously to treating others in the same manner is crucial for Dewey, as it would have to be for all moral theorists.

Before leaving this discussion of Kabat-Zinn's book and its relation to Dewey's theory I must include what another philosopher, Richard Shusterman, has recently said about the lesson to be learned from Dewey's association with Alexander. "Dewey's attachment to Alexander should give us pause," he warns. "If philosophy sees itself most broadly as culture criticism, then somatics is an increasingly significant dimension of our culture that is ripe for philosophical critique. Philosophy here can have the role of critically examining such body practices and their attendant ideologies to see what sense or nonsense they make, what good or harm they do, and whether they could profit from a better formulation of aims and methods. It might helpfully disentangle useful technique from misguided theory so as to make these practices more convincing and effective" (Shusterman 1994, 143). Then Shusterman rounds out his vision of philosophy's future.

> Finally, the most radical and interesting way for philosophy to engage somatics is to integrate such bodily disciplines into the very practice of philosophy. This means practicing philosophy not simply as a discursive genre, a form of writing, but as a discipline of embodied life. One's philosophical work, one's search for truth and wisdom, would not be pursued only through texts but also through somatic exploration and experiment. By acute attention to the body and its nonverbal messages, by

the practice of body disciplines which heighten somatic awareness and transform how one feels and functions, one discovers and expands self-knowledge by remaking one's self. This quest for self-knowledge and self-transformation can constitute a philosophical life of increasing embodied enrichment that has irresistible aesthetic appeal, for one's life becomes a developing work of art. (143–144)

Can bodily disciplines be integrated into the very practice of philosophy? Would the effort to accomplish that condition constitute a philosophical life with irresistible aesthetic appeal? Those, to me, are indeed the questions posed not solely by Dewey's attachment to Alexander but by his philosophy as a whole. Nor is it just bodily disciplines that Dewey asks be integrated into the very practice of philosophy. Rather, he asks that philosophy be practiced whenever and wherever conditions allow, that it be translated into a way of life.

As promising as such a future might sound, it is not exactly new. Pierre Hadot, a distinguished historian of ancient philosophy, sounds much like Shusterman when he speaks of the "abyss between philosophical theory and philosophizing as living action" that exists today. But, he hastens to add, this was not always so. In Greek and Roman times, "philosophizing was a continuous act, permanent and identical with life itself, which had to be renewed at each instant." For the ancients the chief means of that renewal was an alteration of perception, "an orientation of the attention" (Hadot 1995, 268). Even then, he points out, the actual practice of a philosophical perspective, like the ones advocated by the Stoics and the Epicureans, was the exception rather than the rule. The historical record shows that "Already in antiquity people were not conscious of living in the world. They had no time to look at the world, and philosophers strongly sensed the paradox and scandal of the human condition; man *lives in* the world without *perceiving* the world" (258).

Drawing support from modern thinkers such as Henri Bergson and Marcel Merleau-Ponty (while curiously overlooking the additional support that he might easily have garnered from the likes of Dewey, James, and other pragmatists), Hadot calls for a return to something akin to the spiritual exercises practiced by the ancients. What such a return would entail, as he explains, would be an dramatically altered way of perceiving the world, an alteration so extreme as to constitute for most of us "a radical rupture" (254), "a total conversion" (261) of our old ways of seeing and acting. "The utilitarian perception we have of the world, in everyday life, in fact hides from us the world qua world. Aesthetic and philosophical perceptions of the world are only possible by means of a complete transformation of our relationship to the world: we have to perceive it *for itself,* and no longer *for ourselves*" (254).

The transformation that he speaks of, Hadot describes as "a miracle of perception itself, which opens up the world to us" (256). "Yet," he warns, "we can only perceive this miracle by reflecting on perception, and converting our attention. In this way, we can change our relationship to the world, and when we do so, we are astonished by it. . . . At such moments, it is as if we were seeing the world appear before our eyes for the first time" (256).

Another set of terms that Hadot uses to refer to this altered way of looking at things makes it out to be "a disinterested perception of the world" (259). Here is how he describes the attainment of that condition: "What is required is concentration on the present moment, a concentration in which the spirit is, in a sense, without past nor present, as it experiences the simple 'sensation of existence.' Such concentration is not, however, a mere turning in upon oneself. On the contrary: the sensation of existence is, inseparably, the sensation of being *in* the whole and the sensation of the existence *of* the whole" (259). Hadot borrows the phrase "sensation of existence" from Rousseau's *Reveries of the Solitary Walker* (Rousseau [1782] 1979), a book in which Hadot claims "we can see both the echo of ancient traditions and the anticipation of certain modern attitudes" (Hadot 1995, 259). In my own English edition of that work the relevant phrase is translated as the "*feeling* of existence" (Rousseau [1782] 1979, 88, emphasis added), but its essential meaning remains unchanged.

What I find striking about Hadot's historical analysis is the parallel that he draws between modern and ancient conditions and the similarity of philosophy's idealized role in both historical periods. Yet in bringing these similarities to light Hadot does not call for a return to the past. He does not suggest that we can or should seek to revitalize the spiritual exercises of the ancients, along with the wealth of cosmological and theological reasoning that then justified their use. Instead, he recommends a separation of the exercises and their rationale. The former, he believes, can be profitably undertaken without the latter. As he explains, "I think modern man can practice the spiritual exercises of antiquity, at the same time separating them from the philosophical or mythic discourse which came along with them. The same spiritual exercise can, in fact, be justified by extremely diverse philosophical discourses. These latter are nothing but clumsy attempts, coming after the fact, to describe and justify inner experiences whose existential density is not, in the last analysis, susceptible to any attempt at theorization or systematization" (Hadot 1995, 212).

In this regard, it is instructive to note what Kabat-Zinn has to say about the application of the term *spiritual* to the practices that he recommends. "As much as I can," he reports, "I avoid using the word 'spiritual' altogether. I find it neither useful nor necessary nor appropriate in my work. . . . Nor do I find the word 'spiritual' particularly congenial to the way I hold the sharpening and deepening of my own meditation practice" (Kabat-Zinn 1994, 263). In its place Kabat-Zinn prefers the term *consciousness discipline* because "the word 'spiritual' evokes such different connotations in different people. All these connotations are unavoidably entwined in belief systems and unconscious expectations that most of us are reluctant to examine and that can all too easily prevent us from developing or even from hearing that genuine growth is possible" (264). Alexander's second book, the one on which Dewey lavished such praise, was entitled, we will recall, *Constructive Conscious Control of the Individual.*

CORITA KENT AND JAN STEWARD'S *LEARNING BY HEART*

The second self-help book that I came across, *Learning by Heart* (1992), is addressed to people interested in participating in the arts. One of its authors, Jan Steward, was the former student of her coauthor, Corita Kent, who, as Sister Mary Corita, taught art for fifteen years or so—from the mid-1950s through the 1960s—at the Immaculate Heart College in Hollywood, California. Sister Corita's art enjoyed national and even international acclaim before her untimely death in 1986, when plans for this book were already under way. Her manner of teaching and her wisdom as a teacher of art are endearingly described and made available to others in this book.

In essence, the book consists of a mélange of commentary, quotations, and assignments, with many illustrative photographs of artwork, much of it folk art. The commentary is organized around broad topics such as "Looking," "Structure," and "Tools and Techniques." The quotations have varied sources, ranging from Robert Frost and Anaïs Nin to Javanese proverbs, though the bulk of them come from Sister Corita. The assignments suggest ways of putting the book's espoused principles to work.

If there is an underlying theme to the book it has to do with how one looks at things, with what one chooses to look at and what one sees when looking. As Jan Steward writes in the section called "Beginning," "By learning to see the beauty in the world around us, and by looking at many things (not necessarily called art), we can lose our judgmental attitudes about pretty and ugly, good and bad art. We will then be able to find our own visual masters" (Kent and Steward 1992, 9).

The first major section of the book, after the brief "Beginning," is entitled "Looking." Its goal is to goad the reader into taking a fresh look at the world of ordinary objects. To that end, it contains a number of assignments designed to awaken the viewer to aspects of the environment that tend to be overlooked. For example, the reader is encouraged to become aware of the many shadows that traverse the surfaces of his or her immediate environment.

> Begin by looking at the shadows in your room. After about five minutes you will probably think you've seen everything. But then after fifteen or maybe twenty-seven or fifty-eight minutes, it's like an explosion and you see thousands of things you never knew were there. And you know you could go on looking forever and never see it all—the rich texture of that same old wall, the shadowy angles of the window ledge—and everything will always be new. You will make new connections and relationships, and become aware of subtle shading and implications. No amount of reading about looking can do it for you. Do it. Look at those shadows (16).

There follows an weeklong assignment in which the reader is advised to sit for fifteen minutes each day looking at the shadows in one corner of a room. The assignment calls for writing down everything one sees about those shadows— their changes in color, size, and shape.

Another task calls for choosing a single object—the authors suggest a soda bottle—and looking at it very closely for an extended period of time. Indeed, they recommend looking at only the top third of the bottle every day for fifteen minutes and recording all that is seen. As they warn, "This kind of looking requires shutting out everything else, slowing down, and being very patient" (19).

Yet a third set of exercises concentrates on helping readers see the differences between two objects that are very similar. Here is the assignment that accompanies that general advice: "Take something in nature—two dandelions—and look at them for five minutes, listing how they are different from each other. Take two leaves from the same tree and do the same thing. Take two peas from the same pod and do the same thing. Nothing is the same. No thing is the same. Everything is itself and one of a kind. After doing this for a week, look back on these pairs of things again and make a new list. You will find more differences because you have been exercising your powers of observation" (21).

Other recommended exercises could easily be added to the three that I have described, but these suffice to convey the spirit and the content of what *Learning by Heart* has to say about looking. Several aspects of the advice are worthy of further comment here.

To me, many of the assignments in *Learning by Heart,* including those just described, seem very demanding of both time and patience. Though I confess that I have not tried to follow any of the directions to the letter, I find it hard even to imagine doing so. Spending fifteen minutes a day looking at the shadows in one corner of a room and perhaps another fifteen minutes looking at the upper third of a Coke bottle. all the while writing down everything one sees, is daunting in prospect.

At the same time, I must also report that having experimented with several of the assignments, I did find their outcomes to be much as the authors predicted. It was surprising, I found, to take note of the play of shadows in the room in which I was sitting when I first read *Learning by Heart*. Though I did not stay at the task for anywhere near the twenty-seven or fifty-eight minutes that Steward and Kent recommend, I did remain at it long enough to begin to substantiate the authors' claim that one might go on looking at such a scene for a very long time indeed without seeing it all. I also experienced much the same effect while concentrating for a fair amount of time on a single object (I chose a coffee cup). That exercise, too, made me aware of far more detail than I had ever expected to see. Both exercises were as instructive as the authors claimed they would be.

What I have just said about the daunting prospect of following Steward and Kent's assignments to the letter reminds me of something that Dewey wrote in his introduction to one of Alexander's books. Listing a series of questions that might serve as criteria in judging the worth of a training program or set of therapeutic exercises, Dewey asks: "Is it cheap and easy, or does it make demands on the intellectual and moral energies of the individuals concerned?" His point was that unless it does make such demands, it is "but a scheme depending ultimately upon some trick or magic, which, in curing one trouble, is sure to leave behind it other troubles" (MW15, 28).

At first glance the assignments described in *Learning by Heart* do not seem demanding in either intellectual or moral terms. What is there to do, after all, but sit and look and then write down what one sees? Yet so facile a judgment rests on a narrow and outmoded conception of what the terms *intellectual* and *moral* can and should stand for. Remaining attentive to the way shadows play across a room for twenty minutes certainly feels like an intellectual task, as anyone who has tried to do it will readily attest. The concentration that it calls for is what makes it feel that way. It is also morally demanding in the degree of patience that it requires. That, too, becomes evident almost at once. Staring at shadows is not intellectual in the same way as trying to solve a problem in calculus, let us say. Nor is it moral in the same way as trying to decide whether to cheat on income tax. But such stereotypic instances of intellectual and moral effort do not begin to convey the range of human endeavor to which those terms apply.

Dewey surely would have understood the combination of intellectual and moral rigor that such a simple task as looking at the shadows in a room calls for, for he reports being humbled by a similar set of demands while undergoing training in the Alexander Technique. Here is his account. "In bringing to bear whatever knowledge I already possessed—or thought I did—and whatever powers of discipline in mental application I had acquired in the pursuit of these studies, I had the most humiliating experience of my life, intellectually speaking. For to find that one is unable to execute directions, including inhibitory ones, in doing such a seemingly simple act as to sit down, when one is using all the mental capacity which one prides himself upon possessing, is not an experience congenial to one's vanity" (LW6, 318). Dewey's humiliation may or may not have been an intentional outcome of the instruction that he was receiving. But it does underscore the occasional difficulty, as well as the transformative potency, of seemingly simple acts.

The costs and benefits of being attentive to objects and events that have no direct bearing on our immediate needs and interests is a fitting topic on which to end this discussion of Kent and Steward's *Learning by Heart* and its relation to Dewey's theory of experience. If there is anything that the book makes clear, it is that there are both costs and benefits involved in all of our efforts to perceive our surroundings more fully or to view the world more aesthetically. The clearest costs are temporal. It takes time to look closely at shadows or Coke bottles, time that could well have been spent doing something else. So if we wanted to make a strict accounting of the costs involved in our shadow exercise, let us say, we would have to figure in not only how much clock time was spent at the activity but also what the value might have been of our spending the time at something else. We can seldom reckon the cost of opportunities forgone with any degree of accuracy, but the sense of regret that we sometimes feel when struck by the realization that we might have spent our time more wisely serves to remind us that the cost can often be sizeable and real.

Are there costs beyond those of time expended and opportunities foregone? Might there, for example, be genuine disadvantages to becoming more attentive than we typically are? Dewey's criterion of experience as growth makes it difficult to see how there could be. An experience is educative, according to Dewey, to the extent that it increases our capacity for further experiencing. By this criterion alone the kinds of assignments that Kent and Steward recommend are educative in intent, for their goal is the development of habits that promise to enlarge the scope of subsequent experiences.

Could one become so absorbed in the flickering shadows of immediate experience that one became mesmerized by them? Could an increase in the Kent-Steward brand of attentiveness make us dysfunctional? I suppose there is a remote possibility of such a thing happening. Kabat-Zinn, for one, warns of the attractions of excessive meditation. He suggests that the peacefulness of certain meditative states may become so alluring that one makes use of them inappropriately, allowing them to become a kind of escape from reality. Here again, however, we find a built-in warning against such excesses in Dewey's theory of experience. The educative outcome of experience, assuming there is one, is always to return us to the here and now, better equipped than ever to come to grips with reality's demands.

Finally, what of the benefits (as contrasted with the costs) of engaging in the type of exercise that Kent and Steward recommend? Suppose we develop the habit of looking intently at the inconsequential. Let's further suppose that we find there, as predicted, far more complexity than we had ever imagined. So what? What good does it do to have that brought to our attention? Why, in short, should we trouble to perceive the world more closely than our needs and interests dictate?

Such questions doubtless sound silly to some readers, perhaps even exasperatingly so. "If a person doesn't already understand the value of perceiving the world more closely than his needs and interests dictate," I can imagine a disgruntled reader saying to herself, "no amount of reasoning and explanation will suffice to convince him. The value of close, disinterested perception is, or should be, self-evident." That observation mixes truth and falsehood. Its truth lies in the fact that the intrinsic worthwhileness of disinterested perception is indeed perceived to be self-evident, but only by those who have been schooled to look for such things. Another way of putting it would be to say that aesthetic enjoyment in its purest form, which constitutes the emotional aspect of disinterested perception, refers to an achieved condition. It does not come about naturally, even though it may be experienced partially and sporadically long before we consciously seek it out. Dewey calls its fullest attainment "an acquired art. Meaning may *become* purely esthetic," he says, "it may be appropriated and enjoyed for what it is in the having. This also involves control; it is *such* a way of taking and using them as to suspend cognitive reference. This suspension is an acquired art. It requires long discipline to recognize poetry instead of taking it as history, instruction and prediction." "To hold an idea contemplatively and aesthetically," he concludes, "is a late achievement in civilization" (LW1, 220).

How, then, are we to learn to appropriate and enjoy meaning for what it is in the having? Kent and Steward, as we have seen, offer a simple answer. We learn, they tell us, by engaging in the kind of exercises recommended in their book. We come to enjoy the rewards of close perception by the act of closely perceiving, by watching the play of shadows, by studying a coke bottle, and so forth.

"So far, so good," one might say, "but where do we go from there?" Once we have acknowledged that coming to enjoy almost any activity entails active engagement in that manner of doing, and once we have moved forward in that direction with respect to a particular kind of activity, what comes next? Should we continue to look at more shadows and more coke bottles, or should we be doing other things?

What Dewey would want us to understand, first of all, is that the habit of looking closely at objects or of perceiving them more fully, important as such a built-in inclination may be, is in truth not the primary source of the satisfaction that we feel while so engaged. What we come to enjoy or appreciate most is the particular object or event, perhaps also the class of objects or events, on which our attention has been focused. This is not to say that by following Kent and Steward's advice we will come to love the play of shadows as they shift throughout the day. Nor is it to suggest that we will grow attached to top third of coke bottles. Those transient interests and fleeting insights are only the incidental outcomes of exercises designed to teach a lesson of much greater import. Yet Dewey would have us understand that it is out of such close encounters with objects that initially interest us only in instrumental terms that more enduring attachments are born.

Perception, in Dewey's view, is a developmental affair. It emerges in answer to our bodily needs as we go about seeking their fulfillment. That is the condition under which we begin to see the world in meaningful terms. But when operating at that level we are generally in too much of a hurry to allow our perceptual apparatus to function fully. It is only when those needs are temporarily met that we become free, as it were, to look about us with wonder and appreciation. Here is Dewey's description of the process: "Perception is therefore at its lowest and its most obscure in the degree that only instinctive need operates. Instinct is in too much haste to be solicitous about its environing relations. . . . [P]rimitive need is the source of attachment to objects. Perception is born when solicitude for objects and their qualities brings the organic demand for attachment to consciousness. . . . Perception that occurs for its own sake is the full realization of all the elements of our psychological being" (LW10, 260).

The two key points in this statement shed such light on the topic under discussion that they deserve emphasis and elaboration. Dewey's first point is that that only as we come to care about objects (feel solicitous about them) do we begin to perceive them. Perception, in other words, is more than noticing or sensing something. It involves feeling as well as sense. Further on in the same passage, Dewey says, "What is perceived is charged with value" (LW10, 261). His second point is that perception comes into its own or operates at its fullest when we reach the stage of perceiving objects or events for their own sake, when we no longer attend to the role they play in furthering our own ends and purposes. Only then, we are told, do we attain the full realization of our psychological being. I think what Dewey means is that it is during those moments of full perception, when we are totally absorbed in what this object or event or idea is like, that the various components of our psychological being— our ability to think, to feel, to appreciate, to experience through all of our senses—come into play at once. At such moments our various capacities not only are realized (i.e., become real) but are also momentarily fused and unified. Only then do we experience what it is like to be fully human.

How does the Kent-Steward advice fit with Dewey's view of perception? Dewey states that our capacity to perceive objects for their own sake is a learned ability. He suggests that we are pressed in the direction of realizing that ability by an emergent sense of solicitude for certain objects. Beyond that, at least in the statements that we have been drawing upon, he seems to leave open the question of how that learned ability develops.

Kent and Steward advise their readers to focus on ordinary objects and examine them very closely. By so doing, readers presumably come to realize that such objects are far more complex and, therefore, far more interesting (possibly also more beautiful and more valuable) than they first appeared. The chief generalization to be derived from that exercise—the moral of the lesson—is that any and all objects could be treated in the same manner. They all may be said to harbor secrets whose contents are divulged solely through close and patient observation. By virtue of having arrived at that generalization, readers supposedly undergo something like a change of attitude toward perception in general. They now want to observe lots of things more closely than before. A new habit, that of more fully perceiving selected objects and events, has begun to form.

How would Dewey look upon that advice and that likely outcome? Do they fit with his description of how perception develops? Yes and no. They fit with the notion that people learn to perceive objects fully, that they do not develop the habit of doing so automatically or naturally—hence the need for planned exercises and prolonged practice. The advice and the outcome are also in line with the importance that Dewey attaches to the act of looking at things for their own sake, independent of the role the objects might play in furthering personal needs and interests.

The Kent-Steward assignments and the discussion that leads up to them do not address the question of whether looking at objects for their own sake will necessarily engage the whole organism, as Dewey suggests it might, though nothing in what they do say runs counter to such a suggestion. Their advice also contains nothing about the role of attachment and solicitude in engendering close observation. Nor do they have anything to say about the reverse of that process, about the possibility of close observation engendering solicitude, which, it seems to me, Dewey's theory of perception implicitly predicts might happen. (Indeed, several of the exercises that they recommend deal with objects so mundane as to practically rule out such a possibility. It is hard to imagine becoming solicitous about the top third of a coke bottle.)

I conclude, therefore, that Dewey would not object in principle to the recommended assignments of Kent and Steward, though if he himself had been their designer, he might have chosen to have students focus on objects and events that are somewhat worthier of sustained regard than are some of those featured in the Kent-Steward exercises. Yet that judgment may be a bit unfair to both Dewey and the authors of *Learning by Heart.* We must remember that the exercises in that book are essentially for beginners. They are intended to be instructive only in a preliminary way. They are designed to awaken readers to the perceptual complexity and richness to be found in ordinary objects, after which the readers are presumably free to proceed on their own, choosing to examine closely whatever they might wish. The objects mentioned in the exercises are not presented as being of intrinsic value. Indeed, that is the very reason for choosing them. They are objects whose outward appearance we would ordinarily overlook. When we view them contemplatively, however, they become the source of visual patterns (shadows, or the shapes and colors of the bottle top) that turn out to be intrinsically interesting.

We turn finally to the hypothetical questioner who was willing to comply with the assignments in the Kent and Steward book but who wanted to know *Where do we go from here?* His question can be taken in two ways, one positive, the other negative. Interpreted positively, the question expresses a readiness, even an eagerness, to advance to the next stage of perceptual acuity, leaving behind the preliminary step of noting the complexity of ordinary objects. Interpreted negatively, it conveys sarcasm, implying that there probably is no place to go from here.

What might Dewey say to our questioner? Would he share his doubts, or would he see a way out of the difficulty? I picture him as wanting, first of all, to translate the questioner's worries into a problem that could be worked on, if not solved. To do so he would form an image of some kind—a mental picture, let's say—of what someone who made effective use of his or her perceptual capacities looked like. What would such a person do, and how would he or she do it? Once that was accomplished, he would have a crude answer to the question Where do we go from here? "There is where we are headed," he would say, pointing to his formulation of the ideal perceiver. The problem now becomes how to get there, how to build a bridge between the realizations engendered by the Kent-Steward exercises (e.g., that ordinary objects can be fruitfully examined in great detail) and Dewey's own idealized vision of where close looking might conceivably lead.

Is Dewey's way of proceeding a begging of the question? It surely would be if it stopped there. But for Dewey, as we know, the formulation of an imagined goal is but an early step down the arduous path that leads to its successful attainment. The goal itself can only be dimly perceived at the start and is almost bound to change along the way.

Kent and Steward, in the planning of their book, seem to have followed a process very much like the one that I envision Dewey pursuing. In the pattern of their assignments, they, too, move toward a goal that must have been foreseen at least crudely at the start. However, the kind of person they want to bring into being through their exercises differs significantly from the kind implied in Dewey's more generic vision.

Kent and Steward's ideal, which becomes progressively more apparent as one moves through their book, is not just a person who perceives things more closely than most other people do. Rather, it is someone who in addition to being a close observer of things also wants to become an art maker or an art teacher, especially one whose approach to her craft strongly resembles that of the book's authors. Thus, Kent and Steward's assignments move steadily in the direction of having the reader work with an assortment of materials to produce art objects of various kinds—printed textiles, posters, papier-mâché masks. The person who dutifully follows the book's assignments from beginning to end will not emerge from the experience a professional artist but, if I am right about the book's effectiveness, he or she will certainly have taken a giant step toward becoming one.

Dewey's ideal person is not that clearly defined. This is not a criticism of his approach. On the contrary, the unclear definition fits the rest of what Dewey has to say. It matches the level of abstraction at which he pitches his theory.

This high level of abstraction is both a plus and a minus. On the plus side, it leaves plenty of room for working out details and for accommodating alternative modes of striving to reach the same vaguely defined end. This means that anyone who aspires to the ideal implicit in Dewey's writings is free to shop around in books like those by Kabat-Zinn and Kent and Steward, picking and choosing whatever seems helpful while rejecting whatever seems unhelpful. With respect to perception, for example, one of the chief things that Dewey's theory recommends (by implication) is that we develop the habit of pausing to look at things for their own sake How that habit is developed and what things we choose to focus on are not matters that Dewey bothers to address, though his writings do contain strong hints in that direction, as we shall presently see.

On the minus side, Dewey's rarefied vision of where we should all be headed leaves his readers without much to go on when it comes to the practical details of discovering how to get there. As a result, one has no choice but to shop around among the suggestions of others or, failing that, to experiment on one's own. As we saw in the case of Dewey's involvement with F. Matthais Alexander, the option of turning to others was one he made use of himself. Not until he became acquainted with the Alexander Technique did he fully comprehend how certain aspects of his own theory of experience could be translated into practice. For all who subscribe to that theory and to the implicit vision that it contains, the challenge remains one of carrying the task of application forward by whatever means possible. That this task entails risk and the possibility of failure almost goes without saying.

FREDERICK FRANCK'S *ZEN OF SEEING*

The last of the three books that I stumbled on while pondering the question of how Dewey's theory might be put into practice was Frederick Franck's *Zen of Seeing* (1973). Franck's book, like the one by Kent and Steward, invites its readers to engage in the arts directly, though its focus is narrower and its format less explicitly didactic. It restricts itself to one practice alone: freehand drawing or sketching. The author's pen sketches appear on almost every page of the book and are often used to illustrate a point in the accompanying text. The text itself offers a running commentary on the psychological and spiritual advantages of learning to sketch in a particular way.

Franck calls his method SEEING / DRAWING. He speaks of it as "a way of meditation, a way of getting into intimate touch with the visible world around us, and through it . . . with ourselves" (Franck 1973, xi). What it consists of, in essence, is learning how to examine an object very closely with the eyes while allowing the hand holding a pencil or pen to follow what the eye sees. Franck describes introducing a group of newcomers to the process. After distributing pads and pencils and leading the group outdoors he asks them to sit down somewhere on the lawn, keeping at least six feet apart. He gives the following directions.

> Don't talk, just sit and relax.
>
> Now, let your eyes fall on whatever happens to be in front of you. It may be a plant or a bush or a tree, or perhaps just some grass. Close your eyes for the next five minutes.
>
> Now, open your eyes and focus on whatever you observed before—that plant or leaf or dandelion. Look it in the eye, until you feel it looking back at you. Feel that you are alone with it on Earth! That it is the most important thing in the universe, that it contains all the riddles of life and death. It does! You are no longer looking, you are SEEING . . .
>
> Now, take your pencil loosely in your hand, and while you keep your eyes focused allow the pencil to follow on the paper what the eye perceives. Feel as if with the point of your pencil you are caressing the contours, the whole circumference of that leaf, that sprig of grass. Just let your hand move! Don't check what gets onto the paper, it does not matter at all! If your pencil runs off the paper, that's fine too! You can always start again. Only don't let your eye wander from what it is seeing, and don't lift your pencil from your paper! Above all: don't try too hard, don't "think" about what you are drawing, just let the hand follow what the eye sees. (xiv–xv)

If readers follow this method persistently, Franck promises, they not only will become better and better at drawing lifelike figures and objects but will also become more "fully awake and alive." Offering his own experience as testimony, Franck says, "Drawing is the discipline by which I constantly rediscover the world" (6). If they but stick with it, he implies, the same can happen to them. He summarizes the overall benefits of following the method of SEE-ING / DRAWING in these words: "What really happens when seeing and drawing become SEEING / DRAWING is that awareness and attention become constant and undivided, become contemplation. SEEING / DRAWING is not a self-indul-

gence, a 'pleasant hobby,' but a discipline of awareness, of UNWAVERING ATTEN-
TION to a world which is fully alive. It is not the pursuit of happiness, but
stopping the pursuit and experiencing the awareness, the happiness of being
ALL THERE" (8).

Before examining the details of Franck's method of SEEING / DRAWING, I
need to point out that the method itself is not new, nor does Franck claim it to
be. It is a technique that has been used by teachers of art for a long time. Kent
and Steward, for example, call their own variant of the same procedure contour
drawing. Kent and Steward stress that such a procedure is as much a way of
looking as it is a way of drawing. Also like him, they emphasize the importance
of being nonjudgmental about what one draws, and they call attention to the
way this particular method facilitates that essential condition. They further
stress the slowness with which one must proceed if one is to reap the benefits of
this way of learning to draw. Though Franck does not mention the speed at
which his students should work, he, too, it seems clear, does not expect them to
proceed hastily.

Turning now to the relation between Franck's method of SEEING / DRAWING
and Dewey's theory of experience, we should have no difficulty seeing a fair
amount in common between the two, especially in light of points made in
Chapter 1. Both Franck and Dewey, for example, call for living a very different
kind of life than the one that most of us pursue. Each asks that we spend more
time looking at objects and events for their own sake, rather than seeing them as
instruments for the accomplishment of our own ends. For Franck, this basically
means pausing often to sketch objects and scenes that we encounter daily. For
Dewey, at least in *Art as Experience,* it more commonly means pausing to
appreciate the artwork of others, though he by no means overlooks the aesthetic
pleasures that artists themselves enjoy as they go about their work. Nor does he
neglect the delights of nature and the beauty to be found in common objects.
Indeed, one of the strengths of Dewey's theory lies in its inclusiveness. It treats
the creative and the appreciative aspects of both making and consuming art.

Along with the change in the way we look at objects, whether humanly
produced or natural, goes a temporal change. Time slows down for us when we
are fully occupied perceptually. Both Franck and Dewey make note of this. In
the extreme case, time seems almost to stop. Lost in what we are doing or
mesmerized by the object on which our attention is focused, we become
unaware of time. It flies by, yet we seem not to notice.

Another aspect of experience to which Dewey recurrently attends, and one
that Franck also acknowledges to be crucial, has to do with what might be called

the fusion of the senses. For Dewey, this fusion takes many forms; for example, one of the senses can stand in, as it were, for one or more of the others, as when music is heard as "bright" or "smooth" or when colors are seen as "loud" or "soft." In our appreciation of great works of art, Dewey points out, that kind of multiple sensing via a single sense is almost commonplace. For Franck, what supposedly comes together in the activity of sketching is a trio of sensory modalities to which he gives the label eye-heart-hand and which, as the term implies, stands for the essential fusion of vision, feeling, and kinesthetic sense.

Franck also refers repeatedly to a deeper kind of fusion that the artist, even the amateur artist, is said to enjoy on occasion; he implies that some may even experience it regularly. At one level this pleasurable condition registers as a feeling of self and object becoming one or, put somewhat differently, as a state in which self-awareness, at least as commonly experienced, disappears completely. When truly heightened, the feeling of oneness may be extensive and may even seem unbounded. On such occasions the artist experiences a sense of being one with the cosmos, or, as Franck prefers, THE ALL. He also refers to this sense of global unity as the Zen experience (14). Many descriptions of it appear in his book. Here is one of them: "The Zen experience is the overcoming of the hallucination that the Me is the valid center of observation of the universe. It is a momentary, radical turn-about, A DIRECT PERCEPTION OF AND INSIGHT INTO THE PRESENCE, INTO THE TRANSIENCY, THE FINITUDE THAT I SHARE WITH ALL BEINGS. It is a fleetingness that makes this very moment infinitely precious" (14).

The effusiveness of Franck's statement, with its reference to Zen and its blaring use of capital letters to drive home its central point, may make it look and sound miles apart from anything that one might catch Dewey saying or writing. But in discussion what the arts can do for us Dewey does refer on several occasions to subjective phenomena that seem to me to come very close to the condition that Franck aims to describe. On such occasions Dewey's prose takes wing and soars in a manner very un-Deweyan. Several instances of that effusiveness have already been quoted. Here is one of them to serve as a reminder of the others: "Art throws off the covers that hide the expressiveness of experienced things; it quickens us from the slackness of routine and enables us to forget ourselves by finding ourselves in the delight of experiencing the world about us in its varied qualities and forms. It intercepts every shade of expressiveness found in objects and orders them to a new experience of life" (LW10, 110).

Characteristically, Dewey does not allow his prose to stay aloft for long. He soon grounds it in the ordinary and the everyday. He allows for our forgetting ourselves in the delights of art, but the sense of unity occasioned by such an experience has its ultimate payoff, Dewey implies, in the changed self that it leaves behind, a self that, having once been awakened to a new experience of life, henceforth seeks to create conditions that will allow such experiences to be repeated and to multiply.

Another aspect of Dewey's view of perception that is interestingly echoed in Franck's book concerns the connection between perceiving and appreciating, or, more starkly stated, between perception and love. Dewey, we will recall, speaks of perception being born "when solicitude for objects and their qualities brings the organic demand for attachment to consciousness." He does not directly say that the process is reciprocal, that the closer we look, the more we come to care about objects, but that inference is easily drawn from what he does say.

Franck explicitly makes the connection between his method of SEE-ING / DRAWING and a solicitous, one might even say loving, attitude toward the object or scene being drawn. He encourages his students to look upon the object that they are drawing as "the most important thing in the universe" (xiv). He invites them to feel as if the points of their pencils were "caressing the contours" of the object. "Just let the hand follow what the eye sees," he advises. "Let it caress" (xv). Here, too, we find it strongly implied that the act of seeing and drawing in the manner that Franck recommends, which resembles in many ways what Dewey calls full perception, will generate, or forthwith deepen and intensify, the student's feeling of affection and concern for the object.

Powerful support for a causal linkage between perception and the growth of positive feelings toward the object perceived also appears in the writings of the moral philosopher and novelist Iris Murdoch, whose essay "The Idea of Perfection" not only lends credence to such a linkage but also argues for the primacy and centrality of attention in the development of human virtue. "Where virtue is concerned we often apprehend more than we clearly understand and *grow by looking*," she says (Murdoch 1970, 31).

Although Murdoch is by no means Deweyan in her philosophical orientation, she does, like Dewey, stress the formative potency of ordinary experience. She also appreciates, as does Dewey, how long it takes for such changes to occur. "Moral change and moral achievement are slow," Murdoch insists. "We are not free in the sense of being able suddenly to alter ourselves since we cannot suddenly alter what we can see and ergo what we desire and are compelled by" (39).

The reason we cannot suddenly alter what we see, according to Murdoch, is that not all forms of seeing are the same. There is seeing in the crude sense of taking visual note of something, as when we see the winged object that flashes by our window. Murdoch reserves the term *looking* for that kind of sight. But there is also a richer and fuller form of seeing, one that Murdoch calls *attention,* a term whose specialized sense she borrows from Simone Weil. (The distinction between these two kinds of seeing resembles Dewey's now-familiar contrast between recognizing and perceiving.) Attention, Murdoch explains, entails "a just and loving gaze directed upon an individual reality" (34). To look upon an object, a person, or a situation in this manner, Murdoch insists, is to adopt a moral posture.

An interesting aspect of Murdoch's treatment of attention, one that distinguishes it from Dewey's handling of a like set of ideas, lies in the way she links the fundamental notion of attention to the derivative ideas of freedom and choice. For Murdoch, unlike those who adhere exclusively to a rationalist model of decision making, most of the choices that we make do not entail pondering and weighing the pros and cons of alternative actions. Instead, she points out, we make choices constantly as we go about the ordinary business of paying attention to things and to other human beings in their contexts. The choices that we make under those ordinary conditions, however minuscule they might be, serve to narrow the range of choices that we might subsequently be called upon to make.

> If we consider what the work of attention is like, how continuously it goes on, and how imperceptibly it builds up structures of value round about us, we shall not be surprised that at crucial moments of choice most of the business of choosing is already over. This does not imply that we are not free, certainly not. But it implies that the exercise of our freedom is a small piecemeal business which goes on all the time and not a grandiose leaping about unimpeded at important moments. The moral life, on this view, is something that goes on continually, not something that is switched off in between the occurrence of explicit moral choices. What happens in between such choices is indeed what is crucial. (37)

Another crucial concept for Murdoch she encapsulates in the phrase "contexts of attention." By this she means something close to what Dewey would call the situation. For Murdoch, as for Dewey, the objects, persons, and events that we might choose to look upon attentively are never seen in isolation. They are always contextualized or situated, not only physically but ideationally as well. To know them as objects or as persons is to know about them, to understand something about their connections to other objects, persons, and events and possibly something about their relations to their own past and future. In the case of objects being sketched or drawn, such as those that Franck directs his students to gaze upon, knowing about them chiefly means coming to know something about what goes with what internally, how the parts fit together to form the visual whole.

When we look at objects and persons in this attentive way, Murdoch tells us, we gradually develop a language (she calls it a vocabulary) that allows us to share our knowledge with others. Those with whom we might wish to share it may include the person or persons we have chosen to observe. For Franck's students the language of observation is visual. Their drawings represent what they have come to feel and to know about whatever they have chosen to draw. Murdoch's personally preferred mode of knowing about, at least when she is functioning as an artist, takes the form of literature, a novel depicting a set of characters and events and the way they relate to each other over time.

DEWEY AS OBSERVER AND COMMUNICATOR

What of Dewey himself? Was he, too, attentive in a manner analogous to that of Franck and his students or Murdoch the novelist? I know practically nothing of Dewey's perceptual habits as they relate to his immediate physical and social world, save that he is rumored to have been somewhat absentminded from time to time, the way professors are stereotypically alleged to be. The more extreme rumors make him out to be relatively unobservant, even to the point of being almost callous. One such tale has him so caught up in conversation with a friend that he fails to note that a small boy who approached him on the street and asked for money and whom he takes to be a street urchin was actually one of his sons.

It is hard to know how much truth to ascribe to such stories, yet even if they were largely true, I would still want to claim, overall, that Dewey was extremely attentive and was so in many of the ways we have been speaking of here. What perhaps makes that difficult for some to see is that the objects, the individual realities toward which he typically directed a just and loving gaze, tended to be more ideational than physical. Dewey's own brand of attentiveness shows up best in his writings, particularly in his major works. There we see him being attentive as he best knows how to be: turning an idea around, the way a jeweler might examine a gem, looking at it first from this angle and then from that, examining its depths, testing its instrumental worth, pursuing its connections with other ideas and with the world of action, moving close to it, then backing away for a view from afar, even abandoning it for a time, the way an artist might temporarily lay a work aside, only to return to it with renewed energy on another occasion.

Dewey's roundabout manner of examining ideas and of writing about them is not everyone's cup of tea. Friend and foe alike have complained about Dewey's expository prose, sometimes acerbically. Arthur C. Danto, for example, whose writings I referred to extensively in Chapter 2, is one of those who confess to disliking the way Dewey writes. He explains why. "I like things to be clear, I like connections to be clear, and I like to see structures, whereas with Dewey it's an unstructured world in which you sort of move through a fog" (Borradori 1994, 90). But then Danto hastens to forgive Dewey for his fogginess, at least partially. "However, I feel that you can, from a certain distance, begin to see where Dewey replaces structure with fog. And you can understand why he does it, what the systematic reasons are, and if you take a sufficiently distant view of that, you can see that the lack of structure is one of the great historic alternatives to clarity. But it is not the way I would want to do philosophy" (91).

Whether or not we share Danto's opinion of Dewey, we have to acknowledge that he is not alone in holding it. Dewey's way of attending to the ideas that concern him is almost antithetical to the highly structured and systematic presentation that Danto, along with many others, would doubtless prefer. Yet even among his critics, as Danto's hasty retraction also makes clear, Dewey's patient and probing exploration of human experience, his talent as a close observer of ideas, wins him, in the end, wide respect, if not grudging admiration.

This digression into the subject of Dewey's style as a thinker and a writer helps to make clear two important points. The first is that Dewey's manner of writing reveals that perceptual attentiveness of the kind advocated by Kabat-Zinn, Kent and Steward, and Franck need not be confined to physical objects and events. Even if we extend that way of looking to complex human situations, as Murdoch recommends, we still will not have reached the limits of its applicability. Ideas are objects, as Dewey was fond of reminding his readers. They, too, bear close and repeated scrutiny. His own ruminative style illustrates again and again just how objective and attentive a person can become about ideational matters.

The second point is that Dewey does much more than attend, however closely, to the ideas that concern him. He doesn't just mull them over in private. He writes about them. He communicates his thoughts to others. For Dewey, it seems, thinking and writing, observing and communicating, were sufficiently intertwined to be practically coterminus activities. They moved along in tandem, much like the eye-hand coordination that Franck urges upon his students. They almost had to do so, given the sheer amount that he wrote. His collected works alone, we must remember, take up thirty-seven volumes. His vast correspondence adds significantly to that total.

In criticizing the perceived lack of structure in Dewey's writings, Danto refers to Dewey's philosophic style as one of the great historic alternatives to clarity. Harsh though that judgment may sound, it does ring true when applied to much that Dewey wrote. His writings seldom exemplify the virtues of brevity and crystalline clarity. Even his most ardent supporters must readily concede as much. But there are other virtues that a person's writing can exhibit, and Dewey's was by no means devoid of virtue, as even Danto somewhat reluctantly allows. Nor should Dewey's alternative way of writing, if that is the word for it, be read as a purposeful attack on clear thinking and plain prose. Dewey never sets out to mystify, nor does he delight in making simple ideas obscure.

If, as Danto charges, Dewey sometimes replaces structure with fog, he usually does so for good reason, as Danto himself acknowledges. Danto does not say what those reasons might be, but it strikes me that Dewey's prose becomes foggiest when the notions that he is writing about lack sharp boundaries and explicit connectedness with adjacent ideas. Those conditions are seldom of Dewey's own making. He does not, therefore, replace structure with fog so much as he reports on an intellectual landscape that is already foggy. But even that revision needs correction. What Dewey does is to enact in the writing itself several of those very qualities upon which he is reporting—that things fit together organically rather than mechanically, for example, or that endings and beginnings are arbitrary designations rather than definitive ones. Those attributes then become for his readers part of the qualitative immediacy of the reading experience.

Alfred North Whitehead is reported to have said, "The art of literature, vocal or written, is to adjust the language so that it embodies what it indicates" (Auden 1968, 13). It would be going too far, I suspect, to credit Dewey with consciously adjusting his language so that it embodies what it indicates. His essays seldom give the impression of having been written with such a goal in mind. Yet it is not too much, I would argue, to credit him with having been sufficiently responsive to his subject matter to allow its attributes to shine through between the lines.

If a single virtue is exemplified in Dewey's writings, it has to be that of someone trying in all earnestness to address the grand themes of human conduct, describing them at the highest level of generalization, without at the same time losing sight of their embodiment in ordinary affairs. Danto complains that "from the very beginning I thought he was just awful, just muddy, like a preacher, portentous and uninteresting." But then he says, "I still think a lot of that is true, but I think analytic philosophy enables one to see Dewey as one of the main systems, a somewhat 'holistic' system" (Borradori 1994, 90). Perhaps it was that striving to make things whole, to bring together the lofty and the mundane, that Oliver Wendell Holmes detected in his reading of Dewey's *Experience and Nature* and famously commented on: "But although Dewey's book is incredibly ill written, it seemed to me after several rereadings to have a feeling of intimacy with the inside of the cosmos that I found unequaled. So methought God would have spoken had He been inarticulate but keenly desirous to tell you how it was" (Dykhuizen 1973, 214).

Whether we take Danto's or Holmes's depiction of Dewey's style to be the more accurate matters less than that we see them both as balancing criticism with praise. In that respect they resemble most other critics of Dewey's work. That combination of praise and criticism leads us to ask whether a portion of Dewey's difficulties as a stylist may have been at least partially an outgrowth of his vaulting intellectual ambitions. Could he have been more articulate with those goals and subject matter? My tentative answer is no, he could not have been, though that answer bears further investigation—but elsewhere, not in this book.

DEWEY, SELF-HELP, AND SOCIAL CONSCIENCE

We must touch on one additional matter before taking leave of our discussion of how Dewey's theory of experience might be of help to us as individuals. This last matter has to do in part with the jarring incompatibility between Dewey's staid and measured voice as a philosopher and the enthused and somewhat emotive language of the self-help and how-to books that we have been discussing. Dewey, I sense, would never have turned to such books himself and likely would have disapproved of their effusiveness. Alan Ryan, author of a recent intellectual biography of Dewey, puts his finger on why and, in so doing, manages to raise the discussion from the level of noting linguistic preferences. "Dewey's interest in problem solving was unlike that of 'how to' writing. He was skeptical of technical fixes because he supposed that what most needed fixing was people's attitudes toward themselves and one another, and he was uninterested in either his own or other people's private miseries. He would have detested what Christopher Lasch has aptly described as the culture of narcissism and the New Age self-help and psycho babble in which it trades" (Ryan 1995, 366). Ryan then explains why Dewey would have detested much that falls under the heading of self-help: "It would have seemed a retreat from the world, doomed from the outset because it separated people from one another rather than helped them live more interestingly with one another" (367).

I believe that Ryan is right. Dewey would surely have reacted negatively to the form of writing that we today call psychobabble. Yet we must not lose sight of the fact that Dewey was not above seeking help from others to alleviate his own private miseries. His many sessions with F. Matthais Alexander and Alexander's brother, A. R., plus his recurrent testimony regarding the efficacy of the treatment that he received from the Alexanders, should give us pause whenever we picture Dewey coming down hard on the literature of self-help.

Where, then, does Dewey stand with respect to the efforts of all of us who seek to put his outlook to work in our lives? Would he think such efforts misguided because they are too self-absorbed? Might he go on to caution us against being coached in meditation by the likes of Kabat-Zinn or against staring at a blade of grass and trying to sketch it the way Franck recommends?

As I have already suggested, I doubt that Dewey would speak out harshly against such practices. And I am confident that he would never do so solely because they happen to be popular or because certain of them may have acquired a cult following (in the heyday of its popularity the Alexander Technique could have been described in those terms). Instead, I think he would force us to consider where such practices lead.

If meditation leads only to more meditation, or if learning to draw a blade of grass results solely in our becoming more proficient at drawing, I suspect Dewey's reaction, on the whole, would have been condemnatory. If, on the other hand, mediation leads to an altered conception of the self, or if learning to draw a blade of grass conduces to a deepened appreciation of the physical world (as Franck claims it does), I believe that Dewey would have had no difficulty whatsoever in endorsing such practices.

Again, I think Ryan is right when he points out that for Dewey what most needed fixing was people's attitudes toward themselves and one another. Such attitudes—or dispositions, as Dewey sometimes called them—are more important than are isolated habits or skills, because attitudes govern a broad range of human conduct, whereas habits have a much narrower jurisdiction. Thus, to followers of Dewey the relevant question becomes not simply Where does this practice lead? but Where does it lead with respect to instilling and nurturing a set of enduring and positive attitudes toward oneself and others? The more specific question is seldom easy to answer, for the enduring attitudes that need be instilled are of an unknown number and are sufficiently general in character (e.g., open-mindedness and wholeheartedness) to allow for competing, and sometimes conflicting, ideas about how they might be established.

Ryan makes yet another observation that points to the direction in which Dewey's theoretical outlook propels the individual. He says, "The individual in Dewey always seems to be going outward into the world; 'the bliss of solitude' is not a Deweyan thought, even though Wordsworth was one of his favorite poets" (Ryan 1995, 368). This observation, like Ryan's earlier one, strikes me as true, though it contains a contradiction. Dewey does seem to be consistently outward in outlook. He also seems unattracted to the kind of introverted pleasures associated with Wordsworthian nature walks and autobiographical reminiscences. That, too, seems accurate. I am sure that Dewey did enjoy nature, for he arranged to spend much time in the country even while a full-time resident of New York City, but I somehow find it difficult to imagine him wandering lonely as a cloud. Instead, I picture him lost in thought. But the thoughts occupying him, even when alone and when the scene was desolate, would seldom have been self-centered. They would instead have been thoughts about the world and about others. And therein lies the latent contradiction in Ryan's observation.

Dewey delighted in physical solitude, contra Ryan, voluntarily spending a large portion of his life alone, but not because it afforded him the opportunity to indulge in narcissistic remembrances or to dream of an impossible future. He spent time alone or relatively oblivious to the company of others in order to think and to write. The individual in Dewey does seem to be going outward, into the world, as Ryan says, but he chiefly does so on the wings of thought, rather than on foot or by means of public conveyance. That stay-at-home mode of travel suited Dewey to a tee. His was the life of the mind.

Let me turn to Dewey himself for a final word on the subject. He knew, better than did most figures of his day, what it took to blend the public and the private in a way that would preserve the integrity of each. Near the end of his academic career he chose to express that knowledge in a memorable metaphor, that of a gardener whose labors may begin at home but soon extend, almost inevitably, to adjoining lands. Paradoxically, the move outward leaves the inner self richer and more integrated than before. "To gain an integrated individuality, each of us needs to cultivate his own garden. But there is no fence about this garden: it is no sharply marked off enclosure. Our garden is the world, in the angle at which it touches our own manner of being. By accepting the . . . world in which we live, and by thus fulfilling the precondition for interaction with it, we, who are also parts of the moving present, create ourselves as we create an unknown future" (LW5, 122–123).

Chapter 4 Some Educational Implications of Dewey's Theory of Experience

I turn, finally, to the question of how Dewey's theory of experience, particularly his view of the arts, might be put to work in schools and classrooms. Before getting under way, however, I need to repeat the warning made at the start of Chapter 3: My treatment of this important topic must not be read as a full-scale examination of Dewey's educational thought. Readers seeking a balanced and judicious overview of Dewey's vast educational ruminations are advised to turn directly to Dewey's writings. His two early educational treatises, *The School and Society* and *The Child and the Curriculum,* written while Dewey was still directing the University of Chicago Laboratory School, would be good places to start. Other single-volume works devoted exclusively to education include his *Schools of Tomorrow* (with Evelyn Dewey), *Democracy and Education,* and *Experience and Education.* Briefer monographs and articles on educational topics are scattered throughout his collected works.

My chief reason for not undertaking a broad examination of Dewey's educational writings here is that most were written before his theory of the arts had fully developed. Consequently, he did not himself have much to say about how the arts in general might inform educational practice. He certainly made a place for them in the curriculum of his own school—that much is certain—but not a central place, not nearly as central as geography, for instance, or the sciences. The model for Dewey's experimental school, we must remember, was a laboratory, not a studio.

In his Laboratory School, Dewey placed considerable emphasis on the practical arts of cooking, gardening, weaving, and carpentry, especially in the lower grades. He did so, however, without underscoring their status as arts. He treated them, instead, as occupations. His focus was far more on the connection between such activities and life outside the school than it was on the artistic nature of experience that such activities might ideally engender.

What might have happened if Dewey's interest in the arts had developed earlier and was present at the start of his educational experimentation? One can only guess. Might he have granted a larger place for the arts in the curriculum of his school? I think that likely, but who can say for sure? Might the institution that he founded have gone down in history as the Studio School? I find that unlikely. Laboratories were and are far more prestigious than studios in the university setting in which Dewey worked. Even if Dewey had been enamored of the arts at that time, he would have had a hard time selling their paramountcy to the those in control of the purse strings.

It is more edifying to imagine how the educational legacy that we today ascribe to Dewey—the prominence of his famous "learn by doing" motto, for example—might have turned out differently had he concentrated more fully on those aspects of experience featured in such later works as *Experience and Nature* and *Art as Experience*. One reason for pursuing such a hypothetical question is that several of the educational battles that Dewey fought so valiantly around the turn of the century are still being waged today. A vigorous dispute continues, for example, over how best to educate children of the poor. We also continue to argue over the place of the classics in general education and the job placement payoff of vocational training. The pros and cons of curriculum differentiation based on class, race, or ethnicity are at least as hotly debated today as they were in Dewey's day. Any light that a retrospective look at Dewey's early practices might shed on such issues would more than repay the effort.

There is yet another reason for looking at Deweyan practices. As an educational theorist, Dewey was about as forward-looking as one could get. As a thinker, he was quite radical, or so many thought. As a teacher—that's another story. Standing before his own students, he reportedly behaved not at all as his theories might lead one to expect. If such reports are accurate, why the discrepancy between theory and practice? What, if anything, might the discrepancy have to do with Dewey's theory of the arts? Might the arts have come to Dewey's rescue as a teacher? Could his mature view of them have become his pedagogical salvation? Might it become ours?

Here, then, are two sets of questions and two tales to be unfolded, each a mix of reality and conjecture. The first begins in Chicago near the turn of the century, long before Dewey's philosophical interest in the arts had begun to flourish.

THE RATIONALE FOR THE CURRICULUM OF DEWEY'S LABORATORY SCHOOL

The social and intellectual climate of Dewey's Chicago years was one of change. The turmoil within society at large as well as within the narrower intellectual circles of academia—particularly within the emerging biological and social sciences—was so revolutionary in character and so wide-ranging in its impact that Dewey saw the need for an equally revolutionary change in the conduct of schooling. Modest improvements in the status quo were insufficient, he believed, to meet the present challenge.

Socially and economically, the event of note was the industrial revolution and the factory system devoted to the production of material goods. That change was socially disruptive in at least two major ways. First, it hastened the demise of the kind of community life that had previously characterized the households and neighborhoods of the small towns and villages of America. As Dewey reminded the small audience attending the first of the three lectures that later became *The School and Society,* "Those of us who are here today need go back only one, two, or at most three generations, to find a time when the household was practically the center in which were carried on, or about which were clustered, all the typical forms of industrial occupation" (MW1, 7). The educational challenge implicit in the loss of community was how to make the school itself "a genuine form of active community life, instead of a place set apart in which to learn lessons" (MW1, 10).

A second form of social disruption brought about by the rise of industry and its concentration in northern cities like Chicago was created by the sudden and massive influx of immigrants to those cities, creating ethnic enclaves that were set apart physically and culturally from each other. Dewey feared the consequences of that separation. He saw it as constituting a serious threat to the American democratic way of life. He also worried that the public schools might inadvertently reinforce the status quo and perhaps even widen the gaps that already existed. They could do so in one of two ways: either by failing to attract and retain the offspring of the new arrivals or by offering them vocational training aimed exclusively at preparing them for the deadening routines of factory work. Either outcome was fraught with danger, Dewey believed. He voiced his concern at the very start of his lectures. Even without the sound of his voice, his words convey a sense of heartfelt conviction that must have stirred his audience. "What the best and wisest parent wants for his own child, that must the community want for all of its children. Any other ideal for our schools is narrow and unlovely; acted upon, it destroys our democracy" (MW1, 5).

Taken out of context, that statement may sound as though Dewey was calling for a uniform curriculum, one that was as well suited to the sons and daughters of the new immigrants as to the children of the well-to-do. In point of fact he did emphasize the importance of a common set of experiences for all students. But the commonality he sought was not that of having everyone study exactly the same thing. Instead, he wanted schools in which students worked and played together, forming small communities whose members helped one another live and learn together.

Dewey's reference to what the best and wisest parent wants for his own child was certainly not a call for the kind of bookish curriculum that those same parents had themselves undergone. The new education that Dewey enthused over was to be new for everyone, not just for newcomers to the system. It was to be new in both content and method.

When Dewey delivered the lectures, around 1900, the schools served but a small fraction of the school-age population. Only 5 percent of that population reached high school, Dewey reports; fewer than half went beyond fifth grade (MW1, 18). The bulk of the children who left school early differed psychologically from those who stayed on, or so Dewey asserts. The early leavers, Dewey reports, were chiefly interested in practical affairs, whereas the stayers were more interested in intellectual matters. The former wanted to make and do things, rather than simply studying or hearing about them, as typically happened in school. This state of affairs led Dewey to conclude: "If we were to conceive our educational end and aim in a less exclusive way, if we were to introduce into educational processes the activities which appeal to those whose dominant interest is to do and to make, we should find the hold of the school upon its members to be more vital, more prolonged, containing more of culture" (MW1, 19). The appeal that the activities of making and doing might have for a certain segment of the school population was by no means Dewey's sole reason for advocating them. He saw such activities as benefiting all students because they were consonant with what modern psychology revealed about the human condition.

According to Dewey, educational practice in his day was dominated, as it had been for centuries, by a psychology radically different from the one whose influence was beginning to be felt in the waning years of the nineteenth century. In the "old" psychology, as Dewey liked to call it, the mind was a blank slate, passively accepting whatever experience might write on it. The "new" psychology did away with that conception of mind. Humans were portrayed as active rather than passive, impelled to move about and explore their world rather than being prodded into action by external stimuli. The old psychology was chiefly concerned with the acquisition of knowledge and with the development of intellect; the new psychology took into consideration emotional and physical needs as well as intellectual ones. The old psychology was fundamentally individualistic; each person was seen as inhabiting a subjective world of thoughts and feelings, a world that was inherently private and could not be shared with others. The new psychology was intrinsically social; humans were seen not solely as individuals but also as group members, as being shaped and molded as much by their contacts with others as by their interactions with the physical world.

Dewey's espousal of the new psychology afforded him yet another reason (and an intellectually respectable one) for advocating the overthrow of many practices current in his day and for including among its beneficiaries students who were already in the educational system and who were more intellectually inclined, as well as students who were newcomers to the system and who might be inclined to making and doing.

In summary, Dewey had three goals for education at the turn of the century: (1) he wanted to see created within the nation's schools a kind of community life that would compensate in some measure for the gradual disappearance of viable communities within society at large; (2) he wanted to see the schools become broader in their appeal, potentially serving all of the school-age population and not just children from well-to-do families and those headed for intellectual and professional careers; and (3) he wanted to see educational practice reflect an up-to-date understanding of what the fledgling science of psychology had begun to reveal about childhood and about human conduct.

To move in those directions, Dewey and his teachers at the University Elementary School (as it was initially called) devised an innovative curriculum. A small number of "active occupations" were at its center. As Dewey explained, "By occupation I mean a mode of activity on the part of a child which reproduces, or runs parallel to, some form of work carried on in social life. In the University Elementary School these occupations are represented by the shop-work with wood and tools; by cooking, sewing, and by . . . textile work [weaving and spinning]" (MW1, 92).

The attractiveness of this setup lay in its economy of function. In a single stroke it advanced schooling in the direction of all three of Dewey's goals. It engaged the students in cooperative undertakings, thus helping to foster a community spirit within the classroom and the school. Each undertaking offered a variety of things to do, thus providing something for almost everyone, regardless of inclinations and acquired interests. It emphasized activity over passivity, thus helping to effect a shift from learning by listening to learning by doing. Dewey summarized those advantages in this way.

> The fundamental point in the psychology of an occupation is that it maintains a balance between the intellectual and the practical phases of experience. As an occupation it is active or motor; it finds expression through the physical organs—the eyes, hands, etc. But it also involves continual observation of materials, and continual planning and reflection, in order that the practical or executive side may be successfully carried on. Occupation as thus conceived must, therefore, be carefully distinguished from work which educates primarily for a trade. It differs because its end is in itself; in the growth that comes from the continual interplay of ideas and their embodiment in action, not in external utility. (MW1, 92)

The point of an occupation-oriented curriculum is not to prepare students to become weavers, cooks, or carpenters. Rather, it is to show them how weaving, cooking, and carpentry (or any other useful craft) requires the continual interplay of ideas and their embodiment in action. The scope of that interplay extends far beyond the confines of household pursuits, as older and more advanced students come to appreciate. Interplay operates as a principle in the formal study of biology, chemistry, history, geology, and all the other academic subjects of the higher grades and beyond.

Dewey sought to enliven what had typically gone on in school by bringing it closer to what went on outside school in order to prevent it from being the dull and deadening experience that it had become for so many students. He and his teachers strove to effect this transformation in a variety of ways. They introduced into the classroom activities that allowed students to leave their seats and work together on group projects. They insisted that such projects lead some-where, that they be neither isolated intellectual exercises nor mere fun and games; instead, the activities were to bear a clear and direct relation to matters that the students understood and cared about as young people while at the same time connecting to activities of significance in the adult world outside the school.

They also opened the doors of the school to that world. By making a shop, a kitchen, and an outside garden integral parts of the school, they saw to it that rudimentary forms of adult occupations (such as the production of cloth and the preparation of food) became the focus of a portion of the students' experience. This change alone, Dewey reports, was electrifying in its effect. "The difference that appears when occupations are made the articulating centers of school life is not easy to describe in words; it is a difference in motive, of spirit and atmosphere. As one enters a busy kitchen in which a group of children are actively engaged in the preparation of food, the psychological difference, the change from more or less passive and inert recipiency and restraint to one of buoyant outgoing energy, is so obvious as fairly to strike one in the face. Indeed, to those whose image of the school is rigidly set the change is sure to give a shock" (MW1, 10).

EARLY DIFFICULTIES ASSOCIATED WITH MAKING AND DOING

Dewey's decision to center the elementary school curriculum around the study of occupations made a lot of sense in light of his conception of what was wrong with society. His emphasis on group projects and joint activities did likewise. There were difficulties, however, with both strategies. One recurrent worry, especially on the part of parents, was over how well Dewey's students would do in their mastery of basic skills. Some also worried that the time spent on making and doing would cause students in the upper grades to fall behind in the conventional school subjects of history, geography, mathematics, and the rest.

Dewey repeatedly sought to allay those fears. Addressing the small but select audience of parents and friends who came to hear the three lectures that became *The School and Society,* he assured his listeners that the new education would "supply the same results, and far more, of technical knowledge information and discipline that have been the ideals of education in the past" (MW1, 37). A year or so later in an article appearing in *The Elementary Record* he repeated that assurance, although he did by then acknowledge that the problem was a real one and had not yet been solved. "The common complaints that children's progress in these traditional school studies is sacrificed to the newer subjects that have come into the curriculum is sufficient evidence that the exact balance is not yet struck." He claimed that for students in the Laboratory School, involvement in "the more direct modes of activity, constructive and occupation

work, scientific observation, experimentation, etc.," provided "plenty of opportunities and occasions for the necessary use of reading, writing (and spell-
ing), and number work." The problem, as he saw it, was mainly one of taking
advantage of those opportunities and occasions in "a systematic and progressive
way" (MW1, 78). He further pointed out that when conventional subjects, such
as reading and writing, were fully integrated into meaningful activities of the
kind that occurred in his Laboratory School, they typically took less time to
learn. Under such conditions, he asserted, "the final use of the symbols,
whether in reading, calculation, or composition, is more intelligent, less mechanical; more active, less passively receptive; more an increase of power, less a
mere mode of enjoyment" (MW1, 79).

Was he right? Did students at the Laboratory School attain the same results,
and far more, of technical knowledge information and discipline that have been
the ideals of education in the past? From our present vantage point we have no
way of knowing, and it seems almost certain that no one could have said for sure
back in Dewey's day. Standard achievement tests, of the kind that we would use
today to examine such a claim, were unknown at the time. Even had they been
available, their use may not have settled the matter. What Dewey means by
achieving the same results, and far more, is not at all clear. He did go to some
lengths in his lectures to present examples of students' work—drawings and
quotations from essays—obviously intending to impress his audience. But
there is no way to judge the performance of the student body from such isolated
examples. All they reveal is that some students performed impressively on tasks
that resemble some of the things that go on in traditional classrooms.

In fairness to Dewey, I should point out that he understood that the younger
students' involvement in the cruder forms of making and doing could not go on
forever. He knew that all students must ultimately come to appreciate school
subjects in the manner of those who call themselves expert. "*The* problem of
teaching," he candidly acknowledges in *Democracy and Education,* "is to keep
the experience of the student moving in the direction of what the expert already
knows" (MW9, 191, emphasis added). He also saw that the expert's point of
view was not the end of things either. In the final analysis it was to serve as the
means to a richer and fuller life.

Having established that Dewey was not opposed to students gaining mastery
of the conventional school subjects, I must acknowledge that such was not the
picture that many people came away with after listening to Dewey or casually
reading what he said. His big message, as it was widely understood by supporters and critics alike, has little to do with the delights of mastering a subject

matter. Instead, what a lot of people heard (or wanted to hear) from Dewey was that such traditional studies are downright stultifying and should take a back seat to a far more active and engaged form of teaching and learning, one in which sitting and listening to a teacher or reading from a book have little place.

Is that popular conception off the mark? Could his critics as well as many of his supporters have been misreading him all these years? I fear not, or at least not completely, though I must say that a failure to look closely at what he said has doubtless contributed to the popular view. Regretfully, however, I hold Dewey himself partially responsible for some of the extreme views associated with his name.

To his credit, Dewey did come to recognize, albeit belatedly, the increasing frequency of such misinterpretations and the danger of some of the educational practices committed in his name. He sternly warned against them in his small volume *Experience and Education,* published in 1938. "There is always the danger in a new movement that in rejecting the aims and methods of that which it would supplant, it may develop its principles negatively rather than positively and constructively. Then it takes its clew in practice from that which is rejected instead of from the constructive development of its own philosophy" (LW13, 7). He then grew more specific in his complaints: "Yet I am sure that you will appreciate what is meant when I say that many of the newer schools tend to make little or nothing of organized subject-matter of study; to proceed as if any form of direction and guidance by adults were an invasion of individual freedom, and as if the idea that education should be concerned with the present and future meant that acquaintance with the past has little or no role to play in education" (LW13, 9).

Dewey's warning is clear enough. By that time, however, thirty-eight years after the publication of *The School and Society* and twenty-two years after *Democracy and Education,* his cautionary words were long overdue. In several of the so-called progressive schools of the day the situation with respect to students' freedom of choice and the absence of adult guidance was almost out of hand. Many of the newer schools, Dewey informs us, had already gone overboard in their rejection of organized subject matter.

Why did Dewey wait so long to issue his warning? He didn't, some might argue. His cautions were there all along for those who read his works carefully. There is much truth in that claim, as I have already remarked. Yet it leaves the basic question unanswered. Even if he did tuck in admonitions here and there, he did not emphasize them as fully as he might have done.

Dewey failed to issue his warning in stronger language, I would guess, because he was caught up in the excitement and promise of the educational experiment that he had undertaken. The need for change was so great, or so Dewey believed, that he likely give scant attention to the possibility of the excesses that would ultimately temper and even undermine that initial enthusiasm. As Alan Ryan observes, "Dewey's rhetoric was always situational. He wrote against what he supposed was the contemporary exaggeration that most needed to be combated" (1995, 350).

Throughout *The School and Society* the young students at the University Elementary School are pictured as being engaged in all sorts of making and doing, both inside and outside the classroom. Even the physical arrangement of the traditional classroom proved to be unsuitable for the kind of education that Dewey sought to provide. In fact, the standard arrangement, with desks bolted to the floor and facing front, epitomized everything that was wrong with the old way of education. To dramatize the problem that he faced in trying to change such arrangements, Dewey offered the following story. "Some few years ago I was looking about the school supply stores in the city, trying to find desks and chairs which seemed thoroughly suitable from all points of view—artistic, hygienic, and educational—to the needs of the children. We had a great deal of difficulty in finding what we needed, and finally one dealer, more intelligent than the rest, made this remark: 'I am afraid we have not what you want. You want something at which the child may work; these are all for listening.'" The moral of Dewey's adventure is evident, but to drive the point home, he wryly added, "That tells the story of traditional education" (MW1, 21).

Dewey continued to emphasize the importance of hands-on activity (making and doing) in *The Child and the Curriculum* and throughout his stay at the Laboratory School. In the years immediately following his departure from Chicago his interest in education remained high, as did his enthusiasm for getting students out from behind their desks and actually doing something. His book *Democracy and Education,* published in 1916, twelve years after his move to Columbia University, contains his fullest treatment of educational matters and, on his own account, his most up-to-date exposition of his total philosophy. Here, too, the emphasis on activity and on learning by doing remains prominent, though not as dramatically so as in *Schools of Tomorrow,* the book he wrote with his daughter Evelyn in 1915. That book's illustrations, which consist of twenty-seven photographs taken at the various schools that Dewey and his daughter visited, speak louder than do words about what the Deweys would like to have seen happening in schools. The students in the pictures are engaged in all kinds of activities, both inside and outside the classroom (chiefly outside).

They are cooking food, building houses, dancing, putting on plays, working in fields, cobbling shoes, and more. Even when the setting is a traditional classroom with its fixed desks and ready blackboards (only two of the twenty-seven photographs depict such a conventional scene), the accompanying captions describe the students as singing songs and playing games. The message to the reader is unmistakable: In the schools of tomorrow, no matter where a visitor might look, he or she will be apt to see students up and about—moving from place to place, singing, dancing, constructing objects, experimenting—and having a good time in the process—rather than sitting, passive and dull-eyed, reading a textbook or listening to the teacher, as students supposedly do in the schools of today.

In the text of *Schools of Tomorrow* the Deweys qualify the vision of the future created by the book's illustrations. They caution that the emphasis on activity "does not mean that the textbook must disappear." That recommendation, they concede, would be far too extreme. But, they quickly add, in the schools of tomorrow the function of the textbook is changed. "It becomes a guide for the pupil by which he may economize time and mistakes. The teacher and the book are no longer the only instructors; the hands, the eyes, the ears, in fact the whole body, become sources of information, while teacher and textbook become respectively the starter and the tester" (MW8, 255).

In the very next paragraph of text the Deweys repeat their caution about not going too far, but then, as so often happens in the book, they qualify what they have said in a way that dilutes its cautionary force. "Learning by doing does not, of course, mean the substitution of manual occupations or handwork for textbook studying. At the same time, allowing pupils to do handwork *whenever there is an opportunity for it,* is a great aid in holding the child's attention and interest" (MW8, 255, emphasis added). But the teacher who is advised to allow her students to do handwork whenever there is an opportunity for it is to be forgiven, we might suppose, if in following that advice she gives short shrift to corresponding opportunities for textbook studying.

Toward the end of *Schools of Tomorrow* the Deweys once again acknowledge their bias in favor of an activity-based curriculum and their relative lack of interest in more traditional forms of instruction. They say, "And except as their work illustrates a larger educational principle, very little attention has been given to the work of individual teachers or schools in their attempt to teach the conventional curriculum in the most efficient way" (MW8, 388). They explain that "while devices and ingenious methods for getting results from pupils often seem most suggestive and even inspiring to the teacher, they do not fit into the plan of this book when they have to do simply with the better use of the usual material of the traditional education" (MW8, 388).

In other words, Dewey and his daughter were far more interested in the total reform of the schools than in the incremental improvement of ongoing practices. The reform that they sought was so broad-gauged and so visible that even the most casual observer could not fail to take note of it. Dewey the philosopher valued scholarship highly and did so throughout his life. Dewey the schoolman continued to look upon the expert or the specialist in the various domains of knowledge as charting the overall direction in which all formal instruction, even that of the youngest students, should eventually move. Yet during the years when his educational influence was at or near its peak, Dewey all too frequently choose to emphasize only one side of the story. His sensible defense of scholarship as a form of activity to which all learners might aspire was too often muted and at times virtually drowned out by the rhetoric of his call for an activity-based curriculum. Before long, that much overworked phrase "learning by doing," a mantra that even Dewey recited almost ritualistically from time to time, came to be seen as capturing the essence of all he stood for as an educator. More than a slogan, it encapsulated for many of Dewey's admirers the totality of what they needed to know in order to follow in the master's footsteps. For his critics it became a convenient target of scorn. The three words are easy to remember yet burdensome when used to summarize a complex vision of how education might be improved. By the mid to late 1930s Dewey had become keenly aware of the magnitude of that burden.

WAS DEWEY'S WARNING NECESSARY? IS IT STILL NEEDED?

Looking back on the educational scene of the mid-1930s, some may find it hard to imagine the situation that caused Dewey to issue the warning contained in *Experience and Education*. Little remains today of what was then the progressive school movement. Such schools have virtually vanished from the educational landscape. So, too, have most of the laboratory schools of the kind that Dewey himself started at the turn of the century.

Given the disappearance of the progressive education movement, it may seem as though Dewey's worry about schools that paid insufficient attention to organized subject matter needn't have been expressed. Such schools, hindsight informs us, were on their way out anyway. If Dewey had waited a few years, he might have saved himself the trouble of going public with his concern. We must remember, of course, that Dewey's warning was itself a contributing factor in that chain of events and helped lead to the schools' demise.

But what of today? Is that warning only of historical interest? Now that the Progressive Education Association has been disbanded and progressivism as a ideological doctrine has nearly disappeared, may we safely assume that its excesses have disappeared as well? It would be comforting to believe so, yet dangerous.

Dewey's call for more hands-on activity in classrooms and his insistence that school learning be connected to students' lives outside school are two recommendations that large numbers of today's teachers take to heart. Might they do so with greater enthusiasm than even Dewey would have urged? Have these lessons from the past been accepted too uncritically by some? More than a hint that such may be the case is revealed in a recent article on teachers' descriptions of what they do to arouse interest among their students (Zahorik 1996). The study, conducted by John Zahorik, of the University of Wisconsin at Milwaukee, pertains so directly to the topic at hand that I must describe it in some detail.

Zahorik asked sixty-five teachers in three sections of a graduate course on teaching methods to write an essay on each of the following four topics: (1) qualities of a good learning experience, (2) a very interesting activity I have used, (3) how I create interest and what I do to avoid disinterest, and (4) subject-matter facts and concepts I have found to be interesting to students. Thirty of the teachers taught in elementary schools, the remainder in high schools. The essays were not a required assignment and were not used to determine course grades.

The essays revealed the teachers' preference for "engaging students in *hands-on activities*" when the goal was to generate an interest in learning. All sixty-five teachers reported making use of such activities, and "nearly every teacher" saw them "as critical to establishing and maintaining student interest." The hands-on activities the teachers described using were striking in their variety. They included "the use of manipulatives such as pattern blocks in mathematics; playing games of all kinds; participating in simulations, role playing and drama; engaging in projects such as growing seedlings in science or making television commercials in Spanish; and solving problems such as determining the sugar content of chewing gum" (Zahorik 1996, 555).

Within that list of activities, together with others that Zahorik mentions, we can identify several that might as readily have been employed by teachers working at the turn of the century in Dewey's University Elementary School as by teachers studying for advanced degrees in yet another midwestern city nearly a century later. Having students grow seedlings, discuss their experience of tornadoes, engage in debates—all of these and more sound like activities that Dewey's teachers might have arranged. The chief difference between then and now would seem to be in the relative novelty of the undertaking. What today would strike a classroom observer as commonplace may well have seemed unusual to a visitor looking in on Dewey's Laboratory School a hundred years ago.

But after listing and analyzing the reported classroom activities, Zahorik sounds a sour note. "Of the interesting activities that were described, at least one-third were hands-on activities that seemed gratuitous in whole or in part. They probably generated much interest, but whether they led to the acquisition of important learning is unclear. Hands-on activities appeared to be only loosely related to content objectives" (556). For an example, he describes the teaching of a fifth-grade social studies unit in which students seeking to develop an understanding of the decade of the 1950s, were led "to sing Elvis songs, impersonate Elvis, write essays speculating on whether Elvis was still alive, and critique Elvis movies" (556). Zahorik observes, "These activities could have launched a historical study of this period but they seemed to be the only focus of the unit" (557). Other examples are equally disquieting. Of a sixth-grade teacher who took students on a field trip to a nature center, Zahorik says: "In this lesson . . . students were asked to role-play various animals such as the 'radar-eared grass nibbler' and the 'long-legged fish nabber' while the teacher, wearing an official-looking costume, role-played the mayor of a hypothetical community. Using written cues suspended from trees, each 'animal' was to find a home in which it could survive" (557). Zahorik comments that "since natural environments with real plants and animals can provide considerable situational interest, the role-playing activity may not have been needed. But, more important, the chance to engage in activities in which a biologist or scientist might engage and thereby experience both the content and process of science was lost" (557).

Zahorik next turns to the activities that teachers report avoiding, because they supposedly generate disinterest among their students. Here is how he describes them. "The behaviors and tasks that teachers saw as harmful to interest were lecturing, explaining, giving directions, reviewing, taking tests, reading textbooks, doing workbooks, and taking notes." With these behaviors, as one teacher said, "learners are not motivated because they are not actively involved." Another remarked in relation to science, "They don't like it if they can't see it or do it." Still another said, "Math worksheets in class often bore my kids" (557).

Once again, it is not hard to imagine Dewey's teachers also preferring hands-on activities to the more old-fashioned methods of lecturing or relying exclusively on the use of textbooks. Having acknowledged that to be so, one cannot help but wonder how far the similarity extends. Could anything like the Elvis impersonations or the role-playing of fictitious animals in a genuine out-of-doors nature study have taken place in Dewey's school? Possibly so. Yet the eventuality seems remote. Zahorik helps to explain why.

When his teachers were asked to discuss subject-matter facts and concepts they found to be interesting to students, they ran into difficulty. One-third of them wrote exclusively about hands-on activities. Zahorik expresses his surprise: "They didn't mention content or subject matter in any form!" (558). There was a strong tendency to talk about content or subject matter in tandem with hands-on activity. Though asked to concentrate exclusively on the former, fully half of the teachers discussed activity as well. Only ten of the sixty-five teachers, Zahorik reports, "solely discussed interesting content" (558).

Summing up the major conclusions of his study, Zahorik writes that they "suggest that teachers assume that content is intrinsically dull, that facts and concepts in the required curriculum in social studies, science, language, and the other disciplines are unappealing to students. . . . The means they most often select [to create interest] are whatever is perceived as fun. Fun, especially to children, is the opposite of sitting and listening. It is being active in the form of playing games, manipulating objects, constructing models, acting out events, conducting experiments, and the like. . . . [M]aking learning fun is a driving force in teaching" (561).

Read as a portrayal of how today's teachers might actually behave, Zahorik's study is disquieting, even damning in its import. We must be careful, however, to keep its several limitations firmly in mind. It is, after all, a study of only sixty-five teachers, and it deals exclusively with essays written by them, not with their classroom behavior. The essays were written to order. And though Zahorik assures his readers that participation in the study was voluntary and that the results were never used for grading purposes, the possibility remains that some of the respondents were trying to impress their instructor by telling him what they believed he wanted to hear. Above all, we must avoid looking on Zahorik's report as constituting a blanket indictment of today's teachers. His study is provocative and interesting, but we must take care not to read more into it than is there.

The principal service that Zahorik's study performs for us here is to indicate the attitude of many contemporary teachers with respect to the place of interest-generating activities in the classroom. The teachers' essays, written quite recently, strongly confirm what many critics have known all along, which is that organized subject matter is not assigned a back seat just in progressive schools. The same can happen in the school down the street.

A goodly number of teachers, it would seem, have become far more intent on keeping their students engaged in a lively physical sense than in helping them become engaged in the more sedentary and emotionally cooler processes of thought and reflection. It is as though they have taken to heart Dewey's advocacy of learning by doing without at the same time heeding his insistence that "the problem of teaching is to keep the experience of the student moving in the direction of what the expert already knows" (MW9, 191).

Dewey, as I have tried to show, cannot be vindicated of contributing to this unfortunate state of affairs, though it doubtless would have pained him to acknowledge his part in it. Teaching was a serious business for Dewey. It was a lot more than fun and games. He never allowed himself to forget that, although he may have inadvertently made it easier for others to forget it.

Our question now becomes, What might Dewey have done differently if he had come to his interest in the arts *before* he began work at the Laboratory School rather than years later? Might he have gone less overboard in his advocacy of learning by doing? Might he have issued his 1938 warning many years in advance?

I would like to think that he might have done both of those things. I agree with Ryan that Dewey's rhetoric was often situational. He was a man of his times—far more so than many academics of either his day or ours. His enthusiasms as well as his occasional distempers matched the social conditions of the age in which he lived. I therefore do not imagine that he would have changed his tune dramatically even if his interests had already turned to the arts. He would have had the same set of worries about the schools not serving a significant portion of the school-age population. He still would have been concerned about the mass migration to the city and the drift away from community life. He likely would have remained intrigued by the findings of the new psychology.

The possible differences that an earlier arrival at a sustained look at the arts might have made in Dewey's educational outlook are encapsulated for me in the title of his small 1938 book, *Experience and Education,* which was written after both *Experience and Nature* and *Art as Experience.* The word *experience,* common to all three titles, does not appear in any of Dewey's other books on education. It does show up in the title of one chapter in *Democracy and Education,* and it appears often within the text itself. But it was not joined with the word *education* and raised to the level of a book title until after Dewey thought long and hard about the generic traits of *an* experience and about the place of the arts in human affairs. I believe that the timing of its appearance is significant. Unfortunately, *Experience and Education* is not one of Dewey's major works. It was initially a set of lectures written and delivered at the request of the Executive Council of Kappa Delta Pi, an honorary society in education. Dewey himself refers to the book as a "little volume" and to its contents as an "essay" (LW13, 4). Though somewhat longer than a single lecture in its printed version, it contains no index. It cannot be read as a full account of how Dewey looked on education after steeping himself in the arts. It does, however, reveal the primacy of experience as an analytical category in Dewey's thinking.

Experience, for Dewey, is more fundamental than democracy, for, as he points out, if we ask why we prefer "democratic and humane arrangements to those that are autocratic and harsh," "can we find any reason that does not ultimately come down to the belief that democratic social arrangements promote *a better quality of human experience,* one which is more widely accessible and enjoyed, than do non-democratic and anti-democratic forms of social life" (LW14, 18, emphasis added)? Dewey is careful not to equate experience and education, because not all experiences are educative. Yet he does make clear that the question of what constitutes an educative experience is the most important one that an educator can ask. Raised to the level of philosophical abstraction, the question receives its best and fullest answer not in *Experience and Education,* where, based on title alone, we might expect to find it, but in Dewey's most mature discussions of experience, particularly in his ruminations on the arts.

Had Dewey put all of his belatedly acquired insights to work in designing the Laboratory School or in giving educational advice to others, the results might not have looked much different on the surface from those that occurred. Yet the approach would have been different, of that I feel certain, and so would its final outcome. The difference would lie in the details of how things were done. There would have been an increased emphasis on the qualitative immediacy of experience, on its unity and wholeness, on its emotional underpinnings, on the temporal unfolding of events, on expressive meaning (as contrasted with meaning of a more instrumental sort), on the way perception gradually develops, on the style and manner of undertaking a task, on the care with which things are done. In short, there would have been greater attention given to almost all of the distinctions discussed in this book. Those subtle changes would surely add up to a whole greater than the sum of its parts. They might have prevented some of the excesses discussed here.

Why might attention to such matters have had such a beneficial effect? Because it would have kept that attention where it belongs: on the crafting of experiences akin to those undergone in the creation and enjoyment of works of art.

DEWEY AS TEACHER: ANOTHER APPLICATION FOR ART'S LESSONS?

Anyone who casually wandered into one of Dewey's classes at either the University of Chicago or Columbia University expecting to witness learning by doing in the hands of a master was in for a big surprise. So, too, the visitor who hoped to learn how the famous professor who wrote and lectured about "interest in education" would manifest responsiveness to his own students' needs and interests. In fact, all whose expectations were formed by having read one or more of Dewey's educational treatises faced a disappointment. The Great Educator, in the opinion of many, was not the greatest of teachers.

Sidney Hook, who, as a graduate student, had been one of Dewey's most ardent admirers and who went on to become a close intellectual companion, writing extensively on Dewey's philosophy, recalled what it had been like to sit at the feet of the master.

> As a teacher, Dewey seemed to me to violate his own pedagogical principles. He made no attempt to motivate or arouse the interest of his auditors, to relate problems to their own experiences, to use graphic, concrete illustrations in order to give point to abstract and abstruse positions. He rarely provoked a lively participation and response from students, in the absence of which it is difficult to determine whether genuine learning or even comprehension has taken place. . . . Dewey spoke in a husky monotone, and although there was a sheet of notes on the desk at which he was usually seated, he never seemed to consult it. He folded it into many creases as he slowly spoke. Occasionally he would read from a book to which he was making a critical reference. His discourse was far from fluent. There were pauses and sometimes long lapses as he gazed out of the window or above the heads of his audience. (Ryan 1995, 38)

Another former student, Harold Larrabee, who studied with Dewey at Columbia around the time of World War I, offers a description that largely corroborates Hook's account, though its harshness is modified by one or two details that make Dewey seem rather charming despite whatever pedagogical shortcomings he might have had.

In the classroom, Dewey seemed to possess almost none of . . . [the customary] pedagogical essentials. There were none of the recommended "lecture techniques" or histrionic devices of the education courses, to say nothing of today's "battery of visual aids to instruction." His appearance was farmer-like, weather-beaten, and utterly unpretentious. Some of his women students said that they found it hard, occasionally, to repress a desire to straighten up his neckties. He remained seated throughout the hour and seldom seemed to be looking directly at his audience. Often he would turn in his chair and glance sideways, as if half-looking out the window and half-absorbed in his private thoughts. His facial expression was solemn, though it lighted up at times with something like a chuckle, and occasionally his hand would ruffle his shock of hair or tug at his moustache. Questions from the floor were not exactly discouraged, but they were not invited. . . . It is almost comical to measure Dewey against some of his own followers' standards for college teaching, such as: a magnetic, outgoing personality; evident enthusiasm for his subject; a master of his craft; a clear speaking voice; a fluent command of English; the ability to hold the attention, arouse the interest, and enlist the active participation of the student. (Larrabee 1959, 379)

Yet a third student of Dewey's, Irving Edman, who went on to become a well-known philosopher and, in fact, one of Dewey's revered colleagues at Columbia, begins his account with a description that echoes those offered by Hook and Larrabee. Though it repeats much that the earlier accounts contain, its revealing and somewhat amusing comments about Dewey's verbal habits make it worth quoting at length.

This famous philosopher who had written so much on "Interest in Education," as the essence of the educational process, could not, save by a radical distortion of the term, be said at first hearing to sound interesting. He had none of the usual tricks or gifts of the effective lecturer. He sat at his desk, fumbling with a few crumpled yellow sheets and looking abstractedly out of the window. He spoke very slowly in a Vermont drawl. He looked both very kindly and very abstracted. He hardly seemed aware of the presence of a class. He took little pains to underline a phrase, or emphasize a point, or, so at first it seemed to me, to make any. Occasionally he would apparently realize that people in the back of the room might not hear his quiet voice; he would then accent the next word, as likely as not a preposition or a conjunction. He seemed to be saying whatever came into his head next, and at one o'clock on an autumn afternoon to at least one undergraduate what came next did not always have or seem to have a very clear connection with what had just gone before. The end of the hour finally came and he simply stopped; it seemed to me he may have stopped anywhere. (Edman 1946, 196)

Had Edman ended his description here, he would have added but another piece of testimony to the already ample supply that makes Dewey out to have been a dull and boring teacher. Fortunately, however, he goes on. As he does, the picture changes. What changes is not so much Dewey's style of teaching as it is Edman's perception of that style. Referring to Dewey's habit of meandering without purpose from one remark to another, he reports,

> But I soon found out that it was my mind that had wandered, not John Dewey's. I began very soon to do what I had seldom done in college courses—to take notes. It was then a remarkable discovery to make on looking over my notes to find that what had seemed so casual, so rambling, so unexciting, was of an extraordinary coherence, texture, and brilliance. I had been listening not to the semi-theatrical repetition of a discourse many times made—a fairly accurate description of many academic lectures—I had been listening to a man actually *thinking* in the presence of a class. (196)

For Edman, that experience, repeated almost daily, grew to be unforgettable.

> As one became accustomed to Dewey's technique, it was this last aspect of his teaching that was most impressive—and educative. To attend a lecture of John Dewey was to participate in the actual business of thought. Those pauses were delays in creative thinking, when the next step was really being considered, and for the glib dramatics of the teacher-actor was substituted the enterprise, careful and candid, of the genuine thinker. Those hours came to seem the most arresting educational experiences, almost, I have ever had. One had to be scrupulously attentive and one learned to be so. Not every day or in every teacher does one overhear the palpable processes of thought. (196–197)

Larrabee too, as it turns out, came to appreciate the same aspects of Dewey's teaching style that Edman found so admirable. The two of them, as Larrabee informs us, were by no means alone. "His students came to recognize that an hour listening to Dewey was an exercise in 'man thinking.' They saw a well-stocked and original mind, remarkably free from any sort of bias or prejudice, engaged in the patient and honest exploration of 'whole situations' in experience with the aid of penetrating distinctions and a full-fledged 'theory of inquiry'" (Larrabee 1959, 380).

Larrabee's description of what went on during the course of a typical class session adds significantly to Edman's account. His perspective is that of a student trying to follow the course of Dewey's extemporaneous form of reasoning.

> In the classroom, the student's experience went something like this: The hour opened with a half-revealed abstract pronouncement, an apparent platitude, seldom affording any great air of mystery or suspense. Then would follow a painstaking development of the idea, during which the student was sometimes lulled almost to

slumber by the lecturer's snail-like deliberation in getting to the point. But, just as the end of the hour was well in sight, Prof. Dewey would unfold some hitherto-concealed and unexpected practical consequence of his train of thought. Whereupon the student, now completely awake, would curse himself for his inattention and resolve that next time he surely would hang upon every word. One rarely left the classroom without the conviction that something intellectually *and* practically important had been said, no matter how uncertain one was about the precise steps in the argument. (Larrabee 1959, 380)

Both Edman and Larrabee ascribe their ultimate fascination with Dewey's teaching style to the opportunity that it provided them to witness at first hand a person deeply engaged in thought. "A man thinking in the presence of a class" is the way Edman sums it up. "An hour listening to Dewey was an exercise in 'man thinking,'" Larrabee says. Edman adds that in Dewey's classes one was able "to overhear the palpable process of thought." For both of them, over time, Dewey the teacher became, in effect, Dewey the thinker. They both learned to value not only the substance of Dewey's classroom pondering but the process by which that substance was shaped and given point. In fact, in their retelling of the experience, it is the process far more than the substance that stands out and that appears to have stayed with them.

Dewey himself would be among the first to point out that substance and process are inseparable. They can be pried apart analytically when we have a special reason for wanting to do so, true enough, but in reality they are one. To treat either in isolation is to ignore the other. One of Dewey's many ways of making this point was to insist that there is no such thing as thinking. There is only thinking *about,* he would declare, and whatever we think *about* must inevitably influence the way we *go about* thinking.

Importuning of this sort, familiar enough to all who have read Dewey, help to keep us mindful of the fact that when former students such as Edman and Larrabee use a phrase like "man thinking" to characterize Dewey's classroom behavior they have reverted to a level of abstraction that leaves reality far behind. Moreover, it is not substance alone that gets cut from the picture; their own emotional involvement as students gets excised as well.

No matter how lost in thought Dewey may have appeared to some or all of his students, those among them who came to appreciate his air of absorption and what it stood for surely understood that he was doing more than merely thinking. After all, a person trying to figure out how to fix a flat tire could also be described as absorbed in thought. Dewey, they had to have realized, was not just "thinking"; he was thinking about matters of consequence and doing so successfully. Nor was Dewey just trying to extricate himself from whatever intellectual quandary he happened to face. He was struggling on behalf of others as well—his current students most immediately but also the invisible audience of future students and scholars who stood to benefit from the outcome of his ruminations. His thinking, in other words, was steeped in social significance. While making use of the ideas of others (Larrabee calls his mind "well-stocked"), he also sought to contribute to that store of ideas.

Dewey's students (at least the more appreciative ones) must also have come to realize that what Dewey was trying to do was difficult. It was not something that they could easily do themselves. As the testimony of Edman and Larrabee reveals, Dewey's thinking was often subtle and hard to follow. It was, in a word, sophisticated, the thought of an expert, taxing to the attentiveness of the neophyte.

The more alert of Dewey's students could hardly have missed the purposefulness of Dewey's ruminations. He was not just rummaging about in thought, flitting from one idea to the next. His thoughts had direction, Edman discovered. They went somewhere. They also had structure. They were held together by a tight inner logic. And they did not trail on endlessly. They came to rest now and again. The resting places—the conclusions reached—were usually satisfying intellectually and were at times striking in their originality. Edman lauds the process as a whole, calling it creative thinking. Dewey doubtless would have been pleased by the compliment but he likely would have proceeded to point out that all genuine thought *must* be creative, at least for the individual thinker. If it is not, it is little more than the discharge of old habits or the mechanical recall of what others have thought. When it turns out to be either of those, Dewey would say, it hardly deserves to be called thinking.

THE EXPERT AS ARTIST: LEARNING BY DOING AS AN INTELLECTUAL ENDEAVOR

Edman's choice of the phrase "creative thinking" to refer to Dewey's behavior as a teacher does more than pay Dewey a compliment. It invites a fresh look at the relation between Dewey's teaching and his theorizing, a look that yields substantially different results than do the damning judgments passed along by many of Dewey's former students. It does so by focusing on the originality of Dewey's thought. What Dewey was doing in the classroom, Edman's portrayal tells us, was fashioning new ideas, answering questions that were vexing to him, working out solutions to problems that stymied his own intellectual progress. He was forging tools of thought, instruments that he anticipated putting to use as a practicing philosopher, ones he readily shared with others for their future use. At the same time he was demonstrating how such instruments are made, showing what it takes in the way of prior knowledge and current disposition—the importance of personal qualities such as persistence, open-mindedness, perceptual acuity, and so forth—to fashion intellectual products of enduring worth.

Another way of depicting Dewey's modus operandi as a teacher is to see it as an enactment of what it means to behave as an expert. Typically we define the expert in epistemological terms. We see him or her as someone who knows a lot about a particular topic or subject. Dewey, with his well-stocked mind ranging over a wide array of philosophical issues, meets that criterion with ease. But his deployment of expertise goes well beyond the narrow boundaries of epistemology. He shows what it means to put knowledge to work, using it not just as a storehouse of information to be drawn upon when needed (as might the teacher who simply lectured, let us say) but as a repository of ideas to be examined and criticized, ideas providing a foundation upon which to build, as all foundations are meant to be, yet one in need of constant surveillance and repair. As an expert reporting on the ideas of his philosophical predecessors, Dewey was capable of speaking with confidence and authority. He could and did offer public lectures that were no different in style from those of most other lecturers. When contributing to knowledge, however, which is the role in which both Edman and Larrabee depict him, a change overcomes his more public self. His manner becomes diffident and cautious, his voice close to inaudible. But, diffidence and caution aside, there was nothing meek or mild about the conclusions he reached, as the testimony of both Edman and Larrabee attests.

Yet a third way of making sense of Dewey's classroom performance is to view it as a form of artistic endeavor. The adjective *creative* in Edman's description of Dewey's thinking points the way. It highlights the originality of many of the ideas that Dewey presented in class. But there is far more to artistry than originality, as Dewey made clear in his own writings and as I have underscored in this book.

At the heart of artistry lies a process resembling alchemy. Beginning with materials that are raw and crude—pigments, sounds, blocks of stone—the artist creates a finished product, an object or a performance that is at once satisfying, polished, and complete. Dewey speaks of the transformation as entailing a qualitative shift from "material" to "medium." As a result of the artist's labor, what initially was dumb gains a voice. It becomes a vehicle of meaning. It takes on significance. It begins to make sense. Moreover, the artist's raw material, the stuff with he or she works, includes more than physical matter. It embraces everything that the artist brings to the situation—personal skills, plans, motivations, attitudes—as well as everything ideational that emerges serendipitously in the process of creation—the insights, the shifts of attention, the fortuitous associations, the unforeseen opportunities and promises instantly perceived. Ideas, feelings, and insights, we need to recall, were no less real for Dewey than were rocks and trees.

A miniature version of this creative process is nicely encapsulated in Larrabee's account of Dewey's typical behavior in class. Dewey began, Larrabee tells us, with material that seemed very unpromising at the start: a half-revealed abstract pronouncement, an apparent platitude. There was seldom, he says, any great air of mystery or suspense at the beginning. Following such an unauspicious launching, Dewey would set to work in a manner so painstaking in its deliberation and so snail-like in pace (and, I might add, he would be so seemingly oblivious to those present) that the ill-prepared student was sometimes lulled almost to slumber. But then, as the hour wore on, something magical happened. Just as the session was about to end, Dewey would unfold some hitherto-concealed and unexpected practical consequence of his train of thought. Presto, change-o! What had been dull and boring suddenly sprang to life. The student, now wide awake, would belatedly curse himself for his inattention and resolve that next time he surely would hang upon every word.

Of the many noteworthy elements of Larrabee's account one of the most striking is that both the raw material and Dewey's way of handling it were initially perceived as being dull and uninteresting to at least some students, if not to the majority of those present. Dewey apparently did little or nothing to modify that state of affairs. He did not, for example, announce at the start where he was headed, thereby building a sense of anticipation before he began. Nor did he issue warnings about the slow pace at which he would have to proceed. He seems to have taken for granted his students' faith in the importance of the undertaking as well as their willingness and capacity to follow dutifully along. More puzzling perhaps, he seems not to have cared very much whether they were following along. If we can believe Edman and Larrabee, he even avoided eye contact with his students much of the time, preferring to look over their heads or to stare out the window.

Yet, relying on the account we have read, a significant portion of his students *did* come to appreciate the importance of what their teacher was up to in the classroom. They came to be fascinated as much by his methodical way of working as by the content of his thoughts. Dewey, they came to realize, was doing more than teaching philosophy as a body of knowledge. He was showing them what it was like to do philosophy, what it meant to be a philosopher. In his bumbling and fumbling manner he was offering his students a living instantiation of the principle that lay at the core of his own educational perspective. He was, of all things, *learning by doing,* pushing as far beyond the known as his expertise and his own intellectual powers allowed, attending to detail and respecting the materials with which he worked, the way an artist might, arriving at conclusions that he himself had not foreseen, as befits a discoverer. To top things off, he was managing to do all of this in the immediate present. His was not a performance that had been rehearsed the day before. This was the philosopher-in-action. Small wonder that Edman, Larrabee, and no doubt countless others came wide awake once they caught on to what they were witnessing through their half-closed eyes.

TEACHING AS THINKING ALOUD: DOES IT SUFFICE?

The image of Dewey as teacher that the awakened Edman and Larrabee leave us with is laudable in many ways. It is also sentimentalized, no doubt, as is the elaboration of it given here. Dewey must have had his bad days as a teacher, as all teachers do. The bad days may even have far outnumbered the good ones. For the sake of discussion, however, let us accept the picture as presented. Let us allow Dewey to be the intrepid philosophical explorer in the classroom that Edman and Larrabee depict. How does this presentation bear on Dewey's reputation as a teacher? Would it cancel out the negative qualities (the un-Deweyan aspects of Dewey's performance) remarked on by the same two witnesses and by others?

I fear not. Larrabee seems to have feared so as well, for he concludes: "The enigma is not easy to solve. Student after student will tell you that Dewey's teaching changed the course of his or her thinking fundamentally. But each one also will regale you with tales of his dullness as a lecturer" (Larrabee, 1959, 379).

Larrabee's sense of an enigma to be solved is surely correct. His depiction of its character, however, strikes me as misleading. It may well be that many of Dewey's former students would testify to the powerful impact that Dewey's teaching had on them, as well as to his dullness as a lecturer. But if their accounts are anything like Larrabee's own (or Edman's), the two judgments—of impact and of dullness—did not occur simultaneously. They arose at different times in the history of each student's experience in Dewey's class, and they constitute distinct phases of that experience. What typically happened, apparently, was that the style and content of Dewey's teaching was initially seen as dull and uninteresting but subsequently came to be perceived otherwise. As those students began to appreciate the subtlety and significance of Dewey's manner of thinking aloud, they overcame their boredom and found themselves hanging on his every word. Therefore, the enigma that needs solving, I would say, is not how a famous professor could be boring and interesting to the same student at one and the same time. That possibility, as we have seen, is self-contradictory. Nor is it even how the same professor could be boring to some students and fascinating to others? That answer to that question lies chiefly in intellectual and psychological differences among students. Rather, what remains puzzling is this: Why did Dewey seemingly do so little to help his students reach the level of understanding and appreciation that Edman and Larrabee finally attained? Why didn't he liven things up, invite more questions, tell more anecdotes, use more examples, speak more clearly? Why, in heaven's name, did he not even bother to look his students in the eye?

The easy answer to such questions and possibly the final one has to lie in Dewey's personality. That is just the way he was. Dewey the man and Dewey the teacher are identical. Take one and you get the other.

There is surely more than a modicum of truth in that answer. We know, for example, that Dewey was a shy and modest person, not much given to emotional outbursts and displays of affection. The public side of teaching did not come easily to him. But those personal qualities hardly excuse Dewey from his pedagogical responsibilities. For a teacher to think aloud regularly in the presence of his students, and little more than that day after day, presumes a lot about those who witness the performance. It presumes they are already interested in what one is thinking or will readily and spontaneously become so. It presumes they are able to follow one's thinking without individual attention and help. It presumes that the task of following along in thought is not only educative but is the best method available under the circumstances.

Edman's and Larrabee's testimony makes clear that for some of Dewey's students that set of presumptions was either fully justified or almost so. What it leaves unanswered, however, is the question of how many others were like the two of them. Was everyone present in the same state of mind? That seems unlikely. Dewey surely must have known that not all of his student were with him all of the time. Why didn't he take the possibility into account and adjust his teaching methods accordingly?

All of the explanations that come to mind are even more un-Deweyan than the behavior that they seek to explain. I reject them for that reason. Someone might suggest, for example, that Dewey cared only about those students who were quick to catch on to his way of teaching. The others—the sleepers in the back row—he may have been quite willing to overlook, even hoping perhaps that they might physically withdraw from his class. But this explanation runs so counter to everything else that Dewey stands for—in particular, his democratic impulses—that I find it impossible to take seriously. Other explanations fare no better. I conclude, therefore, that Dewey's un-Deweyan behavior has no good explanation. Yet it still calls for further speculation.

Should Dewey have been more mindful of his students? Should he have been more outgoing in his manner of teaching? Speaking as a teacher, I do not hesitate to answer yes to both questions. In fact, I suspect that Dewey himself would have answered the same. In a speech that he gave in 1938 to an audience of educators interested in dance, Dewey describes a condition that sounds like his own. "It is extraordinary how much we lose our powers of direct observation, more than observation I mean our sensitiveness, our responsiveness, to the world of persons and objects and natural events about us because we fall into certain routines or because of our occupations we have certain ends more or less remote that control our thought and attention, and we become oblivious to a great deal of the human scene around us" (LW13, 366).

The compulsion that I sense Dewey being under as he droned on in class, lost in his own thoughts, has its analog in the absorption of the artist, the writer, the scientist in what he or she is doing, the fierce concentration and loss of self-consciousness that leads to missed appointments and a rumpled appearance and that causes some professors to be referred to as absent-minded. Yet as admirable and even as endearing as such qualities might be under certain circumstances, they have little place, it seems to me, in the classroom.

Dewey once characterized the polarities of teaching as the Child (i.e., the Student) and the Curriculum. These poles exert a magnetic pull on all who enter the field of teaching. The closer one gets to one pole or the other, in the sense of centering one's attention on it, the stronger its attraction becomes and the weaker the tug from the opposite end. Teachers of young children tend to gravitate toward one pole, whereas teachers of older students and adults tend to gravitate toward the other. Nothing is wrong in principle with such proclivities. The danger arises when those perfectly natural tendencies become excessive, as one of them appears to have done for Dewey.

How might such excesses be avoided? Is there a way for college and university professors to avoid becoming classroom Deweys? Conversely, must teachers of the young become so intent on keeping their pupils interested and active that they lose sight of the larger goals toward which they should be headed? Might Dewey's analysis of the arts be of some help in both instances? I think it might.

It is easy enough to say what is wrong with the extremes that we have been discussing. Each leaves something out. The student-centered extremist leaves out subject matter or tends to downplay its importance. The subject-centered extremist leaves out the the student. The remedy looks simple enough: stern warnings along the lines of "Don't forget the subject matter! Don't forget the students!"

The trouble with that simple solution is that it doesn't take into account what Dewey teaches us about the nature of experience. Issuing stern warnings makes it sound as though the problem is fundamentally one of memory. Dewey's analysis shows it to be much more complicated than that. The two types of teachers that we have been talking about have not just forgotten what to do. If they have forgotten anything, it would perhaps be more accurate to say that they have forgotten what they are about or, even more sharply said, what education is about. For a teacher to forget this is to commit the greatest pedagogical sin.

Was Dewey guilty of that sin as a teacher? From the evidence at hand, I would say that he was from time to time. But then, isn't every teacher? Keeping a strong sense of what education is all about clearly and constantly in mind is almost impossible for any teacher. That being so, the best teachers can do is to become increasingly aware of pedagogical shortcomings and try to correct them. How might teachers go about doing that? There are dozens of ways, I am sure. One is through exposure to the arts and through reflection on what that exposure reveals about the meaning of education—in other words, through the kind of analysis of art-centered experiences that Dewey offers.

Dewey's failings as a teacher, if they can be called that, might have been substantially lessened by a healthy dose of his own medicine. Indeed, maybe he did swallow his own pills, and they failed to do any good. I am more inclined to believe that he never applied his ideas to his teaching, or never tried hard enough. Whatever the explanation for his failure, it is worth asking what such reflection might ideally have yielded if it had been undertaken.

Imagine Dewey asking: "How should I improve my teaching in the light of my own theory of human experience and especially in light of my growing awareness of the exemplary nature of experiences involving the arts?" The question is awkwardly phrased, I grant, and not one that Dewey would likely have asked. Why not? Mostly because it comes out of the blue. It lacks continuity. It presupposes that Dewey was aware that his teaching was in need of improvement, and I have no evidence to suggest that he was. Nonetheless, it is the question that I would like to have seen him ask, so I will proceed as though he had. Here is a summary of what I would have said to him.

As Dewey's friendly advisor, I would begin by pointing out that his chief difficulty as a teacher appears to center on his lack of sensitivity toward the students sitting in front of him. He almost seems to be unaware of them. To draw upon a distinction that Dewey himself often used, the students are part of his *surroundings* but not part of his *environment*. They do not constitute a force (or set of forces) that causes him to vary his actions, save in the most minimal sense. He does not quite turn his back on them, completely removing them from sight, but he comes close to doing so, if reports are to be believed. To the objection that Dewey was no more remote from his student audience than are most good lecturers, I would reply that the information on which I have relied suggests otherwise. It depicts Dewey as mumbling, as staring out the window, as fiddling with his notes, as leaving little room for questions. That is hardly the way effective lecturers behave, in my experience.

Dewey's classroom behavior resembles that of a writer or even a visual artist more than that of a teacher. He does seem intent on organizing his thoughts and conveying them to an audience. But that audience, as we can judge from Dewey's behavior, is more imaginative than real. It may include, in an abstract sense, the students sitting before him, but it does not include them as living creatures, as people with puzzled expressions on their faces, with raised hands or drooping eyelids. Dewey, one might say, is all but alone in the classroom, almost as he was in his study at home. Incidentally, it is rumored that Dewey was capable of working contentedly at home with several of his young children running about the room, occasionally tugging at his sleeve or climbing onto his lap. The image is an endearing one for all who have heard of Dewey's reputed love for children. It also reveals an enviable power of concentration on his part. The same power to become oblivious to what is going on two or three feet away is not quite as admirable, however, when the setting is a classroom.

Dewey's problem with respect to his students was not that he didn't see them in a physical sense. He knew they were there, but he didn't go beyond seeing. He recognized them but did not perceive them, as he himself might have said. He did not give them sufficient attention in a Murdochian sense. He thus remained *unattached* to them, emotionally distant. These are harsh things to say. I must be overstating what went on in Dewey's classroom. I leave the harsh edge, however, in order to bring out the forcefulness of Dewey's concepts and categories when applied in a classroom situation.

Yet another way of describing Dewey's pedagogical shortcomings, this, too, drawing upon distinctions made in *Art as Experience,* is to say that Dewey seldom treated his students as though they were material resources, part of the stuff with which he was working. That may sound like an odd way of referring to the relationship between a teacher and his students. It is only so, however, if we fail to recall the peculiar status that the concept of material has in Dewey's thought, the way that it becomes infused with meaning in a work of art. Students are hardly the artist's dumb objects of paint and stone, awaiting transformation into a medium. But for teachers, students are as fundamental in determining what moves to make in a classroom as raw materials are in determining an artist's endeavors. The teacher who ignores them does so at her peril.

The harshest way to speak of Dewey's detached aloofness as a teacher is to charge him with failing to appreciate his students. That accusation would surely have pained him, for he was keenly aware of the importance of appreciation in human affairs. He occasionally referred to it as "a realizing sense," a phrase we don't hear much anymore. Here is his definition: "In colloquial speech, the phrase a 'realizing sense' is used to express the urgency, warmth, and intimacy of a direct experience in contrast with the remote, pallid, and coldly detached quality of a representative experience" (MW9, 241). He continues: "The terms 'mental realization' and 'appreciation' (or *genuine* appreciation) are more elaborate names for the realizing sense of a thing" (MW9, 232). He explains that "it is not possible to define these ideas except by synonyms"—as in "coming home to one" or "really taking it in"—the reason being that "the only way to appreciate what is meant by a direct experience of a thing is by having it" (MW9, 232–233). He also points out that "appreciation is opposed to depreciation. It denotes an enlarged, an *intensified* prizing, not merely a prizing, much less—like depreciation—a lowered and degraded prizing" (MW9, 237).

Did Dewey not prize his students? Did he not appreciate them? Did he not have a realizing sense of them? I hint at the possibility in order to show how Dewey might have made use of his own set of categories to call into question aspects of his teaching that had gone unheeded and that needed repair.

But Dewey was not led by his own theory to bring those aspects of his teaching into question, at least not so far as we know. Does that failing invalidate the meliorative potency of his conceptions? I can't think how. There is nothing in Dewey's theory (or any other that I know of) that requires it to come to its own rescue. Theories are tools, nothing more. That, too, is one of Dewey's prime points. They must be employed in order to work, as must lessons culled from the arts. Referring to the arts, Dewey says, "They are not the exclusive agencies of appreciation in the most general sense of that word; but they are the chief agencies of an intensified, enhanced appreciation. As such, they are not only intrinsically and directly enjoyable, but they serve a purpose beyond themselves. They have the office, in increased degree, of all appreciation in fixing taste, in forming standards for the worth of later experiences." He spells out how that happens: "They arouse discontent with conditions, which fall below their measure; they create a demand for surroundings coming up to their own level. They reveal a depth and range of meaning in experiences which otherwise might be mediocre and trivial. They supply, that is, organs of vision. Moreover, in their fullness they represent the concentration and consummation of elements of good which are otherwise scattered and incomplete. They select and focus the elements of enjoyable worth which make any experience directly enjoyable" (MW9, 246).

I believe that, in the main, Dewey sought to live by those words. I have no idea why he was not more attentive as a teacher than he seems to have been, nor why he chose not to wield for his pedagogical improvement, and for the benefit of his students, the intellectual tools that he himself forged over the years, nor, yet again, why he failed to apply the standards nurtured in him by the arts. I do know that he left behind a rich legacy of insights for teachers and nonteachers alike, a veritable tool chest of helpful ideas awaiting our use. What he left undone, for whatever reason, we still may undertake ourselves.

References

In the body of the text all references to Dewey's writings are keyed to his Collected Works published by the Southern Illinois University Press. The abbreviations EW, MW, and LW, followed by specific volume and page numbers, stand for Early Works, Middle Works, and Later Works within that series of publications. To aid readers who may not have easy access to those standard volumes, I have listed below all of the original texts by Dewey that I have drawn upon. Each of those bibliographic entries is followed by a notation indicating its location within the Collected Works.

Abrams, M. H. *The Mirror and the Lamp: Romantic Theory and the Critical Tradition.* New York: W. W. Norton, 1953.
———. *Natural Supernaturalism.* New York: W. W. Norton, 1971.
Alexander, F. Matthais. *Man's Supreme Inheritance.* New York: E. P. Dutton, 1918, with an introduction by John Dewey (MW11, 350–352).
———. *Constructive Conscious Control of the Individual.* New York: E. P. Dutton, 1923, with an introduction by John Dewey (MW15, 307–315).
———. *The Use of the Self.* New York: E. P. Dutton, 1932, with an introduction by John Dewey (LW6, 315–320).
———. *The Universal Constant in Living.* New York: E. P. Dutton, 1941.
Alexander, Thomas M. *John Dewey's Theory of Art, Experience, and Nature.* Albany: State University of New York Press, 1987.

Aristotle. *Nicomachean Ethics.* Indianapolis: Bobbs-Merrill, 1962.

Auden, W. H. *The Dyer's Hand and Other Essays.* New York: Vintage Books, 1968.

Bates, Milton J. *Wallace Stevens: A Mythology of Self.* Berkeley: University of California Press, 1985.

Beardsley, Monroe C. *Aesthetics from Classical Greece to the Present.* University: University of Alabama Press, 1966.

Bishop, Elizabeth. *The Complete Poems: 1927–1979.* New York: Farrar, Straus and Giroux, 1980.

Bloom, Harold. *The Ringers in the Tower.* Chicago: University of Chicago Press, 1971.

———. *The Visionary Company: A Reading of English Romantic Poetry.* Ithaca, N.Y.: Cornell University Press, 1971.

Borradori, Giovanna. *The American Philosopher.* Chicago: University of Chicago Press, 1994.

Cassirer, Ernst. *The Philosophy of Symbolic Forms.* Volume 3, *Phenomenology of Knowledge.* New Haven: Yale University Press, 1957.

Cook, Reginald L., editor. *Ralph Waldo Emerson: Selected Prose and Poetry.* New York: Holt, Rinehart and Winston, 1965.

Cremin, Lawrence A. *The Transformation of the School: Progressivism in American Education.* New York: Knopf, 1961.

Danto, Arthur. *After the End of Art: Contemporary Art and the Pale of History.* Princeton, N.J.: Princeton University Press, 1997.

———. "Response and Replies." In *Danto and His Critics,* edited by Mark Rollins, 193–216. Cambridge, Mass.: Blackwell, 1993.

———. "The Artworld." *Journal of Philosophy* 61 (1964): 571–584.

———. *Beyond the Brillo Box: The Visual Arts in Post-Historical Perspective.* New York: Farrar, Straus and Giroux, 1992.

———. *Embodied Meanings: Critical Essays and Aesthetic Meditations.* New York: Farrar, Straus and Giroux, 1994.

———. *Encounters and Reflections: Art in the Historical Present.* New York: Farrar, Straus and Giroux, 1990.

———. *The Philosophical Disenfranchisement of Art.* New York: Columbia University Press, 1986.

———. *The Transfiguration of the Commonplace.* Cambridge: Harvard University Press, 1981.

Dewey, John. *Art as Experience.* New York: Capricorn Books, 1934. (LW10)

———. *The Child and the Curriculum.* Chicago: University of Chicago Press, 1900. (MW1)

———. *Democracy and Education.* New York: Free Press, 1916. (MW9)

———. *Essays in Experimental Logic.* New York: Dover, 1916. (MW4, MW10)

———. *Experience and Education.* New York: Macmillan, 1938. (LW13)

———. *Experience and Nature.* New York: Dover, 1958. (LW1)

———. *How We Think.* Lexington, Mass.: D. C. Heath, 1933. (LW8)

———. *Human Nature and Conduct: An Introduction to Social Psychology.* New York: Modern Library, 1922. (MW14)

———. *Logic: The Theory of Inquiry.* New York: Henry Holt, 1938. (LW12)

———. *Philosophy and Civilization.* New York: Minton, Balch, 1931. (LW3, 5)

————. *The Quest for Certainty.* New York: G. P. Putnam's Sons, 1929. (LW4)

————. *The School and Society.* Chicago: University of Chicago Press, 1900. (MW1)

Dewey, John, and Evelyn Dewey. *Schools of Tomorrow.* New York: E. P. Dutton, 1915. (MW8)

Dillard, Annie. *Pilgrim at Tinker Creek.* New York: Harper, 1974.

Dunkel, Harold B. "Dewey and the Fine Arts." *School Review* 67 (Summer 1959): 229–245.

Dykhuizen, George. *The Life and Mind of John Dewey.* Carbondale: Southern Illinois University Press, 1973.

Edman, Irwin. "Columbia Galaxy." In *Great Teachers,* edited by Huston Peterson, 187–201. New York: Vintage Books, 1946.

Emerson, Ralph Waldo. *Essays and Lectures.* Edited by Joel Porte. New York: Library of America, 1983.

Franck, Frederick. *The Zen of Seeing.* New York: Vintage Books, 1973.

Garrison, Jim, editor. *The New Scholarship on Dewey.* Boston: Kluever, 1995.

Gilman, William H., editor. *Selected Writings of Ralph Waldo Emerson.* New York: New American Library, 1965.

Giroux, Robert, editor. *One Art: Selected Letters of Elizabeth Bishop.* New York: Farrar, Straus and Giroux, 1994.

Hadot, Pierre. *Philosophy as a Way of Life.* Cambridge, Mass.: Blackwell, 1995.

Herwitz, Daniel. *Making Theory / Constructing Art: On the Authority of the Avant-Garde.* Chicago: University of Chicago Press, 1993.

James, William. *The Principles of Psychology.* Volume 1. New York: Henry Holt, 1890.

Kabat-Zinn, Jon. *Wherever You Go, There You Are.* New York: Hyperion, 1994.

————. *Full Catastrophe Living.* New York: Delta, 1991.

Kalstone, David. *Becoming a Poet.* New York: Farrar, Straus and Giroux, 1989.

Kent, Corita, and Jan Steward. *Learning by Heart.* New York: Bantam Books, 1992.

Kostelanetz, Richard. *Conversing with Cage.* New York: Limelight Editions, 1988.

————, editor. *John Cage: An Anthology.* New York: Da Capo Press, 1991.

————, editor. *John Cage: Writer.* New York: Limelight Editions, 1993.

Kupfer, Joseph H. *Experience as Art.* Albany: State University of New York Press, 1983.

Kuspit, Donald. "Concerning the Spiritual in Contemporary Art." In *The Spiritual in Art: Abstract Painting, 1890–1985,* edited by Maurice Tuchman, 313–325. New York: Abbeville Press, 1986.

————. *The Cult of the Avant-Garde Artist.* New York: Cambridge University Press, 1994.

Lamont, Corliss, editor. *Dialogue on John Dewey.* New York: Horizon Press, 1959.

Larrabee, Harold Atkins. "John Dewey as Teacher." *School and Society* 87 (1959): 378–381.

Leonard, George J. *Into the Light of Things: The Art of the Commonplace from Wordsworth to John Cage.* Chicago: University of Chicago Press, 1994.

Meyer, Leonard B. *Emotion and Meaning in Music.* Chicago: University of Chicago Press, 1956.

————. *Music, the Arts, and Ideas.* Chicago: University of Chicago Press, 1994.

Mitchell, Stephen, editor. *The Selected Poetry of Rainer Maria Rilke.* New York: Vintage Books, 1989.

Moore, Richard. "Elizabeth Bishop: 'The Fish.'" *Boston University Studies in English* 2, no. 4 (1956): 254–259.

Murdoch, Iris. *The Sovereignty of Good.* London: Routledge and Kegan Paul, 1970.

Read, Herbert. *Education Through Art.* London: Faber and Faber, 1943.

Revill, David. *The Roaring Silence: John Cage: A Life.* New York: Arcade Publishing, 1992.

Rousseau, Jean-Jacques. *Reveries of the Solitary Walker.* New York: Penguin Books, [1782] 1979.

Ryan, Alan. *John Dewey and the High Tide of American Liberalism.* New York: W. W. Norton, 1995.

Schapiro, Meyer. *Modern Art: Nineteenth and Twentieth Centuries.* New York: George Braziller, 1982.

——. *Theory and Philosophy of Art: Style, Artist, and Society.* New York: George Braziller, 1994.

Schiller, Friedrich. *On the Aesthetic Education of Man.* Edited by Elisabeth M. Wilkinson and L. A. Willoughby. New York: Oxford University Press, 1967.

Shusterman, Richard. "Dewey on Experience: Foundation or Reconstruction?" *Philosophical Forum* 26, no. 2 (Winter 1994): 127–148.

——. *Pragmatist Aesthetics: Living Beauty, Rethinking Art.* Cambridge, Mass.: Blackwell, 1992.

Spiegelman, Willard. "Elizabeth Bishop's 'Natural Heroism.'" In *Elizabeth Bishop and Her Art,* edited by Lloyd Schwartz and Sybil P. Estess, 154–171. Ann Arbor: University of Michigan Press, 1983.

Stevens, Wallace. *Opus Posthumous.* New York: Vintage Books, 1990.

Taylor, Mark C. *Disfiguring: Art, Architecture, Religion.* Chicago: University of Chicago Press, 1992.

Travisano, Thomas J. *Elizabeth Bishop: Her Artistic Development.* Charlottesville: University Press of Virginia, 1988.

Wilson, Malin, editor. *The Hydrogen Jukebox: Selected Writings of Peter Schjeldahl.* Berkeley: University of California Press, 1991.

Wollheim, Richard. *Painting as an Art.* Princeton, N.J.: Princeton University Press, 1987.

Wordsworth, William. *The Oxford Authors: William Wordsworth.* Edited by Stephen Gill. Oxford: Oxford University Press, 1984.

——. *The Norton Anthology of Poetry.* 3d edition. New York: W. W. Norton, 1983.

——. *The Prelude, 1799, 1805, 1850.* Edited by Jonathan Wordsworth, M. H. Abrams, and Stephen Gill. New York: W. W. Norton, 1979.

Zahorik, John. "Elementary and Secondary Teachers' Reports of How They Make Learning Interesting." *Elementary School Journal* 96, no. 5 (May 1996): 551–564.

Index

A

Abrams, M. H., 72, 75, 76
Aesthetic experience, 29, 33, 34–35; internal organization of, 43–43; as perception, 57
Aesthetic form, 43, 44; formal conditions of, 45–56
Alexander, F. Matthias: Alexander technique, 137–139, 143, 145, 146, 162
Alexander, Thomas, 56
Andre, Carl, 90–91, 96, 102, 108, 109
Anticipation, as formal condition of aesthetic form, 45, 47, 52–54
Appreciation, by cultivated taste, 63
Art, as source of exemplary experience, 5
Art appreciation, 51, 63
Art-centered experience, 35, 112, 119–120; introduced, xiv, xv; properties of, 36; selective attention in, 36–40;

place of chance in, 39–40; anticipation as part of, 53

B

Balance, in aesthetic experience, 43–44
Bates, Milton, 52
Beardsley, Monroe, 11
Bishop, Elizabeth: "The Fish," 96–108, 110
Bloom, Harold, 72, 75, 76

C

Cage, John: *4′ 33″*, 70, 75, 78–87, 94, 106, 108, 109
Carlyle, Thomas, 74
Coleridge, Samuel: "Kubla Khan," 5
Completeness, as generic trait of *an* experience, 7–8

Conservation, as formal condition of aesthetic form, 45, 47, 48, 49; of energy, 48–49; of meaning, 48, 49–50
Continuity, as formal condition of aesthetic form, 45; contrasted with flux, 45
Cumulation, as formal condition of aesthetic form, 45, 47, 48

D

Danto, Arthur C.: end-of-the-arts argument, 69–71, 77; reaction to Warhol's *Brillo Box*, 88–91, 94–96, 99, 109, 110, 114, 117; on Dewey, 159–160
Dewey, Evelyn, 165
Dewey, John: method of abstraction, 33–34; as writer, 46, 159; studies with F. Matthais Alexander, 137–139; goals for education, 169; view of "old" psychology, 169; warns of progressivism's excesses, 173; favors activity-based curriculum, 175; as teacher, 182–195; characterization of polarities of teaching, 191. Works mentioned: *Art as Experience*, xi, xii, xiv, xv, 1, 33, 35, 43, 44, 71, 113, 122, 166, 180, 194; *The Child and the Curriculum*, 165, 174; *Democracy and Education*, 172–174, 181; *Experience and Education*, 173, 176, 180, 181; *Experience and Nature*, 2, 166, 180; *The School and Society*, 165, 167, 171, 173, 174; *Schools of Tomorrow*, 174–176
Dillard, Annie, 17–19
Dunkel, Harold B., 122–123

E

Edman, Irving, on Dewey as a teacher, 183–186, 189, 190

Emerson, Ralph Waldo, on art, 73–74, 75, 76
Emotions: primary and secondary, 12; subconscious, 13
Energy, as force within experience, 48
Events, as objects, 24
Existences, transformed into objects, 23
Experience: generic traits of, 1, 5, 7, 14, 34; *an* experience, 4–5; and meaning, 4, 14–34; temporality of, 4, 44; as educative and miseducative, 5–6; primacy of ordinary experience, 6; completeness of, 6–7; consummatory nature of, 8; uniqueness of, 8; immediacy of, 9; emotion as unifying, 10–12; unity of (mailbox example), 12–14; single pervasive quality within, 20; integral nature of, 51; intellectual, 51; field of action, 56; dynamics of, 56; discontinuity of, 106; conservation of, 110; cumulation within, 110; tension within, 110; as artifice, 124; as interaction, 124; continuity of, 124; unity of *an* experience, 124; framing experience, 125; crafting of, 128
Expressiveness: of objects, 26–27; as meaning, 27
Extrinsic versus intrinsic meaning, 14, 28. *See also* Meaning

F

Franck, Frederick—method of SEEING / DRAWING, 152–156; related to Dewey's theory of experience, 154; related to Zen, 155, 159
Fulfillment, as characteristic of aesthetic experience, 45

G

Glass, as material and medium, 41–43

Growth, as criterion of judgment, 47

H

Habit: as inner material, 45; in aesthetic experience, 46
Hadot, Pierre, 141–142
Heizer, Michael, 92–95, 108–110
Herwitz, Daniel, 81–84 passim, 87
Holmes, Oliver Wendell, on Dewey's writing style, 161
Hook, Sidney, on Dewey as teacher, 182–183

I

Imagination, and the construction of meaning, 27–28
Immediacy: qualitative, 21, 53: of existences, 26
Intellectual experiences, 51

J

James, William, 121

K

Kabat-Zinn, Jon: mindfulness meditation, 130–140, 142–143, 159
Kalstone, David, 104–105
Kaprow, Allan, 80, 83, 84, 87, 88, 90
Kent, Corita, and Jan Steward: *Learning by Heart*, 143–152, 159
Kostelanetz, Richard, 82, 87
Kupfer, Joseph, 123, 128
Kuspit, Donald: concept of "silent art," 114–115, 117–119

L

Larrabee, Harold, on Dewey as teacher, 182–189, 190
Leonard, George J., 69–78 passim, 86–89, 102

Lowell, Robert, 105, 107

M

Material, inner versus outer, 43
Meaning: intrinsic and extrinsic, 14, 28; extrinsic primary, in reflection, 15; taken up by objects, 22; as inexhaustible, 24–25; as inference, 27–28; divorced from use, 29; in use, 29; breakfast teaspoon example, 29–33; expressive, 32, 41
Means, two kinds of, 40–41
Media, transformation of physical materials into, 40
Meyer, Leonard, 127
Moore, Marianne, 105, 106, 108
Moore, Richard, 101, 103
Murdoch, Iris, 156–158

N

Natural Supernaturalism, 75, 76, 83, 86
Nims, John Frederick, 107–108

O

Objects: emergent within field of observation, 22; as product of inquiry, 23; as events, 24; as abstractions, 25; perceived as unique, 26

P

Perception: temporal nature of, 57; versus recognition, 57; relational character of, 59; correlative with object, 60; as redemptive, 61; experiential extension of, 63; contribution to meaning, 64; in use, 65–67; for its own sake, 65, 148; of art objects, 113; full, 60, 112, 130, 149
Philosophical fallacy, 2
Progressive Education Association, 177

R

Rauschenberg, Robert, 79, 89
Read, Sir Herbert, xii
Realizing sense, 194
Reconstruction of habit, 46
Rhythm, in aesthetic experience, 44
Rousseau, J. J.: *Reveries of the Solitary Walker,* 142
Ruskin, John, 74, 75, 76
Ryan, Alan, 161–163, 174, 180

S

Schapiro, Meyer, 114, 115–119
Schjeldahl, Peter, 90–92, 94, 95, 96, 99, 110
Sense of a situation, versus significa-tion, 20. *See also* Realizing sense
Shusterman, Richard, 140–141
Situations, 15–22; as systems of mean-ing, 15; containing objects and events, 16; controlling terms of thought, 16; proleptically described, 17; as problematic, 56
Spiegelman, Willard, 100
Stevens, Wallace, vi, 52
Steward, Jan, and Corita Kent: *Learn-ing by Heart,* 143–152, 159
Suzuki, Daisetsu Teitaro, 78
Symmetry, in aesthetic experience, 43–44

T

Taylor, Mark C., 85–86, 110, 114–115; visit to Heizer's *Double Negative,* 92–95, 97

Teachers, on classroom practices, 177–180
Temporality of experience, 44
Tension: as formal condition of aes-thetic form, 45; involving compres-sion and release, 50–52
Thoughts, as rational objects, 23
Travisano, Thomas, 100–101, 105
Tudor, David, 79–80

U

Uniqueness, of *an* experience (birth-day party example), 7
University Elementary School, xii, 165; curriculum of, 167–175; making and doing as classroom activities, 171; worries about students' mastery of basic skills, 171
University of Chicago Laboratory School. *See* University Elementary School
Use: as instrumentality, 25; its comple-mentarity with enjoyment, 25

W

Warhol, Andy: *Brillo Box,* 70, 71, 88–89, 91, 94, 102, 108, 114
Whitehead, Alfred North, 160
Wordsworth, William, 58, 69, 72–77 passim, 87, 163

Z

Zahorik, John, 177–180